Crank it up

Crank it up

Jason Statham: star!

Edited by Steven Gerrard and Robert Shail

Manchester University Press

Copyright © Manchester University Press 2019

While copyright in the volume as a whole is vested in Manchester University Press, copyright in individual chapters belongs to their respective authors, and no chapter may be reproduced wholly or in part without the express permission in writing of both author and publisher.

Published by Manchester University Press
Oxford Road, Manchester M13 9PL
www.manchesteruniversitypress.co.uk

British Library Cataloguing-in-Publication Data is available

ISBN 978 1 5261 4277 1 hardback
ISBN 978 1 5261 6394 3 paperback

First published by Manchester University Press in hardback 2019

This edition first published 2022

The publisher has no responsibility for the persistence or accuracy of URLs for any external or third-party internet websites referred to in this book, and does not guarantee that any content on such websites is, or will remain, accurate or appropriate.

Typeset by Newgen Publishing UK

Contents

Figures vii
Contributors ix
Acknowledgements xiii

Introduction 1

Part I: Statham and (reframing) masculinity

1 Reframing the British tough guy: Jason Statham as postmodern hero *Robert Shail* 15
2 'I'm certainly not Tom Cruise or Brad Pitt': Jason Statham, fandom and a new type of (anti) hero *Renee Middlemost* 29
3 The power of Statham *Paul Feig* 45
4 'It's that peasant mentality': the cult persona of Jason Statham, Hollywood outsider *Jonathan Mack* 56
5 A balancing act(or): Jason Statham and the ensemble film *Sarah Thomas* 71

Part II: Statham and genre case studies

6 Blagging it both ways: *The Bank Job* (2008) and the British heist movie *James Chapman* 99
7 Jason Statham in *Spy*: subverting genre and gender *Clare Smith* 113
8 Arthouse Statham *Martin Carter* 127

Part III: Rebranding Statham

9 Transporting Jason Statham: national identity in
   The Transporter trilogy   *Jennie Lewis-Vidler*   151
10 The avatar hero: exploring the virtualisation of the
   Statham brand   *Dean Bowman and Erin Pearson*   169
11 Ageing Statham: expendable Expendable?
   Natasha Parcei   185
12 Crank it up! Scoring Statham   *Shelley O'Brien*   198
13 Clothes make the man: Jason Statham's
   sartorial style   *Steven Gerrard*   211

   Conclusion   227

Select bibliography   231
Jason Statham filmography   236
Index   249

Figures

1–3	*The Transporter* (Corey Yuen: 2002) EuropaCorp, TF1 Films Production, Current Entertainment, Canal+	86
4–6	*Transporter 2* (Louis Leterrier: 2005) EuropaCorp	87
7–9	*Transporter 3* (Olivier Megaton: 2008) EuropaCorp, TF1 Films Production, Grive Productions, Apipoulai Entertainment, Canal+, CineCinema	88
10–11	*Crank* (Neveldine/Taylor: 2006) Lakeshore Entertainment, @radical.media	89
12–13	*Crank* (Neveldine/Taylor: 2006) Lakeshore Entertainment, @radical.media	90
14–15	*Crank* (Neveldine/Taylor: 2006) Lakeshore Entertainment, @radical.media	91
16–17	*Crank* (Neveldine/Taylor: 2006) Lakeshore Entertainment, @radical.media	92
18	*Crank* (Neveldine/Taylor: 2006) Lakeshore Entertainment, @radical.media	93
19	*Crank: High Voltage* (Neveldine/Taylor: 2009) Lakeshore Entertainment, @radical.media	93
20–21	*Crank: High Voltage* (Neveldine/Taylor: 2009) Lakeshore Entertainment, @radical.media	94
22–23	*Crank: High Voltage* (Neveldine/Taylor: 2009) Lakeshore Entertainment, @radical.media	95
24	*Crank: High Voltage* (Neveldine/Taylor: 2009) Lakeshore Entertainment, @radical.media	96
25	*In the Name of the King: A Dungeon Siege Tale* (Uwe Boll: 2007) Boll KG Productions, Herold Productions, Brightlight Pictures	96
26	*In the Name of the King: A Dungeon Siege Tale* (Uwe Boll: 2007) Boll KG Productions, Herold Productions, Brightlight Pictures	140

27	*The Bank Job* (Roger Donaldson: 2008) Mosaic Media Group, Relativity Media LLC, Skyline (Baker St) Productions	140
28–29	*The Bank Job* (Roger Donaldson: 2008) Mosaic Media Group, Relativity Media LLC, Skyline (Baker St) Productions	141
30	*Death Race* (Paul W. S. Anderson: 2008) Relativity Media, Cruise/Wagner Productions	141
31	*Death Race* (Paul W. S. Anderson: 2008) Relativity Media, Cruise/ Wagner Productions	142
32–33	*Blitz* (Elliott Lester: 2011) Davis Films, Lipsync Productions	142
34–35	*Killer Elite* (Gary McKendry: 2011) Omnilab Media, Ambience Entertainment, Current Entertainment, Sighvatsson Films, Film Victoria, Wales Creative IP Fund, Agora Films, International Traders, Mascot Pictures Wales	143
36	*The Mechanic* (Simon West: 2011) Millennium Films	143
37–38	*The Mechanic* (Simon West: 2011) Millennium Films	144
39	*Hummingbird* (Steven Knight: 2013) IM Global, Shoebox Films	144
40–41	*Hummingbird* (Steven Knight: 2013) IM Global, Shoebox Films	145
42	*Parker* (Taylor Hackford: 2013) Incentive Filmed Entertainment, Sierra Pictures, Sidney Kimmel Entertainment	145
43–44	*Parker* (Taylor Hackford: 2013) Incentive Filmed Entertainment, Sierra Pictures, Sidney Kimmel Entertainment	146
45	*Spy* (Paul Feig: 2015) Chernin Entertainment, Feigco Entertainment, TSG Entertainment	146
46–47	*Spy* (Paul Feig: 2015) Chernin Entertainment, Feigco Entertainment, TSG Entertainment	147
48	*The Meg* (Jon Turteltaub: 2018) Warner Bros. Pictures, Gravity Pictures, Flagship Entertainment, Apelles Entertainment, Di Bonaventura Pictures, Maeday Productions	147
49–50	*The Meg* (Jon Turteltaub: 2018) Warner Bros. Pictures, Gravity Pictures, Flagship Entertainment, Apelles Entertainment, Di Bonaventura Pictures, Maeday Productions	148

Contributors

Dean Bowman's work at University of East Anglia studies the unique narrative potential of videogames through a combination of interviewing designers and audience reception analysis. He has a degree in English Literature (also from UEA), a Master's in Film Studies from the University of Edinburgh, and his PhD is nearing completion. He is the deputy editor of www.ready-up.net, a large and well-established community blog where he writes on videogames and board games, and co-hosts a weekly podcast called the Sixty-Two Cast.

Martin Carter is a keen cineaste and loves all forms of cinema. He works as Principal Lecturer at Sheffield Hallam University, where his specialisms include cinema preservation and archival film restoration. He has lent his vocal talents to radio programmes and been interviewed on BBC One's *The One Show*, where he talked about the Sheffield Photographic Company's 1903 film, *Daring Daylight Robbery* – the first UK-produced film reel.

James Chapman is Professor of Film Studies at the University of Leicester and editor of the *Historical Journal of Film, Radio and Television*. His research explores the cultural histories of British cinema and television, and his books include *Hitchcock and the Spy Film* (I. B. Tauris: 2018), *Swashbucklers: The Costume Adventure Series* (Manchester University Press: 2015), *War and Film* (Reaktion: 2008), *Inside the Tardis: The Worlds of 'Doctor Who'* (I. B. Tauris, 2006; 2nd edition 2013) and *Saints and Avengers: British Adventure Series of the 1960s* (I. B. Tauris: 2002). In between writing a history of the fiscal politics of the post-war British film industry, he is also preparing a third edition of *Licence to Thrill: A Cultural History of the James Bond Films* (I. B. Tauris).

Paul Feig is an American actor, producer, screenwriter and film director. Specialising in comedies, his work includes creating *Freaks and Geeks* (1999–2000) and *Other Space* (2015). He has directed for both TV and cinema, with *The Office* (2005), *Arrested Development* (2006), *Mad Men* (2007), *Bridesmaids* (2011), *The Heat* (2013), *Ghostbusters* (2016) and the Jason Statham comedy *Spy* (2015) in his oeuvre.

Steven Gerrard is Reader in Film at The Northern Film School, Leeds Beckett University. A lifelong fan of the *Carry On* films, he has written a monograph about those ribald British comedies for Palgrave Macmillan. He has also written about *The Modern British Horror Film* for Rutgers University Press. He is co-editor for Emerald Publishing's *Gender in Contemporary Horror* series, and editor of their *Gender in Contemporary Horror TV*. A lifelong *Dr Who* fan, not only does Steve want to be the Timelord, he would also like to be *Status Quo*'s rhythm guitarist. He will have a very long wait.

Jennie Lewis-Vidler teaches at the University of Portsmouth and was previously a Karten Doctoral Outreach Fellow for the Parkes Institute in the University of Southampton. The Parkes Institute is one of the world's leading centres for the study of Jewish and non-Jewish relations. Jennie is interested in British racial, ethnic and national identity, the representation of masculinity in sports such as boxing and British fascism primarily the British Union of Fascists. Her PhD thesis is titled 'Traveller, Boxer and Fascist: The Identities of Joe Beckett'. It is a case study on the former 1920s heavyweight champion and how his career in boxing and later fascism represented masculinity and identity in Britain in the twentieth century.

Jonathan Mack is a lecturer and researcher in film and media, primarily focusing on the relationships between medial forms. His work on intermediality in film has been published in *Adaptation* (2016) and *Cinema Journal* (2017), and he has contributed to a number of edited collections.

Renee Middlemost is a lecturer in Film and Cultural studies at the University of Wollongong, Australia. Her PhD thesis was entitled 'Amongst Friends: the Australian cult film experience', which examined the audience participation practices of cult film fans in Australia. Her forthcoming publications reflect her diverse research interests. These include a chapter on cult film and nostalgia for *The Routledge Guide to Cult Cinema*; an article on space and the Australian film industry for *Media International Australia*; and a co-authored chapter on the finale of *Dexter*.

Shelley O'Brien is Senior Lecturer in Film Studies at Sheffield Hallam University. Her interests are the use of sound and music in cinema, and a passion for all things horror and cult in cinema. After gaining her MPhil in 2000, which examined the emergence and evolution of Body Horror Cinema, she has published essays on the directors Herschell Gordon Lewis ('The Gore Auteur') and Tobe Hooper ('One Trick Pony?') for *Directory of world cinema: American independent*, ed. John Berra (Intellect, Autumn 2016); 'The Devil's in the Detail: Musical Form and Function in *Profondo Rosso*', SHU Film Magazine; 'The Void', October 2015 and 'Killer Priests: The Last Taboo?' in *Roman Catholicism in Fantastic Film* (ed. Regina Hansen, McFarland: 2011). She has also delivered academic conference papers, focusing on the diversity of her work, including: Eli Roth's *Hostel*; 'The Art of Sound'; Soundscapes in Nigel Kneale's telefantasy series *Beasts*; Riz Ortolani scoring violence; issues of revenge in *I Spit on Your Grave* (1978).

Natasha Parcei is a PhD student and undergraduate tutor at the Northern Film School, Leeds Beckett University. She earned both her MA in Literary Studies and BA (Hons) in English Literature from the University of Huddersfield. Her current research interests include cultural gerontology, cinematic representations and celebrity culture. An avid conference speaker, Natasha regularly presents her new research on a variety of topics. Natasha has written a chapter for Emerald Publishing's *Gender in Contemporary Horror TV*, where she investigates the role of Jessica Lange in *American Horror Story*.

Erin Pearson's work at University of East Anglia explores the ways that promotional materials work to shape the discursive and physical spaces of American 'indie' film culture. Erin has contributed a chapter focusing on the role of review journalism in structuring indie to the forthcoming *Blackwell Companion to Indie* (ed. Geoff King). She has also written for Intellect's *World Film Locations* and *Directory of World Cinema* series and is editor for the review, *Intensities: The Journal of Cult Media*.

Robert Shail is Professor of Film at the Northern Film School, Leeds Beckett University. He has published widely on post-war British cinema and masculinity. His work includes a full-length study of Welsh star Stanley Baker and essays on Michael Caine and Terence Stamp.

Clare Smith is Heritage Centre Manager for the Metropolitan Police Museums in London. Her publications include her monograph, *Jack the Ripper in Film and Culture: Top Hat, Gladstone Bag and Fog* (Palgrave Macmillan: 2016), a chapter called 'Softly Softly Catchy Ripper – Barlow & Watt and the Investigation of the Whitechapel Murders' in *70s Monster Movie Memories* (WBD Publishing: 2015), and is a regular contributor to The History Press's invaluable work on Jack the Ripper. Clare was also the Collection Manager for the art collection at the National Museum of Wales, Cardiff and was responsible for organising an international loans programme, travelling the world with the works of art to oversee their safe transport and installation in galleries and museums around the globe. Her PhD investigated screen depictions of Jack the Ripper, while her research interests include the visual depiction of narrative and the construction of iconography in painting and film, plus the depiction of crime and murderers in art, film and television.

Sarah Thomas is a Lecturer in Media and Communication at the University of Liverpool. She is the author of the monographs *James Mason* (BFI Film Stars: 2017), *Peter Lorre – Face Maker: Stardom and Performance Between Hollywood and Europe* (Berghahn: 2012) and co-editor with Kate Egan of *Cult Film Stardom: Offbeat Attractions and Processes of Cultification* (Palgrave Macmillan: 2013).

Acknowledgements

This book would not have been possible without the invaluable help of a number of people. Matthew Frost and his design team at Manchester University Press, for not only believing in the project but also offering advice, guidance and certainly patience to the editors; also, staff at the Northern Film School and Leeds Beckett University for their disbelief that we could find something academic to write about The Mighty Jason Statham. Praise goes to Mr Steve Chasman, Jason Statham's friend and producer, who telephoned Steve in the office and questioned him about the project, where the words 'Jason is intrigued about your book' were etched into his memory. Mr Paul Feig contacting Steve was a brilliant bonus, both on a personal level and for this collection. Finally, acknowledgements must go to the book's contributors, who have not only delivered their manuscripts (mostly) on time, but shared their incredible enthusiasm for the project.

I love Jason Statham. When I first thought of the possibilities of this edited collection, I didn't realise quite what a journey it would take me on. I spoke to Jason Statham's agent, discussed the book with a major Hollywood director, and saw numerous people who looked bemused at the project, but then smiled and thought it was a great idea. The first group of dedications go to my friends, Phil, Griff and particularly Nick, who watched every Statham movie with me provided I supplied him with pasties, chips and cheap, fizzy lagers. Then there are my mum and dad, who during the editing of this book were badly injured in a road traffic accident. That they survived was a miracle. And, that they are so strong and resilient in both character and fortitude remains stunning to me. I love them both. Finally, there is one man that this book needs to be dedicated to, if only for his one-liners like 'Chicken and broccoli', 'Bonjour, douchebag', 'What are you? A pair of Sausage Nigels?' and 'Juice me!' – Jason Statham. Thanks for being brilliant.

Steve Gerrard

I would like to dedicate this collection to my very good friend of many years, my co-editor Steve Gerrard. Without his belief, dedication and sheer hard work it would never have happened.

Robert Shail

Introduction

Steven Gerrard and Robert Shail

In August 2018, Warner Brothers released their $130-million production *The Meg*. Based on Steve Alten's bestselling book *Meg: A Novel of Deep Terror* (1997), and directed by Jon Turteltaub, the film sees the main character – Jonas Taylor, a deep-sea diver working for the American navy – battle a 75-foot long, 20-million-year-old megalodon shark that has been revived from its deep slumber. The film, a co-production between American and Chinese companies with a *Jaws*-meets-*Jurassic Park* advertising campaign, starred British film actor Jason Statham. The aim of this edited collection is to introduce, survey and develop various critical analyses of Statham across not only his film work but his work away from cinema and across a variety of transmedia.

Film stars are often the mainstay of academic and lay discussion about the latest films and cinematic fads. While genres may fluctuate in fortune, the film star remains arguably the most important of all cinematic commodities. Film stars *sell* movies. But they don't only do this. Over the last twenty years, and since Richard Dyer's work in *Stars* (1998), the study of film stars, celebrity and stardom has become the centre for much critical argument. According to Dyer (1998: 1–4), these critical arguments have usually taken on two perspectives: the social/cultural context, and the semiotic. He argues that these two approaches, where stars are seen as a social phenomenon *and* that the star is important only because of the film(s) that they appear in, have formed the backbone to much that has been written about movie stars. However, he does concede that while investigations can focus on either one of these approaches, and that their results can certainly comment on the nature of film stardom and production modes of representation, it is of more use to combine the two: that is, the star and the films remain interlocked, and by adopting this process of analysis, so the 'overall' construction of a film star and the films they appear in (and beyond those films into other media) can offer richer rewards for the investigator.

Interestingly, Dyer's work here clearly assumes that stars are dealt with in terms of their signification, and not as 'real' people, and that 'we' will never know the 'real' 'them'. As an audience we are presented with a media-controlled image and persona, and the real person remains hidden. Even when appearing on chat shows, film stars remain part and parcel of an identity construction, and although they may laugh and joke or talk about their latest film promotions, they remain still the 'film star'. Therefore, this duality – both 'real' and 'fake' – does open up ideas about identity and persona.

Dyer takes this idea further. He argues that film stars are not only a social phenomenon, but that they reflect ideological stances within both 'themselves' as stars *and* the work they create. For the purpose of this collection, ideology remains a key theme of each chapter. As Dyer (1998: 2) states: 'Ideology is a characteristic of all human societies, but a given ideology is specific to a particular culture at a particular moment in history.' If this is the case, then film stars (and their oeuvre) can be, and are, laden with ideological approaches, either found directly within the text or hidden as a subtext and found upon further investigation. Of course, there is a counter-claim to be made here. Ideologies are only (mostly) found upon investigation. The average cinemagoer does not muse on the notions that the film they just watched is all about the predominant ideological stance at the time. Rather, films are meant – in the main – for enjoyment and leisure.

For the purpose of this collection, the chapters that are included here do offer some ideological approaches of how Statham 'reflects' the contextual world around him. For example, in Parcei's chapter, she eruditely argues that Statham's natural ageing is both accepted and rejected by those watching *The Expendables* trilogy in which Statham plays a soldier-of-fortune, Lee Christmas, as a norm of the Western culture that produced it. Lewis-Vidler's argument, that Statham's Gallic Britishness in the *Transporter* franchise is a heady mix of UK, European and American ideological stances (Statham as 'British'; France as a backdrop; the USA represented through its set pieces) are 'melded' together to produce an altogether new version of action hero clearly has ideological approaches at its heart. This ideological approach lies so fascinatingly within the 'limits' of Statham and his work. He is a new type of British star, both reliant on past traditions and celebrating newer ways of promoting his 'brand' through a variety of multimedia platforms. As you will see, this collection focuses on numerous aspects of Statham's work across his career.

While Dyer primarily focuses on American film stars such as John Wayne and Jane Fonda, it is clear that his approach to stardom is both satisfying and infuriating. On the one hand, he sets out his stall early on, by discussing the role of the star as a 'social phenomenon' created by the film studios, the actor and the films that they appear in. Yet, there are contradictions here. The individual, and that includes the writers and readers of this tome, will look at Statham from their own particular viewpoint, and even though they may not readily accept Dyer's views, their own views remain steadfastly important. The individual may look at Statham from contextual, sexual, political and gendered points of view. But this is the point of investigating someone like Statham: he is both old-fashioned and new.

In an era of mass communication across multimedia platforms, Jason Statham remains noticeable not only through his work on-screen, or various tabloid stories that focus on his private life and views, but in an increasingly bewildering range of media forms. This forms an important part of this edited collection. Not only does Statham appear in films, he has appeared in pop videos, catalogues, fashion magazines, and has branched out into the area of video gaming. This intertextuality through a panoply of media sources shows just how important he is to the idea that the 'new' film star of the post-millennial era both harks back to the past – through the films he makes – and towards the present/future areas of video gaming, graphic novels, etc. This is where the collection highlights these areas of 'new' mixed with 'old' concepts, and the interdisciplinary nature of the book's content, coupled with in-depth analysis of moments from Statham's films, fills a gap that is noticeable in the study of film stars. Admittedly, the stars of the past may not have had the variety of mass media through which they could be propelled out into their demanding public's gaze; but those film stars did have magazine circulations, TV programmes and radio shows to help them. Statham has taken this further. His approach to these media-varieties has certainly not only shown a remarkable trajectory from pop video dancer to international megastar, but also that he is prepared to accede that he *needs* other forms of media through which to form the Statham brand.

However, this does not diminish his importance as a bona fide British film star who has 'made it' in Britain, Hollywood and other lucrative markets. According to Dyer in his still-essential work on film stardom, the film star fulfils three roles: the first is the star as a 'construction', whereby the 'star' is built through advertising, films, magazines and such like; the second is where the star becomes a 'commodity' – that is, the monetary value of the star (as a 'star' and as a business); and finally, and arguably, as far as this book is concerned, most importantly, the ideological importance of the star. In other words, Jason Statham as a performer, actor, *star*, contains across his persona, his private and public life, a range of ideologies that can be 'read' to reflect and comment upon the world around us. As a consequence of these ideologies, fans could dress like Statham, share similar views, and identify with his constructed persona. But here lies the paradox of the notion of the 'star' and Statham: the traditional film star must be both 'ordinary' and 'extraordinary'. They must be both relatable and idolised by their audience. Likewise, they must be both 'present' and 'absent'. In the case of Statham, his audience interacts with him through various media platforms, yet at the same time he remains unobtainable, and therefore 'absent'.

For Dyer, the historic construction of a star persona was particularly reliant on the intersection between key texts – films – and secondary media outlets such as advertising and personal appearances. Dyer's work focuses on the idea that the films come first. However, Statham is particularly interesting for the way in which this balance has been altered. Of course, the films are still crucial, but in the construction of Statham's persona via his non-filmic texts have taken on an increasing prominence, a feature more and more prevalent in contemporary stardom. This fracturing and multiple dimensionality of his stardom reflects a key trend. This existence across a number of platforms invites a plurality of ideological meanings – something reflected in the diverse range of chapters in the edited collection. Statham's rise to prominence invites an analytic response which recognises the changing nature of stardom and its response to the nature of our postmodern culture. He really is a phenomenon of these times.

Following on from O. E. Klapp's work on 'social types' (1962), Dyer argues that male film stars typically occupy one of three 'types': Good Joe; Tough Guy; or Rebel. While each contains inherent ideological implications for both the performer and the audience, they become useful in providing a recognisable set of values and beliefs that then radiate out from their films and other media to create a persona. This persona is a combination of materials (film, advertising, magazines, etc.) that have selling points which create an overall 'product'. In the case of Statham, this persona might have such components as toughness, agility, humour and fashion style. All of which are reflected through his films, but also through the cross-pollination of his various multimedia platforms whereby he is also seen as a devoted partner and father. The complexity of these constructions indicates a fundamental shift in Dyer's model, where the categories need re-evaluation; Statham might easily qualify for one of Dyer's female types – the Pin Up. Again, the issue of typologies is tackled in many of the essays in this collection. Here, the editors make no apology for accepting Dyer as the 'role model' for his work on film stars. Admittedly, there are other academic writings that focus on film stars in general, including Gedhill's excellent *Stardom: Industry of Desire* (1991), Fischer's *Stars: The Film Reader* (2004), Willis's *Film Stars: Hollywood and Beyond* (2004), and Shingler's *Star Studies: A Critical Guide* (2012). Likewise, there are those tomes dedicated to single film stars. One that is closely linked to the subject of this collection is Holmlund's (2014) *The Ultimate Stallone Reader: Stallone as Star, Icon, Auteur*, that focuses on the academic analysis of this American star, which clearly shows that the idea of film stars, stardom and celebrity is a fascinating area to investigate. For the majority of the chapters in this collection, Dyer remains at the cornerstone of investigations, but obviously there will be areas where this work is critiqued, and alternative viewpoints offered.

Before we begin, it is perhaps wise at this point to introduce the main focus of this book: Jason Statham.

Statham, well known for his mock-cockney accent, tough guy persona, and films that range from the low-budget *London*

(2005), cult movies like *Crank* (2006), and franchises such as *The Transporter* (2002–2008), *The Expendables* (2010–) and *Fast and Furious* (2001–), headlined 2018's *The Meg* to massive box office success. For the first time in his career, he headlined a $100million+ co-production, and throughout the advertising campaign was promoted as *the* star, in a series of adverts which focused on his 'cool', 'calm' and 'hero' personas. While he had been the lead in over twenty movies, this was the first time that Hollywood had given him a chance to headline a major movie. It appeared that Jason Statham had 'made it'.

However, his rise to stardom had taken time. He was born in Derbyshire, England in 1967. His parents, Eileen and Barry were a dancer and lounge singer/street seller respectively. After leaving school and selling perfume to the tourists of London, Statham's dedication to his love of diving (which resulted in him being chosen to compete with the National Swimming Squad at the age of twelve) paid dividends. He competed for the squad at the 1990 Commonwealth Games. However, his career as a diver faltered following an average performance at the event. Despite this, he was spotted by the Sports Promotions agency, and was signed to undertake modelling work for clothing companies such as Tommy Hilfiger and Levis. Unlike the industry's quickly dating fashion lines, Statham's physique and rugged looks caught the eye of pop video directors who put him – as a gyrating Adonis – in pop promos for The Shamen ('Coming on Strong' 1993), Erasure ('Run to the Sun' 1994) and The Beautiful South ('Dream a Little Dream' 1995).

It was while working as a model for French Connection that he was asked to audition for the role of Bacon in Guy Ritchie's *Lock, Stock and Two Smoking Barrels* (1998). His school friend, Vinnie Jones, had put him forward for the part. Although only on-screen for a few minutes, his screen presence was noticeable. Following on from this, he worked with Ritchie again in *Snatch* (2000) which earned over $80million at the American box office. From these two films he worked for John Carpenter on the ill-fated *Ghosts of Mars* (2001) and then broadened his appeal with the martial arts, science fiction movie *The One* (2001). It was, however, with the success of the international co-production *The Transporter* (2002) that Statham began to receive wider attention. His role as Frank Martin, a hired driver who asks no questions, became his signature role: lean, muscular, skilled in martial arts and almost always quiet, Martin battled against Asian businessmen, American kidnappers and a French police inspector who eventually became his friend. The role took him outside of the British cultural frame of reference on which his star persona had previously been based.

Statham certainly has audience appeal. His fanbase grew, and while *Crank* and its sequel saw Statham's character Chev Chelios in full-on, rampant mode, other movies like *Parker* (2011) – a remake of *Point Blank* (1967) and *Payback* (1999) – and especially *Hummingbird* (2013) saw him take on much more complex roles, which clearly showed that he was not just an action star but a *film* star and actor. It was with his involvement in both *The Expendables* and the *Fast and Furious* franchises that cemented his box office appeal, having a 2018 box office tally of over $2billon in evidence (see boxofficemojo.com for details). With these films Statham moved up another division in the star rankings, as key support in major, global Hollywood products, while still retaining his cult following.

However, Statham has also branched out into other media platforms: he has provided voices for games such as *Red Faction II* and *Sniper X*; appeared on numerous magazine covers which all advertise his physique, fitness, and 'manliness'; become something of a fashion icon; and inspired the comic book series of *Ultimate Spider-Man*'s artists to draw The Vulture as a Stathamlookalike. Statham has become the subject of tabloid stories but nonetheless remains largely quiet and withdrawn from public life.

Stardom has remained central to the successful commercial production, distribution and exhibition of films. It has also helped to cement a relationship between the 'product' and its consumer. As such, film stars are *the* main marketing tool for an audience. There have been numerous books written about the subject of stardom: Dyer's aforementioned *Stars* gives an excellent overview of what stars and their 'types' mean. Localising the subject, Andrew Spicer's *Typical Men: The Representation of Masculinity in British Cinema* (2003) narrowed the field to British subjects in cinema. Moving towards a singular subject, Robert Shail's *Stanley Baker: A Life in Film* (2008) showed that the focus on one star could yield rewarding results: in this case, Baker was a Welsh actor who started from humble beginnings living in coal-strewn valleys, to one of Britain's most bankable stars. And herein lies the fortune of Statham. He is a modern-day Stanley Baker: an actor, a producer, Good Joe, Tough Guy and a

Rebel – all rolled into one. The tensions between the stable elements of his persona – strength, aggression, dynamism – and his ability to morph into other areas provide a characteristic feature of contemporary masculinity.

This is where this edited collection comes in. Statham is a modern-day movie star phenomenon. His career has embraced bit-parts, cameos, voice-overs, ensemble acting, action pictures, comedies, science fiction, horror, gangster films, art films, pop videos and postmodern ultra-violent fantasies.

The book has been divided into three separate parts, and for very distinct reasons. The first portion of the collection looks at Statham's masculinity, and includes ideas about traditional British film stardom, anti-heroes, and how Statham's mainstream persona has lent itself to cult projects. It also contains a remarkable personal essay from Paul Feig, director of the highly successful Statham comedy, *Spy* (2015). Much has been written about film stars and stardom, notably including hundreds of both official and unofficial biographies of hundreds of actors and actresses. That is not the point here. This opening portion focuses on how Statham remains both anchored in ideas of (British) film masculinity and moves beyond those cultural and contextual confines. Shail's essay, in which he argues that Statham is part and parcel of a British tradition following on from the likes of Michael Caine, Sean Connery and Stanley Baker, clearly sees Statham as a reflection of those, while simultaneously offering the idea that he is a post-millennial new 'type' of actor. In her chapter, Middlemost argues that Statham is an anti-hero for the post-millennial age. By positing the idea that he is inextricably linked to his persona and his fans, she clearly delineates the notion that Statham – again – is a new brand of film star. Paul Feig's essay remains slightly separate from this collection, inasmuch as it is not academically framed. However, it reveals a fascinating insight into what this A-list Hollywood director thinks of Statham and his work. Mack's chapter investigates the idea that Statham has moved – with ease – between both mainstream and 'cult' productions. It is an interesting point to make at this juncture, as there is a clear chain of events that are evident in the subject's career: namely, his breakthrough into cinema via a cult movie and its follow up, and then through films such as *Crank*. To conclude the first part of the collection, Thomas analyses how Statham remains important not through his work as an individual, but through his work as an individual *within* an ensemble piece. Her conclusions, in which she shows that Statham works across both fields with ease, demonstrates that in this day and age of mega-budgeted franchises he remains both part and parcel of individualism and collectiveness in equal measure.

The second part of this collection then focuses on Statham's genre output, including thoughts about his role within British filmic traditions such as the heist movie and the spy film, his work as a 'fish-out-of-water' in the French-based *Transporter* movies, and how he moves between mainstream and arthouse projects. Although 'genre' is not a word that pops up in everyday conversation, for film historians (and the general public) it remains an important part of cinematic history. The film industry thrives on genre productions, where the same generic outing is presented time and time again to an apparently unconcerned public. However, despite these repeated elements (narrative, characters, set pieces, etc.), the fact that Statham works within the 'confines' of genre clearly demonstrate that he remains safely housed within specific genres' walls. For example, in Chapman's investigation of Statham in *The Bank Job* (2008), he gives an overview of the cinematic history of the heist movie, while placing the film into that history. For Smith, Statham's incompetent Rick Ford in Feig's *Spy* is a comic turn that surpasses all expectations of the actor's comedic talents. Yet, it is noticeable that Statham has, on numerous occasions, admitted that he wants to play cinema's ultimate spy, James Bond. That Smith deconstructs Statham through his comedic ways is both enlightening and chastening: would Statham make Bond his own? Perhaps only the future can answer that. The final chapter in this section, Carter's investigation into Statham's move into 'arthouse' cinema, is fascinating. Through the analysis of three movies, Carter argues that while two of the films remain box office misfires, the overarching idea was that Statham was prepared to move between mainstream and arthouse to flex his acting muscles and expand his repertoire.

In the final part of the book, Statham's liminal work is analysed. The first chapter by Lewis-Vidler looks at the *Transporter* franchise, as a way in which Statham both cements and comments upon ideas of a British 'Gallicness' within the three narratives. By analysing the trilogy, the author clearly sees Statham's Frank Martin as a (anti) hero that moves seamlessly across borders and across continents, much in the same way that James Bond has done for over fifty years. In their chapter, Bowman and Pearson open up Statham's work in the burgeoning and lucrative area of video gaming. Statham has used his vocal talents in numerous games, and the authors examine his performance as a voice-over artist for videogames. As with all action heroes, ageing remains an important trope within their career. Stallone and Schwarzenegger, once the bastions of 1980s action movies, have maintained their importance to the genre through films like *The Expendables* (2010) and *Terminator: Genisys* (2015). Parcei looks at Statham's changing role across three *Expendables* movies, and by using the theme of gerontology, she helps us understand Statham's stance as ageing star within his canon. Moving completely away from Statham as an actor, O'Brien's work on the music in *Crank* shows a fascinating insight into how this often-neglected area reflects and comments upon Statham's character (Chev Chelios), while simultaneously arguing that the songs and traditional score lend themselves a form of extra-dimensionality through which audience identification can occur. The last chapter offers up an examination of the way that clothes reflect Statham's career, from pop video dancer, through fashion model and into the world of cinema. Each, in their own way, helps construct a rounded view of many facets of Statham that reflect his position as a modern-day film star, and how his embracing of new platforms showcases his work. The collection together offers a new way of considering stardom and theorising it which reflects the cultural changes of the last twenty years.

At the time of this edited collection going to press, Jason Statham has become arguably Britain's most important male film star of the post-millennium phase. He has tackled a wider range of roles than he is usually given credit for. These roles incorporate broken men, lost professionals, fathers, husbands, soldiers of fortune, gamblers, maniacs, hitmen, spies and assassins. But at their heart lies Jason Statham, an actor and star who rose from obscurity to box office success. Across his career, his almost nonchalant style and charm has swayed the public to look at him with affection, despite the critical mauling he has sometimes had from an unappreciative press. However, it is ultimately audiences who make stars. Like Stanley Baker before him, Statham is now part of a British tradition of actor/stars who, when discussed and scrutinised, analysed and studied, is more than the sum of his parts. There is speculation that he is to be cast as the ultimate male icon, James Bond. Perhaps he will be. Until then, and hopefully beyond any announcements, this book will not only clearly show the importance of Jason Statham to popular culture, it will also celebrate him.

References

Dyer, R. (1998). *Stars*. London: BFI Publishing.
Fischer, L. (2004). *Stars: The Film Reader*. Abingdon: Routledge.
Gedhill, C. (1991). *Stardom: Industry of Desire*. Abingdon: Routledge.
Holmlund, C. (2014). *The Ultimate Stallone Reader: Sylvester Stallone as Star, Icon, Auteur*. London: Wallflower Press.
Klapp, O. E. (1962). *Heroes, Villains and Fools*. Englewood Cliff, NJ: Prentice Hall.
Shail, R. (2008). *Stanley Baker: A Life in Film*. Cardiff: University of Wales Press.
Shingler, M. (2012). *Star Studies: A Critical Guide*. London: Palgrave Macmillan.
Spicer, A. (2003). *Typical Men: The Representation of Masculinity in Popular British Cinema*. London: I. B. Tauris.
Willis, A. (2004). *Film Stars: Hollywood and Beyond*. Manchester: Manchester University Press.

Part I
Statham and (reframing) masculinity

1

Reframing the British tough guy: Jason Statham as postmodern hero

Robert Shail

The tough guy, in one form or another, has been a staple of popular narrative cinema since its beginnings and in particular has been central to key genres such as the gangster film, the western or the contemporary action movie. In his influential study *Stars*, Richard Dyer (drawing on the work of sociologist O. E. Klapp) lists the Tough Guy as one of three dominant star types, along with the Good Joe and the Rebel (Dyer 1998: 48–51). Dyer's definition of the Tough Guy borrows from Klapp's original notion of a deteriorated hero but refines it in a more sympathetic way to understand its audience appeal. For Dyer, the Tough Guy is differentiated from the hero or Good Joe by a level of moral ambivalence or ambiguity: 'he confuses the boundaries between good and bad behaviour, presses the anti-social into the service of the social and vice versa' (1998: 49). At heart, Dyer's Tough Guy serves the moral certainties of the wider society like the hero but his actions, and the type is identified as male, often utilise methods that are anathema to a Good Joe. In straying across the ethical lines to employ the anti-social in the aid of social, the Tough Guy becomes a morally ambivalent figure. But this is also where his appeal to an audience lies. Whereas the certainties of the Good Joe may be alienating to parts of the audience who feel their own inadequacies heightened in comparison with this hero, the Tough Guy represents a figure as flawed as they are, someone who tries to do the right thing and gets there in the end but who may lose his moral compass along the way. This is the appeal of Robert Mitchum as opposed to John Wayne or Bruce Willis rather than Kevin Costner.

The example Dyer gives is James Cagney in his many gangster roles for Warner Brothers from the 1930s. Cagney's persona provided audience excitement and wish fulfilment through his personal dynamism and unfettered ambition but he remains sympathetic despite his capacity for violence. His socially deprived childhood is often sketched in, so that we feel we understand his motivations, as in *The Public Enemy* (1931), or in the final reel where he is redeemed by an apparent act of selflessness, as per *Angels with Dirty Faces* (1938). Audience identification is encouraged despite the moral contradictions of siding with characters on the wrong side of the law, an ambivalence usually corrected by final reel punishment. Another controversial example that illustrates the type and its appeal would be Clint Eastwood in *Dirty Harry* (1971), where the maverick policeman retains the legitimacy of a personal code of conduct but stretches the methods used in its service to such extremes as to divide audiences between those who still find Harry both human and sympathetic and those who see a justification for a near fascist use of violence. Harry's moral code gives him the ethical high ground, while his confusion at the corruption all around him is expressed by his finally tossing aside his police badge, mirroring Gary Cooper's actions at the close of *High Noon* (1952). An additional characteristic that Dyer attributes to the Tough Guy is a specific ability to reflect wider societal anxieties especially in relation to masculinity and violence. These can come to the surface at particular historical moments of collective stress, such as the depression of the 1930s or the political turmoil of 1970s America at the time of the Vietnam War.

The progression of the tough guy in American cinema might usefully be charted from the popular gangster films of the 1930s, through the patriotism of the Second World War, to the post-war pessimism of film noir, and onwards into the crime movies of the 1960s and 1970s, taking in the varying fortunes of the western genre along the way. The prominence of the tough guy in a wave of apparently recidivist action movies in the 1980s attracted considerable scrutiny from feminist scholars. This work was prompted by the popularity of stars such as Arnold Schwarzenegger, Bruce

Willis and Sylvester Stallone appearing in a succession of box office successes such as the *Terminator*, *Die Hard* and *Rambo* franchises, along with the continuing popularity of Eastwood (Dirty Harry became the subject of his own franchise). In the work of Yvonne Tasker and Susan Jeffords, the rise of these ultra-masculine stars is often read as a response to the aggressive foreign policy and free market politics of the Reagan administration, as well as to a male backlash against the perceived influence of Second Wave Feminism in the wider society. The emphasis on polished muscularity and male bonding in these films has also been interpreted in relation to discourses of fetishised power or sublimated homoerotic undercurrents. In *Spectacular Bodies: Gender, Genre and the Action Cinema*, Tasker debates whether this re-emergence signalled an attempt to reassert male hegemony at a point when it appeared to be under threat, or whether it just indicated its final death throes (Tasker 1993: 109–131). Jeffords takes a similar approach in her ironically titled essay 'Can Masculinity be Terminated?' (1993). The recent success of Jason Statham in the new millennium suggests that this form of cinematic masculinity proved more resilient than might have been predicted in the post-Reagan 1990s. The purpose of this chapter is to explore how Statham's particular version of the Tough Guy has negotiated this era and found new ways of successfully mutating.

Dyer's approach occasionally tends towards the broad-brush and often uses Hollywood as a paradigm for its exemplars. Work by scholars within British cinema history such as Bruce Babington (2001) and Andrew Spicer (2001) has suggested that while the concept of a star typology is useful, its exact application needs to integrate a sensitivity to place as well as time. For Babington, 'whatever stars mean in the larger cinema, they signify more complexly in relation to their original environment' (Babington 2001: 22), allowing for the analysis of representational characteristics such as gender, class, ethnicity and national identity. Spicer's study of British male stars, *Typical Men*, fractures and extends Dyer's approach across a number of types which allow the nuances of post-war Britain to be explored over a period of time, charting how the various British types fluctuate and evolve in response to changing social conditions and audience demands. This is a useful construction when considering how Jason Statham's star persona, rooted as it is in a British working-class context, has extended the Tough Guy type in recent years.

Although Statham's career has established him as a key supporting performer and emerging lead actor in major Hollywood films, his early career and star persona remain grounded in British culture. He was born in Shirebrook, Derbyshire in 1967 and grew up in Great Yarmouth in a working-class family. His early career success was as an athlete, which then led to modelling and appearances in music videos, supplemented by occasional work as a street seller like his father. His breakthrough film role in Guy Ritchie's *Lock, Stock and Two Smoking Barrels* (1998) immediately established his public image, one in which a working-class, specifically London-centred persona was fundamental to his appeal. Even later Hollywood films such as *The Expendables* (2010) or *Spy* (2015) continued to play on Statham's established persona and assume the audience's acceptance of his British working-class background in a manner previously established in the 1960s by stars such as Michael Caine, Terence Stamp and Sean Connery. In order to assess Statham's particular modification of the British working-class tough guy, it is helpful to trace this specific 'type', in Dyer's terms, back to its starting point in the late 1950s.

Andrew Spicer suggests that the first British actor to 'forge a consistent persona as the modern tough guy was Stanley Baker' (Spicer 2001: 73). Baker had impeccable working-class credentials as the son of a coal miner from Ferndale in South Wales. After years of taking bit-parts on stage and in British films, alongside some greater success on British television, Baker made his commercial breakthrough with the American director Cy Endfield's *Hell Drivers* (1957), in which his typical star persona is first seen. Baker's British tough guy is an ex-convict trying to go straight. He is certainly brave, resilient and physically strong but he also projects a tenderness in his friendships and restraint in his use of violence which mark him out; he only finally resorts to using his fists after continuous goading by the mildly psychotic Red, played by Patrick McGoohan. His subsequent roles in *Blind Date* (1959), *Hell is a City* (1960), *The Criminal* (1960) and *A Prize of Arms* (1962) further developed the character, whether as policeman or criminal, making him one of the most popular British actors with domestic audiences in the period. His persona combined aspects of the established American tough guy such as Robert Mitchum, unusually for a British star at the time (he did much of his best work for two expatriate American directors – Cy Endfield and Joseph Losey), alongside a soulfulness frequently attributed to his Welsh background, and a keen sense of class resentment (Shail 2008: 50–52). Baker's tough guy also suited the times: 'the new image that he offered to audiences, as a working-class hero with scant respect for authority, chimed perfectly with a transformation that was taking place in Britain itself' (Shail 2008: 62).

Spicer traces the fate of the British tough guy through to the turn of the millennium. He notes the motif of class identity, as well as the impact of challenges to traditional notions of masculinity brought about the wider discourses of feminism and changes in work patterns for men, particularly the decline of working-class employment in the manufacturing industry. He points to an ongoing preoccupation with crime as an outlet for social unease, the focus on rebellion or alienation, and a growing escalation in violence. These features can, nonetheless, be seen as negotiating tropes evident in Baker's persona. A newer characteristic for Spicer is the appearance of a 'damaged' masculinity whereby the working-class tough guy frequently appears as a figure so misshapen by the social upheavals of the last forty years that he has mutated into a dysfunctional relic, as portrayed by actors such as Christopher Ecclestone, David Thewlis, Gary Oldman, Tim Roth and Ray Winstone (Spicer 2001: 195–198). It was just at a point where this trend seemed to have potentially exhausted itself that Jason Statham emerged into British cinema stardom.

The typical characterisation offered by Statham in *Lock, Stock and Two Smoking Barrels* and Guy Ritchie's second successful foray into Britain's crime underbelly, *Snatch* (2000), is markedly different from anything to be found in Baker's films, or even those of Michael Caine or Ray Winstone. The films adopt an irreverent and deliberately ironic attitude to the more familiar generic elements of the crime genre and the tough guy type. It's not stretching credibility too far to suggest that many of the devices employed by Ritchie in his framing of Statham's performances are essentially postmodern in their approach. Susan Hayward's description of the four elements that define postmodernism in cinema are a helpful measure here (Hayward 2000: 277–279). She lists these as simulation, prefabrication, intertextuality and bricolage. Prefabrication refers to the knowing use of many existing motifs taken from the rich past of cinema history, while intertextuality denotes the referencing of other cultural sources from outside of cinema (and particularly from other forms of popular media). Bricolage is a means of assembling these apparently disparate elements in ways that emphasise their collision or which juxtapositions them in unexpected ways. Simulation is a term that unites the other three elements and gives postmodernism its central mode of address, which for Hayward lies in the use of either parody or pastiche. Ritchie's films make abundant use of all these techniques and reflect them through the performances of actors like Statham.

Statham's career has gone on to incorporate these postmodern characteristics repeatedly, whether evidenced by the number of remakes he has appeared in – *Mean Machine* (2001), *The Italian Job* (2003), *Death Race* (2008) or *Parker* (2013) – or the centrality of franchising to his career, as in the *Transporter* films or the *Expendables* series. His performance in *Fast and Furious 8* (2017) caught the amused attention of many critics simply because of the studied humour of his character's relationship with his mother, played by another iconic British performer, Helen Mirren. Nowhere is this deployment of postmodern tropes more apparent than in *Crank* (2006) and its sequel *Crank: High Voltage* (2009). Both films were written and directed by Mark Neveldine and Brian Taylor whose background was in advertising and music promos. Despite rather mixed initial reviews, the first film grossed over $40 million dollars on an estimated $12 million budget (source IMDB.1). The sequel fared slightly less well with takings over $34 million on a budget of $20 million (IMDB.2) and its frequently extreme content divided critics, with some accepting the humorous intent while others found it merely offensive. Although both films were produced and set in America, Statham's performances as Chev Chelios continue to overtly reference him as a British tough guy, both through his accent and his characterisation.

Crank quickly establishes its narrative structure, generic format and style, alongside the characterisation of its central character. Chev Chelios is a British paid assassin working in Los Angeles. In the opening section of the film, he finds himself caught in counterplots between two warring crime syndicates, as well as being targeted by a new aspiring gunman, Ricky Verona (Jose Pablo Cantillo), who wants to usurp him. Verona injects Chelios with a synthetic drug which will inhibit his adrenaline levels, eventually causing heart failure. A jaded Mafia medic, Doc Miles (Dwight Yoakum), advises Chev that he will need to keep his adrenaline levels constantly high through exposure to danger or excitement so that he can have sufficient time to take his revenge on the various hoodlums who have conspired to kill him – there is no antidote. *High Voltage* effectively restages this plot set-up but exaggerates it still further. Following a miraculous reprieve from the end of the first film when our hero seems to have been both poisoned and flattened by a fall from a helicopter, Chev awakes to find that his now legendary heart has been removed and possibly transplanted into the body of an ageing Triad leader (David Carradine). Chelios now has a battery-operated pump keeping him alive which needs regular charging from an electrical source as its battery pack gradually runs down. He has to find various ways to keep his artificial heart going while trying to track down the real one, at the same time evading various characters from the first film who are intent on revenge.

The film's prefabricated elements include the wide-ranging appropriation of generic elements from the action film genre and specifically various examples of earlier tough guy film-making. The essential premise of the first film is taken from *D.O.A.* (1949), itself remade in 1988, a classic post-war film noir directed by Rudolph Maté in which Edmond O'Brien's character has been poisoned with an incurable toxin and has just days to find his own killers and exact justice. As well as the central narrative conceit, *Crank* adopts the headlong narrative drive that made its predecessor's reputation, as well as its low budget, as Chelios chases across the urban landscape from one fraught encounter to the next. Its other major point of cinematic reference is *Speed* (1994) from which it borrows both its frenetic pace and set-piece stunts, as well as the concept of a hero who must maintain his own relentless momentum to avoid death. Other more recent films are directly referenced, as in the sequel where Chev attracts the attention of a prostitute called Ria (Bai Ling) who suggests that as a couple they resemble Whitney Houston and Kevin Costner in *The Bodyguard* (1992). Chev dismisses this suggestion. The cross and double-cross which provides the underlying plot development in both films is a trademark of noir and the action film, as is the array of stock characters lined up for Chelios to fight. In particular, a number of racial stereotypes indicative of the 1980s action movie are brought back against the more progressive, liberal vein of recent mainstream Hollywood cinema. These include the portrayal of grossly caricatured Hispanic and Asian criminals who are portrayed as virtual-cartoons, their potential for giving offence is offset by the irony of their presentation. In the manner of Stallone and Schwarzenegger, Statham's character is an astonishingly skilled combatant able to fend off hordes of inept gangsters in elaborately staged fight sequences, many of which are startlingly violent. Statham's character mimics the hard-bitten one-liners associated with American tough guy characterisations from Clint Eastwood onwards; but here they are inflected with curious cockneyisms which mirror Statham's earlier films for Guy Ritchie and which are frequently in deliberately appalling taste. These have subsequently obtained their own online cult following. *Crank: High Voltage* even references its predecessor by having Chev persistently encounter characters who he thought had been killed in the first film.

Intertextuality is evident throughout both films, from the casting of David Carradine as the master Asian gangster ironically recalling, and inverting, his most famous television role as the stoic, pacifist Chinese monk in the martial arts series *Kung Fu* (1972–1975), to a bizarre sequence in *High Voltage* when a fistfight in an electrical substation becomes a fantasy slow-motion battle deliberately referencing the *Godzilla/Gojira* franchise (1954–1975), specifically *King Kong vs Godzilla* (1962) which it recreates exactly, as well as other Japanese monster movies such as *War of the Gargantuas* (1966), complete with retro special effects and sound. Other knowing cameos include Geri Halliwell of the Spice Girls appearing in a flashback sequence as Chev's mother, country singer Dwight Yoakum as Doc, and a brief appearance by Lloyd Kaufman, CEO of cult low-budget production company Troma. Neveldine and Taylor stated their intention to make 'a film just like a videogame' (Leyland 2006: 49); at the finale of the first film Chelios finally becomes a videogame character, complete with crude pixelation and a panel showing his current game score. His imminent demise is indicated by the diminishing number of heart symbols he has, terminating in the inevitable 'Game Over'. Sequences are continually undercut by comic subtitles or cartoon-like graphics which comment on the action and invite viewers to pick up allusions to other media forms.

Bricolage is apparent in the way both films combine these various elements of intertextuality and prefabrication at great speed, with editing employed to consistently juxtapose the disparate content. There is a barrage of visual effects from slow motion to split screen, through to the use of CCTV footage and satellite mapping. Even shutter speed is manipulated to produce a curious wavering light effect which is used for both action scenes and more startlingly in dialogue exchanges. Spectators are left grasping at the threads of one idea just as another one is rapidly presented. The sheer pace of the sequel is even ironically mocked by an intertitle which tells us 'Nine seconds later'.

Throughout *Crank*, Chelios resorts to increasingly farcical methods to keep his adrenaline running high. This includes downing energy drinks like Red Bull, ingesting cocaine and injecting himself with a hypodermic full of synthetic adrenaline stolen from a hospital. The latter results in a comic book sprint out of the hospital and down a busy street, still wearing his hospital robe, culminating in him standing at a junction waiting to cross the road while speaking on the phone to Doc who is horrified at the dosage he has taken, and then noticing that he has a visible erection. In the second film, Chev's need to charge up his batteries includes shoving his arm into a street-side electrical substation, using jump-starter cables on his tongue, and applying the paddles from a cardiac resuscitation unit to his own chest. Using these cables causes Chev to temporarily catch fire during which time he kisses a female villain thinking she is his girlfriend, Eve, and inadvertently setting her on fire as well, before exiting the scene and giving a middle-finger salute to the audience.

Overarching the films is the deployment of what Susan Hayward describes as simulation, articulated either in the mode of pastiche or parody (Hayward 2000: 277). In arriving at these terms Hayward draws on the influential work of theorist Fredric Jameson, and in particular his study *Postmodernism: Or, the Cultural Logic of Late Capitalism* (1992). She argues that pastiche is essentially a recycling and blending of borrowed elements intended to merely please the audience through playful distraction, pacifying them in the process. This chimes with Jameson's critique of the postmodern condition as one in which the failings and inequality of late-stage capitalism are disguised by an ever-increasing cultural sleight of hand, often achieved in the form of new entertainment media forms like gaming. These forms are characterised by an apparent lack of ideological meaning, but for Jameson they are fundamentally conservative and conformist. Parody, by contrast, offers a potentially more positive interpretation in which, as Hayward suggests, the strategies of postmodernism are used to undermine the certainties of the capitalist ideological system and invite an interrogation of its values. The question arises as to how the *Crank* franchise and Statham's own role can be evaluated in relation to pastiche and parody.

An area where this might be debated is in the deliberate flouting of good taste or political correctness in the films. In *Crank* one method used by Chev Chelios to maintain his heart rate is to have sex in public with his girlfriend, Eve (Amy Smart). They make love in the middle of the street watched by a large crowd of onlookers including a busload of female tourists who cheer them on. Later in the film Eve performs oral sex on Chev in the middle of a car chase. As the reviewer in *Sight and Sound* put it: 'there's something perversely refreshing about a Hollywood action hero so lacking in respectability' (Leyland 2006: 49), further comparing Statham's performance to earlier 'monomaniacal avengers' such as Lee Marvin in *Point Blank* (1967) and Mel Gibson in its 1999 remake, *Payback*. This is continued in the second film where the couple have sex at a racetrack, employing a comic variety of positions, in front of a vast crowd on race day. Other grotesque, politically incorrect jokes in this film include a sequence where a stripper is shot in the chest and bleeds silicone and another where Chev obtains information from a heavy by inserting a greased shotgun barrel into his backside. The film's assault on the audience's moral sensibilities is continued in the relentless cartoon violence with one thug having his elbow sliced off with a machete, while another loses a hand and yet another minion is punished by cutting off his own nipples. This is further supplemented by a number of blatantly racist gags, often at the expense of Oriental characters or Hispanics whose difficulties with English are mocked with exaggerated subtitles. Chev employs a series of homophobic one-liners, and stereotypical character types appear, such as the gay couple in *High Voltage* from whose pet dog Chev steals an electric collar which he then uses to provide extra power for his battery pack. As Kim Newman describes *High Voltage*, the results are deliberately 'callous, energetic, culturally voracious, unashamedly crass, extreme beyond the point of parody and genuinely ingenious' (Newman 2009: 60). The sheer nihilism of the two films, and of Statham's gleefully destructive persona, might even be seen to combine the modes of parody and pastiche as it embraces all the kinetic energy of its various sources and references in an open attempt to provide a deliberately shallow exercise in excess and escapism; the ultimate commentary on our jaded consumerist age. Chev Chelios is the man for the times.

We have come a long way from Stanley Baker's comparatively mild expression of anomie. In my own study of Baker's career, I suggested that the appeal of the star persona he developed in the late 1950s and early 1960s was generated by several key factors including his national identity, class and the complexity of his representation of masculinity (Shail 2008). In relation to national identity, Baker's Welshness was used both to introduce melancholic notes into some of his performances and to offer a critique of dominant English masculine types. For Statham, it is his Englishness which is used to place him as an outsider in the glossy, brittle world of Los Angeles. However, while there is a certain 'otherness' in Statham's oddities of language and his unreconstructed aggression, he seems no stranger than the wildly various multi-ethnicity of the characters around him. There is no real hegemonic dominance for Statham to react against and so his Englishness, and his mock-cockney persona, operate at the characteristic level of pastiche, a source mainly for humour. This seems to be confirmed by his gradual rise through the strata of Hollywood stardom, something Baker never really achieved; a BBC news report in 2012 described Statham as 'a billion dollar box office success' (Jones 2012), while a similar Sky news report referred to him as a 'Hollywood superstar' (Vinnell 2016). In this he seems to mirror Liam Neeson who has risen to major league status in the Hollywood star system largely through action movie roles such as in the *Taken* franchise (2008–2014), films which make little of his Irish background. Class is an even less potent indicator of disruption for Statham's Chev Chelios. In the context of the 1950s and 1960s, Baker's clear working-class credentials and background marked him out as a perceived threat to the middle-class status quo, providing an obvious appeal to an audience majority. For Statham's character, class is always apparent in his accent and manner but is again used only for comedic affect. He is also comparatively affluent and self-confident throughout both *Crank* films, his class background barely causing any ripples of reaction. Class here seems largely irrelevant.

Statham's characterisations in the *Crank* films rarely offer much in the way of internal complexity, nuance or ambiguity; that is not where their appeal lies. The nearest we get to a moment of sentiment or vulnerability is at the end of the first film when Chev phones Eve during his prolonged fall from a helicopter to his apparent death. He offers her a tentative apology for his misbegotten behaviour but we don't see her receive the message, just his voice being recorded on her answering machine. However, this is completely undone in the second film when we discover that she never even got to hear his words as his voice was masked by the sound of the rushing wind as he plummeted to the ground. His confession becomes the basis for another gag. His suggestion earlier in the first film that he has had enough of his murderous lifestyle is soon forgotten as he charges into another ultra-violent melee.

Baker's characterisations, even in the superficially gung-ho heroism of *Zulu* (1964), are often tempered by a questioning of dominant male values. Baker was open in his left-wing political stance, and his roles in films like Joseph Losey's *Accident* (1967) showed an increasing subtlety, depth and willingness to challenge his own star persona. Some critics have noted an indication of greater range in Statham's more recent work as evidenced by *Hummingbird* (2013) or *Redemption* (2013), although both films remain strongly generic. Other critics have noted the increasingly mocking tone of his performances or have speculated as to his ability to escape the straightjacket of his own star persona; a *Huffington Post* report in 2011 was headlined 'Nowhere left to go' (Mendelson: 2011). Advance notices for *The Meg* (2018) in which he tackles a 75-foot-long prehistoric shark seem to confirm the parodic strategy.

If O. E. Klapp's definition of the Tough Guy suggested a 'deterioration' of the mythic hero figure in social interactions, then the cynic might argue that Jason Statham's role as Chev Chelios in the *Crank* franchise provides further evidence of this decline. Dyer's suggestion that the Tough Guy actually provides an opportunity to work through the complexities and contradictions of masculinity holds up well when applied to many classic figures from the American tradition, as well as to Stanley Baker. As film historians like Andrew Spicer have shown, Baker's persona reacted in challenging ways to the specific contexts of time and place. In more recent American cinema this might be seen in the characterisation of Jason Bourne (Matt Damon) in the *Bourne* franchise (2002–2016). When applied to Chev Chelios this form of analysis disappears in gun smoke, or perhaps is exploded. The films make little of such ideological specifics but, in line with

Jameson's notion of the postmodern condition, offer a representation which largely functions through prefabrication, intertextuality and bricolage. If this is pastiche rather than parody, in Susan Hayward's terms, then it is pastiche taken to the ultimate extreme where any notion of a moral compass or an arena of debate relating to male identity has morphed into an elaborate game. In the world of the *Crank* films these things don't seem to matter anymore. If there is an aspect that provides ideological meaning then it is pure nihilism, a sense in which there is little point in striving for meaning when distraction reigns. Perhaps Susan Jeffords was premature and it is only now that masculinity on-screen has been terminated. But then again, there is always time for another sequel.

References

Babington, B. (ed.). (2001). *British Stars and Stardom: From Alma Taylor to Sean Connery*. Manchester and New York: Manchester University Press.

Dyer, R. (1998). *Stars*. London: BFI Publishing.

Hayward, S. (2000). 'Postmodernism', in *Cinema Studies: The Key Concepts, Second Edition*. London and New York: Routledge.

IMDB.1 (n.d.) Box Office Mojo.com. *Crank*. www.boxofficemojo.com/movies/?id=crank.htm

IMDB.2 (n.d.) Box Office Mojo.com. *Crank High Voltage*. www.boxofficemojo.com/movies/?id=crank2.htm

Jameson, F. (1992). *Postmodernism: Or, the Cultural Logic of Late Capitalism*. London: Verso.

Jeffords, S. (1993). 'Can masculinity be terminated?', in Cohan, S. and Hark, I. R. (eds). *Screening the Male: Exploring Masculinities in Hollywood Cinema*. London: Routledge.

Jones, E. (2012). 'Jason Statham: billion dollar man'. *BBC News*. www.bbc.com/news/entertainment-arts-17905818 (03.05.12, accessed 12.12.17).

Leyland, M. (2006). '*Crank*'. *Sight and Sound*, 16(10) (October, 2006).

Mendelson, S. (2011). 'Nowhere left to go: why Jason Statham can't break out of the B-movie action genre'. www.huffingtonpost.com/scott-mendelson/jason-statham-movies_b_988657.html (accessed 30.09.17).

Newman, K. (2009). '*Crank: High Voltage*'. *Sight and Sound*, 19(7) (July).

Shail, R. (2008). *Stanley Baker: A Life in Film*. Cardiff: University of Wales Press.

Spicer, A. (2001). *Typical Men: The Representation of Masculinity in Popular British Cinema*. London: I. B. Tauris.

Tasker, Y. (1993). *Spectacular Bodies: Gender, Genre and the Action Cinema*. London: Routledge.

Vinnell, P. (2016). 'Hollywood superstar Jason Statham reveals his Olympic heartache'. www.skysports.com/olympics/news/15234/10548322/hollywood-superstar-jason-statham-reveals-his-olympic-heartache (accessed 23.08.17).

2

'I'm certainly not Tom Cruise or Brad Pitt': Jason Statham, fandom and a new type of (anti) hero

Renee Middlemost

Diver. Model. Music Video Dancer. Street Hustler. Actor.
While his real-life career choices may be more diverse than his acting roles, Jason Statham's on-screen persona has unquestionably confirmed his role as one of cinema's most successful contemporary action heroes. As his popularity has grown, so too has his reputation as a modern action (anti) hero, and the logical successor to the legacy of Stallone, Schwarzenegger and Willis. Yet in many ways, Statham's tongue-in-cheek acknowledgement that he is no Cruise or Pitt also imbues him with an authentic likeability beyond that of his hardman action roles, with 54 million followers of his Facebook account alone.

By reading Statham through the lens of Richard Dyer's (1998) formative work on star types, this chapter will argue that Statham has leveraged his laconic 'real-life' personality as an untrained actor, but skilled man of action, into an authentic star persona: 'Brand Statham'. This branding is grounded in the performance of uncompromising action and caters to the expectations of his fan base. Statham exemplifies the challenges of contemporary male stardom, by combining the classic action hero role with interventions across multimedia platforms. Ultimately, Statham comes to represent a new type of action hero, who subtly modifies his performance to retain fans drawn to his action persona, thereby avoiding the pitfalls of his predecessors.

Dyer and the male star: the (anti) hero

One of Dyer's key features is the designation of different star types drawn from Klapp's *Heroes, Villains and Fools* (1962). Klapp focuses on three types of star: the Good Joe, the Tough Guy and the Pin Up. Although Dyer critiques the limits of Klapp's designations of type, he discusses them at length as a starting point for reading common characterisations on-screen. If Statham is assessed through this typology, his work falls primarily into the category of the anti-hero – or 'the tough guy' (in Klapp's idiom). For Klapp, the tough guy is problematic when presented as the hero (thus, an anti-hero), due to his 'universal appeal' as one who 'cannot be beaten' which threatens the status quo and suggests the 'collapsing of moral and social categories' (Klapp 1962; Dyer 1998: 55–56). For Dyer, the collapse of moral and social categories allows for the performance and rereading of the 'contradictions of the male role, which are disguised in more traditional types (cowboys, swashbucklers, war heroes)' (1998: 49). The anti-hero is arguably the ultimate contradiction of the male role, as it complicates how we read the male protagonist, whereby 'traditional heroes do not have moral flaws. Anti-heroes do, and these flaws play a role in the unfolding drama. The presence and depiction of these flaws is the defining character feature' (Shafer and Raney 2012: 1030).

Indeed, Statham's recent roles often see him playing the tough guy imbued with various contradictions. In *Hummingbird* (aka *Redemption* 2013) he played a dramatic role as a homeless veteran engaged in a campaign of revenge, with Statham noting that,

> It is different to what I normally do; there are a lot more layers. A lot of the characters I play are invincible in some way. They are not tuned into anxiety and pain. This one still plays to my strengths, though. It isn't light years away from something I thought I could get my shoes on for. (Statham, quoted in Thorpe 2013).

Similarly, *Safe* (2012) also represents a variation of the tough guy role for which Statham is known. While critics such as Patterson (2012) were quick to dub the film: 'Safe by name, safe by nature; don't expect too many surprises from Jason Statham's new movie', others such as Dittman (2012) offered praise for his attempt at a drama/thriller outside of his normal comfort zone. *Safe* presents a contradiction of the typical loner type that Statham depicts by introducing a quasi-paternal relationship with an orphaned Chinese girl, Mei (Catherine Chan). Statham plays an ex-cage fighter whose life is ruined when the Russian mob murder his wife. After discovering that Mei is being forced to work for the same mobsters, he assumes the role of her protector and plots his revenge. Although the role seems consistent to 'Brand Statham', he insisted that 'There is a heart to the movie too, and that's my character's relationship with the little girl' (Statham, quoted in Jones 2012). The most obvious contradiction to his standard type was his comedic performance as Rick Ford in *Spy* (2015). Statham received acclaim from established critics such as Maltin (2015), who wrote: 'I never could have anticipated that this stone-faced action star would become a great comic foil, but Feig has pulled off the casting coup of the year. Statham delivers and provides one of *Spy*'s funniest running gags.' In participating in the parody of his tough guy persona, Statham contradicts the perception that action performers lack the sense of humour required to succeed in comedy.

Dyer notes that these apparent contradictions in type allow the viewer 'to make connections with other specific aspects of cultural meaning and to explore the ideological complications these connections bring with them' (1998: 49). The anti-hero narrative (Shafer and Raney 2012) permits the exploration of contradictions in character type, and how these are impacted by context and cultural meaning. As Shafer and Raney (2012: 1029–1030) write, Statham's frequent portrayal of anti-heroes, is as 'morally complex, or ambiguous protagonists' which allows audiences to interpret modern masculinity as performative and fluid, rather than static and fixed, with them further explaining,

> As protagonists, antiheroes display qualities of both heroes and villains; acting in morally ambiguous, and at times unjustifiable ways, if even to reach noble goals. These characteristics can be embodied in a variety of ways across narratives. Sometimes antiheroes are revenge-seeking loners who thumb their noses at authority. Some antiheroes are well-intending but flawed; others are criminal but redeemable. Regardless of these differences, antiheroes serve as protagonists who generally act in questionable ways; modelling (some) bad behaviour even if for justifiable reasons. But despite clearly doing improper things for (at times)

corrupt reasons, antiheroes still function as 'forces of good' in many narratives. (Shafer and Raney 2012: 1029–1030)

When considering Statham's career to date, his roles as a contradiction of type correlate with the timing of his debut to produce a powerful statement about contemporary masculinity.

Statham's appeal

Statham's acting career as the 'go to' action man is closely linked to the timing of his emergence as an actor. After the dominance of the 'hard body', action stars began to wane, and the 1990s was marked by what Jeffords (1993) has dubbed the 'big switch', where younger, sensitive male protagonists became popular, exemplified by the rise of stars such as Keanu Reeves, Leonardo Di Caprio and Ben Affleck in action roles. Statham emerged with a new crop of British actors marked by a perceived authentic embodiment of the roles they played. Guy Ritchie was the architect of this movement; like Statham, his success with films such as *Lock, Stock and Two Smoking Barrels* (1998) was attributed to their confluence with 'lad culture'. As Gill (2003: 37) observes, the 'new lad' was characterised as anti-aspirational, and seems to owe a lot to a particular classed articulation of masculinity. (whereby) the '"new lad" is a reaction against "new man", as well as a backlash against the feminism that gave birth to him'.

The emergence of Statham, and other authentic (untrained) actors such as Vinnie Jones in *Lock, Stock and Two Smoking Barrels* and *Snatch* (2000), could be considered as a desire to return to a performance of masculinity focused on homosocial relationships, and unconcerned with being politically correct. Gill contends that, as an interpretation of contemporary masculinity the new lad may be more ambiguous – and thus, following from Dyer (1998) representations of lad culture, imply a further contradiction to the tough guy type. Citing Tasker's (1993) observations regarding the polysemic nature of texts, Gill (2003: 47–48) posits the idea that filmic representation of the male action stars of the 1980s (and here it could be suggested, those like Statham who began in the same mould) 'should be understood in terms of the difficulty of maintaining masculine physicality in the microchip era. Thus, the muscular masculinities on offer *simultaneously reassert*, *mourn*, and *hysterically state* male power, whilst also *parodying* it' (emphasis in original).

The timing of Statham's ascent is informed by the debate about representations of contemporary masculinity both on-screen and in the press. At the height of the new lad movement, Statham's appearance in Ritchie's films and resulting popularity proved that audiences were waiting for a new type of action hero to emerge, and Statham appeared to fit that bill.

While not associated with the worst excesses of lad culture, Statham famously gained his role in *Lock, Stock and Two Smoking Barrels* by convincing Ritchie to purchase a fake Rolex during his audition (Jones 2012). Ritchie was seemingly so enamoured with Statham's skills that he was cast immediately. Ritchie's British crime heist films established Statham as the 'go to' actor for street-smart action thrills, while arousing debate over Ritchie's vision of contemporary masculinity, and the lad magazine culture from which it seemed to be derived (Simpson 2000). After a string of supporting roles, Statham headlined *The Transporter* (2002) as a mercenary hired to move goods, and fan favourite *Crank* (2006), a ludicrous, adrenaline-packed action film about a man on borrowed time – or as one critic claimed '*Speed* ... but Statham is the bus' (Corcoran 2006). Statham's choices at this stage of his career hinted at his alignment with 1980s action stars; this compatibility became evident with his addition to *The Expendables* franchise (2010–), a vehicle for an ensemble cast of classic action heroes with Stallone at the helm. Of his role in *The Expendables*, Statham (De Medeiros 2013) remarked:

> It's a huge role. Some people dubbed it a passing of the torch from Stallone. I'm conscious of his endorsement. It couldn't come from a higher place. It's something I really want to fulfil. If he sees me as someone that has the chops to fill that sort of position ... it was one of the greatest compliments I could ever get.

Statham has cultivated a close working relationship with Stallone, which has become a mentorship of sorts. Stallone's regard for Statham culminated in his casting in *Homefront* (2013), in a part he had written for himself. Edwards (2013) suggests that Statham is following the 'Stallone model' of establishing his own production company to develop projects he is interested in, and thus ensuring the longevity of his (action) career. The connection between Statham and Stallone is meaningful when read in terms of academic work on the ageing male action hero.

Gates (2010) and Evans (2015) discuss the distinct challenges faced by the ageing heroes of the 1980s when diversifying beyond the action roles for which they are famous. Gates highlights Stallone's fluctuating capital, contrasting his approach to the ageing male body with that of Clint Eastwood, and the difference in their career trajectories. She believes that: 'Unlike Eastwood, Stallone had not successfully transitioned to the new social climate because he had not embraced aging to add vulnerability and seriousness to his tough guy persona; instead he kept his body pumped up' (Gates 2010: 280). In the press, Stallone has been frank in recognising the difficulty he faced making films in the late 1990s, 'because audiences did not like his attempts to embody contemporary ideals of masculinity that moved him outside of his type: "I'm a stereotype. I can't break away from that"' (Gates 2010: 279). Although Statham is two decades younger than Stallone, his future is potentially problematic if he does not evolve beyond his iconic action roles, as he reflects:

> There's a shelf life for everything, I suppose, but you have to keep people guessing ... As long as you make entertaining films, that's the goal. And as long as people get their money's worth they'll go back, and if they don't you'll be on the shelf like many others. (Statham, quoted in Shoard 2011)

Statham's early career trajectory and alignment with Stallone as both co-star and successor highlights the precarity of the ageing male action star.

Evans (2015: 25) also reflects upon the reappearance of 1980s action heroes and their relationship to time, noting how they are 'not only out of place, but conspicuously out of time'. The resurrection of action heroes (who have clearly aged) in their original franchises (Stallone in *Rocky* and *Rambo*; Willis in *Die Hard*; Schwarzenegger in *Terminator*) disrupts 'adventure time' in which protagonists are 'ageless' (Flanagan in Evans 2015: 26–27). The disruption of adventure time, and discourses around ageing male action heroes is important to the narrative of Statham's rise. By affiliating himself with the style of 1980s action icons, Statham was initially 'out of time' – his immediate popularity with audiences can therefore be attributed to filling the gap left by the hard body action heroes in the late 1990s. This historical context influenced Statham's rise to stardom – and yet, he has continued to successfully bridge the gap as both the natural successor to the action star throne by collaborating in franchises with both action icons (*The Expendables*) and his action contemporaries such as Dwayne Johnson (*Furious 7*;

and forthcoming *Hobbs and Shaw*) to ensure the constancy of his brand.

Statham distinguishes himself from his predecessors for several key reasons. In all of his roles, he appears to share a knowing wink with the audience – he has repeatedly stated that he is not a great actor and has never taken lessons (De Medeiros 2013). Statham is famous for performing most of his own stunts, and has declared that he aims to be great at action:

> Some roles suit me better than others, no doubt about it ... It actually takes time to perfect this genre and to be able to do it with confidence. I'm still working on it ... You're never going to get me in a period drama, put it that way. But I do care about a good script, because all I can do is what is put in front of me, and all I can choose from, role wise, is what I'm offered. (Statham, in Jones 2012)

It is this attempt at portraying, however carefully composed his words might be, a sense of realism, whereby Statham clearly realises his limitations as an actor, that has seemingly led to his popularity with both fans and producers. Executive producer Stuart Ford suggests it is Statham's skill in the action arena, combined with his authenticity that is the reason for his success. 'He's not manufactured, and there's an honesty about him when you watch him. That's partly because he does his own stunts, but I think he's believable emotionally as well ... He has universal appeal and that's why he makes so much at the box office' (Ford, in Jones 2012). The perceived authenticity of a celebrity is, as Dyer (1998) observed, central to their appeal. As previously noted, Statham both exudes and cultivates this authenticity in a number of ways, including his commitment to performing his own stunts, and low-key social media profile. As Marshall contends:

> Fans continue to try to strip away the veneers of performance and publicity to find these true versions of celebrities, and the online world constructs the parasocial interpersonal pathways for an apparent intensified connection. The reading of the 'true' public self through the celebrity is now linked to an audience/user pedagogic function of constructing and producing the self, as well as the continuing celebrity effect of producing emulative desire in an audience. (Marshall 2010: 44)

Like Stallone before him, Statham's true public self is often conflated with the roles he plays. This conflation can be attributed to his minimalist approach to social media, and unwilling participation in the artifice of celebrity,

> I try and keep my stuff private. I don't want to be a part of that world. It's just too much, it's a headache. Once you expose your private life, if you give one little bit, the floodgates are open and everyone's got a free range for you. (Statham, quoted in Shoard 2011)

For this reason, Statham inhabits the traditional 'star' role rather than the 'celebrity'. As Holmes (2005: 9) remarks, the two terms are frequently interchangeable in popular discourse, and she notes the ambiguity of 'celebrity' and how it is structured 'by discourses of cultural value; used to indicate a more fleeting conception of fame [or used] when fame rests predominantly on the private life of the person, as opposed to their performing presence'.

Part of Statham's authenticity as an action star is his commitment to performing most of his own stunts. He has frequently spoken of his respect for stunt coordinators (Pulver 2013), explaining that his childhood dream was to become a stunt man (Chiarella 2015). In recent years Statham has called for an Oscar Award category for stunt coordinators, citing the amount of responsibility they have, where 'for some of the greatest entertainment in action movies … these are the unsung heroes' (Miller 2013). Statham also maintains that despite their popularity, his participation in a superhero franchise is unlikely, as he favours 'true stories' (Shoard 2011). As a fan of action films, and part of his campaign for a stunt Oscar category, Statham has been vocal in highlighting the lack of authenticity in superhero films as a turn off.

> I could take my grandma and put her in a cape, and they'll put her on a green screen and they'll have stunt doubles come in and do all the action. Anybody can do it. They're relying on stunt doubles and green screen and $200 million budgets. It's all CGI created. To me, it's not authentic. (Statham, quoted in Fox 2015)

As an actor who does not actively court celebrity status or popularity, Statham is able to speak freely, retaining his position as a credible everyman for his fans. By constructing an authentic public persona through the techniques identified, Statham inhabits the star role, rather than the celebrity, as outlined by Holmes (2005). In assuming the tough guy 'type' and bridging the gap between classic and modern action stars, Statham has established himself as a new type of action hero in four distinct ways: diversification; participation in franchises; studio support; and multimedia reach.

Diversification

Previous generations of male action stars have found the challenge of revising their persona as the tough guy insurmountable. When director Paul Feig cast Statham in a comedic role in *Spy* (2015), critics were shocked at his hilarious portrayal of Rick Ford, a secret agent that is a caricature of his signature hardman role (Alexander 2015). When explaining his casting decision, Feig emphasised Statham's comedy potential (Chiarella 2015):

> Jason makes every movie better. I hate comedy that's trying to be funny. Jason doesn't have to try. He gets it. In every movie, people pick up on his good-natured ways. And I've known he was funny ever since that first *Crank* movie. *Crank* is ridiculous. He's so good in it.

Statham's performance was regarded as a highlight in a very funny film, and has led to discussions for an expanded role in *Spy 2* (Libby 2017). With his initial foray into comedy Statham has succeeded where most 1980s action heroes have struggled – in branching out and playing against type (Gates 2010; Brew 2015). By playing a caricature, Statham cleverly tests the fan response to a comedic role, as it is not so far removed from the characters that fans love – thus there is not the same backlash that stars such as Stallone and Schwarzenegger received when playing dramatically against type. Statham has also expressed interest in more dramatic film roles like *Hummingbird*; however, he is savvy enough to evolve gradually. 'The dilemma is that you have to do what people want to see' (Statham, quoted in Heritage 2013).

Statham has proven discerning in actively courting the Chinese market for action films. His presence in the Chinese film market began in 2002 with *The Transporter* (directed by Hong Kong filmmaker Corey Yuen), and expanded significantly with the release of *Furious 7* in 2015. Statham's recent role in *The Meg* (2018) is also a diversification of sorts. While Statham portrays the same action-based anti-hero character, this film is a co-production with China. In early 2018 *The Hollywood Reporter* announced that Statham had signed a deal with STX Entertainment and Tencent Pictures to produce and star in a Chinese co-produced action film under development (Brzeski 2018). Statham's move into the Chinese market demonstrates his potential to convert his action persona into a transnational brand.

Statham also ensures his longevity as a star by appearing in successful action franchises. *The Transporter*; *The Mechanic*; *Crank*; *Spy*; *The Expendables*; and *The Fast and the Furious* have all produced sequels, or have sequels in production. In early 2018 it was announced that the on-screen rapport between Statham and Johnson in *The Fate of the Furious* (2017) would result in a spin-off for their characters *Hobbs and Shaw* (2019) (Alexander 2017). Statham has suggested in interviews his willingness to revisit fan favourite Chev Chelios in *Crank 3* (Brew 2015); and Paul Feig is planning an expanded role for Statham's Rick Ford in the mooted *Spy 2*. Statham has also openly expressed a desire to play 'a very, very different' James Bond (Dockterman 2015), should the opportunity arise – but only Bond (not a Bond villain), to expand beyond his portrayal of villainous Deckard Shaw in *Furious 7*. If Statham's Bond becomes a reality, he will ensure his immortality as an action hero in the ultimate action hero film franchise. Statham's participation in franchises illustrates his evolution as a modern action hero; unlike the 'lone wolf' (Moore 2014) roles that marked his early career,

> at the end of the day, the insurance of working with a big, already successful franchise just gives you the chance to do other things, on a more personal level. So without doing the big blockbusters I wouldn't be able to find the money to go after little projects that I want to do. (Statham, quoted in Edwards 2013)

By starring as part of an ensemble cast, Statham has enhanced his status as a box office draw, ensuring the continued support of industry partners.

Although he has been criticised for only playing one type of role (Gabbatt 2015), fans of Statham have fondly labelled him a 'genre all by himself' (Jones 2012). 'We try to give the fans what they want. Let's make a movie, have some fun doing it, visit some nice countries, and give people 90 minutes of entertainment' (Statham, quoted in Alexander 2016). The acknowledgement of the desires of his fan base is central to Statham's appeal. Statham is rare for his ability to inspire a huge home viewing audience, resulting in sequels to films with only mediocre box office success, such as *Mechanic: Resurrection* (2016). Media analyst Paul Dergarabedian from Comscore stated: 'When you drill deeper into the numbers, and tally the additional revenues, it becomes clear that the Jason Statham business is a great business to be in' (Alexander 2016). Film studio Lionsgate have openly stated their support for Statham as one of their most successful performers. In 2012, the BBC reported that his films have grossed over $1 billion worldwide (Jones 2012); Lionsgate, who have produced more than eleven films with Statham declared: 'Every single movie we've done with Jason Statham has been profitable. We're big believers in Jason, and his fan base is getting even bigger' (Constantine, quoted in Alexander 2016). Lionsgate also have a videogame development division to capitalise on the studio's youth-oriented franchises *Twilight* (2008), *The Hunger Games* (2012) and *Divergent* (2014). The connection between Statham and Stallone identified earlier is strengthened by their joint association with Lionsgate. Coincidentally, Lionsgate greenlit *Rocky Balboa* (2006) for Stallone after a lack of interest elsewhere; their rationale was an appeal to the youth market who continue to purchase videogames featuring Rocky (Evans 2015: 30). After releasing *The Expendables* in 2010, Lionsgate appear to be an ally for action stars, and their diversification across platforms; given Statham's existing involvement in videogames, this could represent a further collaboration with the company, and expansion of his brand (Variety 2014).

In line with international viewing trends favouring binge watching and quality television, Statham's next project is an adaptation of novel *Viva La Madness*, acquired on behalf of his production company. Originally conceived as a film, it will now be a ten-part television series, made in conjunction with Netflix and Sky UK (Daniels 2017). *Viva La Madness* is an action/comedy hybrid sequel to *Layer Cake* (2004) that allows Statham to diversify, while retaining his core audience (Leane 2015).

The most notable way in which Statham has diversified across platforms is his participation in multimedia texts. While videogames based on action characters such as the Terminator are common, Statham's level of direct involvement is rare. Prior to his Hollywood ascent, Statham voiced characters in *Red Faction II* (2002, as Shrike) and *Call of Duty* (2003, as Sergeant Waters). These voice roles remain congruous with the Statham persona as a tough guy; thus, he lends the authenticity of his brand to these appearances. His on-screen persona reportedly inspired the rendering of the villain Vulture in *Ultimate Spider-Man* with writer

Brian Michael Bendis instructing artist Mark Bagley to base his drawings on Statham (Potts 2015; Leane 2016). In 2015 Statham became Glu Mobile's first male celebrity partner to have an Android mobile videogame created featuring his name, voice and likeness (following Kim Kardashian, Katy Perry, Kylie and Kendall Jenner, Britney Spears and Nicki Minaj). Statham's partnership with Glu Mobile further diversifies his portfolio, while increasing his fanbase, as Glu Mobile's celebrity gaming titles reach nearly 650 million social followers (Shaul 2015). *Sniper X: Kill Confirmed* invites the player to team with Statham on missions as part of an elite military squad/first-person shooter game, consistent with his most admired film roles. Glu Mobile announced:

> Jason Statham's action persona and strong social following make him an ideal partner for *Sniper X: Kill Confirmed*. We look forward to launching this new title to a global audience of mobile action gaming fans, including Jason's social audience of more than 54 million followers. I'm pleased to welcome Jason to Glu's celebrity portfolio and believe this new partnership will cement Glu's leadership in the Hollywood gaming space. (Shaul 2015)

Although Statham has embraced multimedia platforms, he maintains a connection to stars of the past by cultivating a mystique that few others achieve. While Statham has active Instagram and Facebook accounts, these are updated infrequently, and primarily feature photoshoots, promotional material for upcoming releases and outtakes from behind the scenes, rather than his 'real life'. Statham does not reveal his private life online, he does not use Twitter and partakes in few interviews (Heritage 2013). By maintaining this sense of authenticity as a 'real person' who values their privacy, and minimises use of social media, Statham ensures the interest of his fans remains focused on his tough guy persona, while affording him the possibility of a real life off-screen.

Conclusion

At the beginning of this chapter it was argued that Statham's rise to prominence has been a combination of hard work, authenticity and serendipity. He is now arguably one of the most recognisable action stars internationally for his unique star persona, known as 'Brand Statham'. Despite his global success, Statham insists that

> nothing's really changed, but I hope I am quite approachable, you know? I'm certainly not Tom Cruise or Brad Pitt. And if people

come up and say they like the movies you're in, it's a great compliment. But it doesn't sort of create much of a hindrance to go anywhere, as of now. (Statham, quoted in Head 2003)

This chapter has highlighted the career trajectory of Jason Statham, and how it is heavily imbued with the authenticity of his tough guy persona, as one of Dyer's types. By inhabiting this role throughout his career, fans have grown to rely on the Statham 'genre', despite criticisms that he can only play one type. By creating a reliable brand, Statham has proven himself to the industry as one of their most profitable performers, filling the gap left by ageing action stars. The timing of Statham's ascent coincides with public debate about contemporary masculinities, and the desire of audiences to see a new type of hero, with the best features of the old guard still intact. While filling the action hero role, Statham has ensured his longevity by subtly diversifying his acting roles, appearing in franchises, gaining industry support, and fostering his persona across multimedia platforms. In these four ways, Statham sets himself up to avoid the pitfalls of the 'ageing action star'. By varying his roles in subtle ways that enhance his persona as an authentic everyman, Statham embodies a new type of hero beyond that of the 1980s stars, and perhaps even beyond Cruise and Pitt.

References

Alexander, B. (2015). 'Comedy genius! Even Jason Statham is surprised he delivered funny blows in *Spy*'. *USA Today*. www.usatoday.com/story/life/entertainthis/2015/06/07/even-jason-statham-is-surprised-he-delivered-comedic-shots-to-the-funny-bone-in-spy/77507182/ (08.06.15, accessed 15.02.18).

Alexander, B. (2016). 'Here's why *The Mechanic* was resurrected for a sequel'. *USA Today*. www.usatoday.com/story/life/movies/2016/08/23/why-is-there-a-mechanic-sequel-jason-statham/89110234/?siteID=je6NUbpObpQ-ycaSsOs9Roe6GjTzll6fvQ (24.08.16, accessed 19.02.17).

Alexander, B. (2017). 'Dwayne Johnson, Jason Statham to star in *Fast and Furious* spinoff'. *USA Today*. www.usatoday.com/story/life/movies/2017/10/05/fast-furious-spinoff-2019/737998001/ (10.10.17, accessed 15.02.18).

Brew, S. (2015). 'Jason Statham interview: *Spy, Crank 3, Viva La Madness*'. *Den of Geek*. www.denofgeek.com/movies/jason-statham/jason-statham-interview-spy-crank-3-viva-la-madness (01.06.15, accessed 19.01.18).

Brzeski, P. (2018). 'Jason Statham developing action film with STX, China's tencent pictures'. *The Hollywood Reporter*. www.hollywoodreporter.com/news/jason-statham-developing-action-film-stx-chinas-tencent-pictures-1074928 (16.01.18, accessed 19.02.18).

Chiarella, T. (2015). 'Jason Statham, for your amusement'. *Esquire*. www.esquire.com/entertainment/movies/interviews/a35122/jason-statham-cover-story-0615/ (26.05.15, accessed 15.01.18).

Corcoran, M. (2006). 'Action bloke'. *The New York Times*. www.nytimes.com/2006/09/03/fashion/03NITE.html (03.09.06, accessed 19.02.18).

Daniels, N. (2017). 'Netflix sets up UK shoot for Jason Statham drama'. *KFTV News*. www.kftv.com/news/2017/12/14/netflix-sets-up-uk-shoot-for-jason-statham-drama- (14.12.17, accessed 18.01.18).

De Medeiros, M. (2013). 'Jason Statham in his own words'. *Men's Fitness*. www.mensfitness.com/life/entertainment/jason-statham-in-his-own-words (accessed 19.02.18).

Dittman, E. (2012). 'Action film star Jason Statham is no longer playing it *Safe*'. *Digital Journal*. www.digitaljournal.com/article/331870 (30.08.12, accessed 19.01.18).

Dockterman, E. (2015). 'Jason Statham wants to play James Bond'. *Time*. time.com/3904863/jason-statham-spy-james-bond/ (02.06.15, accessed 14/1/18).

Dyer, R. (1998) *Stars*. London: BFI Publishing.

Edwards, M. (2013). 'Jason Statham interview: *Homefront*, Stallone & more'. *Den of Geek*. www.denofgeek.com/movies/homefront/28436/jason-statham-interview-homefront-stallone-expendables (03.12.13, accessed 29.08.17).

Evans, N. (2015). 'No genre for old men? The politics of aging and the male action hero'. *Canadian Journal of Film Studies*, 24(1), 25–44.

Fox, J. D. (2015). 'Robert Downey Jr, Chris Evans, and Mark Ruffalo are as tough as Jason Statham's grandma, according to Jason Statham'. *Vulture*. www.vulture.com/2015/06/jason-statham-thinks-marvel-movies-are-for-wimps.html (05.06.15, accessed 19.12.17).

Gabbatt, A. (2015). 'Jason Statham: our last action hero (50 million Facebook fans can't be wrong)'. *Guardian*. www.theguardian.com/film/2015/may/20/jason-statham-action-hero-spy (21.05.15, accessed 15.02.18).

Gates, P. (2010). 'Acting his age? The resurrection of the 80s action heroes and their aging stars'. *Quarterly Review of Film and Video*, 27(4), 276–289.

Gill, R. (2003). 'Power and the production of subjects: a genealogy of the New Man and the New Lad'. *The Sociological Review*, 51, 34–56.

Head, S. (2003). 'An interview with Jason Statham'. http://au.ign.com/articles/2003/06/07/an-interview-with-jason-statham (06.06.03, accessed 20.10.17).

Heritage, S. (2013). 'The secret life of Jason Statham'. *Guardian*. www.theguardian.com/film/2013/jun/21/secret-life-jason-statham (21.06.13, accessed 12.12.17).
Holmes, S. (2005). 'Starring … Dyer?: Revisiting star studies and contemporary celebrity culture'. *Westminster Papers in Communication and Culture*, 2(2), 6–21.
Jones, E. (2012). 'Jason Statham: billion dollar man'. *BBC News*. www.bbc.com/news/entertainment-arts-17905818 (03.05.12, accessed 12.12.17).
Klapp, O. E. (1962). *Heroes, Villains and Fools*. Englewood Cliff, NJ: Prentice Hall.
Leane, R. (2015). '*Viva La Madness*: Jason Statham's *Layer Cake* sequel moves to TV'. *Den of Geek*. www.denofgeek.com/tv/viva-la-madness/36989/viva-la-madness-jason-stathams-layer-cake-sequel-moves-to-tv (18.09.15, accessed 24.01.18).
Leane, R. (2016). '*Spider-Man: Homecoming* – just who is Vulture?' *Den of Geek*. www.denofgeek.com/uk/movies/spider-man-homecoming/43278/spider-man-homecoming-just-who-is-vulture (08.09.16, accessed 19.2.19).
Libby, D. (2017). '*Spy 2* is happening, with plenty more Jason Statham, get the details'. *Cinema Blend*. www.cinemablend.com/news/1525979/spy-2-is-happening-with-plenty-more-jason-statham-get-the-details (accessed 29.01.18).
Maltin, L. (2015). 'Melissa McCarthy scores a hit in *Spy*'. http://leonardmaltin.com/melissa-mccarthy-scores-a-hit-in-spy/ (04.06.15, accessed 19.1.18).
Marshall, P. D. (2010). 'The promotion and presentation of the self: celebrity as marker of presentational media'. *Celebrity Studies*, 1(1), 35–48.
Miller, J. (2013). 'Jason Statham says stuntmen deserve Oscars if 'poncy' actors faking it get them'. *Vanity Fair*. www.vanityfair.com/hollywood/2013/11/jason-statham-stunt-oscars (19.11.13, accessed 02.02.18).
Moore, S. (2014). 'The 5 types of action hero, explained'. *Esquire*. www.esquire.com/entertainment/movies/a29702/action-hero-types/ (15.08.14, accessed 24.01.18).
Patterson, J. (2012). 'Jason Statham, he's an unpreposterous action hero'. *Guardian*. www.theguardian.com/film/2012/apr/28/jason-statham-safe-action-hero (28.04.12, accessed 19.02.19).
Potts, M. (2015). '15 things you didn't know about Jason Statham'. *What Culture*. http://whatculture.com/film/15-things-you-didnt-know-about-jason-statham?page=7 (accessed 19.12.17).
Pulver, A. (2013). 'Jason Statham calls for stunt Oscars'. *Guardian*. www.theguardian.com/film/2013/nov/22/jason-statham-stunt-oscars. (22.11.13, accessed 19.12.17).

Shafer, D. and Raney, A. (2012). 'Exploring how we enjoy antihero narratives'. *Journal of Communication*, 62(2012), 1028–1046.

Shaul, B. (2015). 'Glu Mobile launches Sniper X with Jason Statham on mobile'. www.adweek.com/digital/glu-mobile-launches-sniper-x-with-jason-statham-on-mobile/ (accessed 03.01.18).

Shoard, C. (2011). 'Jason Statham: "Me in a cape? Tight tights? Nah!"'. *Guardian*. www.theguardian.com/film/2011/sep/15/jason-statham-interview. (16.09.18, accessed 11.01.18).

Simpson, M. (2000). 'Just what sort of a guy's guy is Guy Ritchie?'. *The Independent*. www.google.com.au/amp/www.independent.co.uk/arts-entertainment/films/features/just-what-sort-of-a-guys-guy-is-guy-ritchie-697331.html%3famp (26.08.00, accessed 11.01.18).

Tasker, Y. (1993). *Spectacular Bodies: Gender, Genre and the Action Cinema*. London: Routledge.

Thorpe, V. (2013). 'Jason Statham breaks into new acting territory with Hummingbird'. *Guardian*. www.theguardian.com/film/2013/jul/06/jason-statham-hummingbird-british-action (06.01.13, accessed 29.11.01.18).

Variety. (2014). 'Lionsgate taps nerdist's Peter Levin to head interactive ventures, games'. https://variety.com/2014/digital/news/lionsgate-taps-nerdists-peter-levin-to-head-interactive-ventures-games-1201167600/ (30.04.14, accessed 19.01.18).

3

The power of Statham

Paul Feig

I know this is a very scholarly book that strives to find intellectual theorems to analyze the never-ending appeal of Jason Statham. But since I'm a neither a scholar nor particularly intellectual, I can only approach the whole topic of Mr. Statham from one angle …
  I love the guy.
  I can't even tell you what was the first Jason Statham movie I watched. It wasn't *Lock, Stock and Two Smoking Barrels* because I didn't end up seeing that movie until years after it came out, once my Statham obsession had led me down the road of watching every single frame of film he's ever appeared in. (Yes, even the Uwe Boll one.) It might have been *Crank* or it might have been *The Transporter*. All I know is that once I saw him kicking ass and commanding the screen, I was hooked. He has a presence that few other actors have. He owns the screen when he's on it. You love to listen to his voice. You can't stop watching his face. You marvel at his physicality. And you weirdly want to be his friend, no matter how tough of a character he's playing.
  In short, he is the very definition of a movie star.
  As a director, pretty much every day of my career, I deal with the question of what makes an audience want to watch an actor. As a filmmaker, I live and die on how effective my actors are in my projects. I have to cast the right person for the right role and if I do it correctly, magic happens and the audience is pulled along with the story. If I do it wrong, the audience doesn't quite

know why but they will begin to have a hard time connecting with the journey I'm trying to take them on. And physical beauty has little to nothing to do with who's right and who's wrong for a role. Even if the role is non-speaking, there is something that is required from every human being who appears up on that movie screen in order to make the movie work its best.

Charisma.

I've been in more casting sessions in my career than I can count. I work with amazing casting directors who bring in a range of performers, from established character actors to up-and-coming future stars to fresh-off-the-bus newbies. Having been an actor for many years and having suffered through thousands of auditions, I try to give all actors I see the maximum amount of latitude and encouragement. Auditioning is a hard and slightly ridiculous process. You stand in a white-walled room across from dispassionate producers sitting in comfortable chairs while a casting director videotapes you as you sit on a hard, folding chair performing lines in which everyone has to imagine you're actually in a realistic setting that will be filmed weeks or months later with full production values. As a fly on the wall, the whole thing looks absurd. But it's in these rooms that charisma makes itself apparent.

When I'm casting, I'm trying to give everyone the benefit of the doubt. So, I attempt to look beyond the strange set-up I'm sitting in and place myself with the actor in the movie. And because I work with the top casting directors who only bring in people they know are good and viable actors, I find myself usually saying to myself after their auditions, 'Yeah, that person could work for this role' or 'Maybe that person could do a good job with this'. And because of this, I'll have a long list of 'maybes.'

But I'm usually not terribly excited about any of them. It's more of an 'if I had to decide on my actors right now, I could live with one of these.' Which is a nice way of saying I'd be compromising.

It's right around this point in the process that an actor will walk in, and she or he will be so good, so perfect, so compelling, so *charismatic* in the role, that she or he will literally blow those other maybes off of my list.

It's all about charisma, that indefinable quality that makes you sit forward when someone appears, makes you listen closer when they talk, makes you care more while you're watching them and makes you want to keep watching them do whatever it is they're doing. But that charisma has to come across on the screen. It's one of the reasons we videotape auditions. Because some people have oodles of charisma in real life. They can walk into a room and light up the place and turn heads. But that doesn't always translate to the movie screen. I've auditioned actors and been blown away in that all-white room and then sent the videotape to my fellow producers and studio executives and had their response be lukewarm at best. Then, confused, I'll watch the tape and see that whatever charisma was there in the room doesn't exist on-screen. The camera didn't pick it up. That's how slippery big screen charisma can be.

It's the same for physicality. We have a saying in the business that certain people's faces just make sense on-screen. It's another way of saying, 'The camera loves you.' I've met people who are quite unremarkable physically but when they step in front of the camera, they suddenly have the most compelling faces you've ever seen. It's all part of a mystical, magical, ethereal stew that can't be predicted and can't be manufactured. As another famous saying goes, 'Either you have it or you don't.' Jason Statham has it. Buckets of it. It's coming out of every pore of his body. It flies off the screen and makes you care about every situation he's in, no matter how insane or sometimes ridiculous it is. It makes him the only person you really watch when he's sharing the scene with other actors. You truly can't stop watching the guy. He commands the screen like the biggest movie legends.

That is the very definition of charisma.

However, it's not the only ingredient for total on-screen success. There's one extra element that, if present, will make a movie star completely beloved by an audience for years to come. To wit ...

My wife and I started to devour all things Statham about twelve years ago. I had a kids' movie I made called *Unaccompanied Minors* that was up for a Taurus stunt award. At the ceremony, they showed clips of scenes from our competitors. One was for a movie called *Crank*. The stunt that was up for an award was Jason Statham in a medical gown standing up on the seat of a motorcycle as it sped down a street. The image was so bizarre (the stunt ended up beating my movie, by the way) that I told my wife, 'We *have* to watch that!' It was later that night as we watched this truly insane (and insanely entertaining) film that it hit me.

Jason Statham is funny.

Or, more accurately, he knows not to take himself too seriously. In *Crank*, he has to keep his heart rate up at insanely high levels or he will die due to a drug that has been injected into him. And so, he spends the movie jacking himself up in all kinds of ways including putting car battery jumper cables on his tongue, having sex in front of a busload of Asian tourists and by the end, falling thousands of feet from a helicopter, landing on the pavement and *still* not dying.

Now, there's no way any movie star could do that and not realize that it's truly ridiculous. Many movie stars wouldn't take the role, fearing for their credibility or Oscar worthiness. They'd worry their gravitas as a serious actor would be damaged. But Jason took the role and he embraced it. He played it real. He committed to it. And there's no way he didn't realize just how funny it all was.

He's willing to laugh at himself, to look at us in the audience and say, 'You and I know this is ridiculous but it's also wildly entertaining and so I'm going to play this like it's the most real thing in the world and you're going to invest in it like it's really happening and we're all going to have a ton of fun and thrills'.

And that, my friends, is what I believe is the power of Jason Statham. He's wildly charismatic on the screen and he knows how to have fun with this fact. He knows he can get away with almost anything on-screen because, in the best sense, we will never really take it too seriously. We will be engaged in it and affected by it and thrilled by it, but we'll never feel like he's lost perspective on it. He seems to be having fun, or at least has no problem with us having fun with what he's doing. We're happy when he's beating up the bad guys. We're thrilled when he saves the day. And we laugh whenever he wants us to.

It was because of all this that I decided to put the Statham magic to the test in my 2015 movie, *Spy*.

In 2013, I took advantage of one of the perks of being a movie director – I set up a general meeting with Jason Statham. A general meeting is just what it sounds like. If there's an actor that you either want to meet or who wants to meet you, you sit down with them and simply get to know each other in a general sense. I really love general meetings because many times I'll get ideas for characters I want to write for the specific actor across from me, once I get to know her or his personality and peccadilloes. I've gone into general meetings with a limited preconception of what that particular actor has to offer and then once I see who she or he truly is, I realize there's other unexpected parts of that actor's personality that I can mine and showcase. There's nothing more fun to me than surprising an audience with a new side of an actor they thought they knew everything about. And so, I love to use these general meetings to discover those epiphanies.

However, with all that said, I set the meeting because I just *really* wanted to meet Jason Statham. I'd been dying to put him in a movie for years but since I do comedy, I knew I had to figure out the perfect role for him, a role that could showcase what I hoped was the sense of humor I was sure he had. So, I set up a general meeting for Jason and me.

As the day approached, I was more nervous than I had ever been to meet anybody in my life. I kept playing out scenarios in my head. What if he's really mean? What if he thinks I'm just some idiot and resents that I summoned him all the way across town to my offices when, with him being the big movie star, I should have driven to *his* house to meet him? What if he beats me up? I didn't know. I had only seen his movies and had never seen him interviewed. Jason Statham could be the exact same guy that he is in his movies, hell-bent on vengeance, and now I was some Hollywood weasel who needed to have vengeance exacted upon me. I could be *Transporter*ed right there in my own office.

My stomach was churning.

When my assistant finally buzzed my office and said, 'Jason Statham is here,' my heart started to pound. This was it. I was going to meet my hero.

My office has mostly glass walls and if I walk to the center of it, I can see who's waiting in our lobby area. I looked and there was Jason Statham sitting in one of our rather garish purple swivel chairs, reading a magazine. His face was set and serious, and I could see the famous Statham scowl as he skimmed the pages of a weeks old *Hollywood Reporter*. This is it, I said to myself. He's already angry and he's just going to stare at me during the meeting and answer my questions with a terse 'yes' or 'no' as he sat there thinking, 'What the fuck am I doing in this Hollywood lightweight's office?' The day of reckoning was here. It was time to pay the price for my summoning of The Great One to my Burbank digs.

I opened my door and walked over to him. 'Jason?' I said, trying to sound both cool and friendly (and not terrified), 'I'm Paul.'

He looked up from the magazine and suddenly the famous deadpan Statham face cracked open into a big toothy smile and he said, 'Hey, Paul! Great to meet you!'

I almost fainted. Jason Statham is nice!

He came into my office and we sat and talked and joked for a good half hour. It was a bit of an out-of-body experience for me because there was never a moment during our discussion that I wasn't extremely aware that I was talking to Jason Statham. How could I not be? The movie star whom I had watched for so many hours on the big screen was sitting across a glass coffee table from me and we were actually talking to one another. And he was as charismatic in real life as he is on the big screen. It was a surreal dream come true.

At the end of the meeting, I went into a gushy proclamation about how I'm dying to work with him and that I'm going to find him the perfect role in the perfect vehicle that he and I could work on together. He was very kind and polite and said that he'd like that too. The meeting ended, we shook hands and he left. And I vowed right then and there that I was going to create a great role for Jason Statham.

Right around that time, as I was in post-production on my movie *The Heat*, I had the idea to do what would basically be my version of a funny female James Bond film. As I started writing the script, I knew I needed a foil for my hero, Susan Cooper, and figured that it would have to be some hardcore CIA agent who resents that someone whom he considers a secretary is now suddenly out in the field doing the same job as him. And so, the character of Rick Ford was born. When I first started writing the role, I didn't really have a specific actor in mind. Rick Ford was more of plot device than a fleshed-out character in my first draft. But as I started rewriting him, I suddenly had an epiphany.

This is the perfect role for Jason Statham.

If he'd do it.

The role was pretty ridiculous. Rick Ford is so full of himself and his abilities that he can't give anyone credit for anything, whether they actually help him or not. He's incessantly mean to Susan and constantly gets in her way. He's pretty much incompetent, or at least he is when his rhythm and judgment are thrown off by having someone he doesn't respect doing the same job that he is *and* doing it better than him. When the studio read the script, they all loved the Rick Ford character and were convinced that I had written it for a comedic actor like Will Ferrell or Ben Stiller. Now, I am a huge fan of both of those gentlemen but I told the studio that, no, I wasn't hiring a comedian for the role. I wanted to hire Jason Statham. They looked at me with blank expressions for several seconds, then all burst out laughing. Not derisive laughter. It was the laughter of realizing just how funny this movie could be with Jason Statham in it.

If he'd do it.

I sent the script to him through his agent and waited on pins and needles to hear what he'd say. I was in New York City at the time directing a pilot for HBO and so I was walking down 32nd Street when my phone rang. It was Jason's agent.

'Jason thinks the script is very funny.'

'What did he think of the Rick Ford role?' I asked, heart pounding. To me, the whole movie hinged on whether Jason would do it or not. I saw him so clearly in the role that I did that thing that you're not supposed to do as a director – I didn't want anyone else to play the role and frankly didn't want to do the movie without him. Which is usually a recipe for not getting a movie made because it's hard to nail down movie stars. Or, if you do cast your second choice, you always feel like you compromised and didn't make the movie you truly wanted to make. As a director, you're supposed to stay flexible when you're casting. But when it came to Jason Statham, I was completely inflexible.

'Well ...' said his agent after a long pause. 'He has some concerns about it. But he also appreciates that you actually came through with a role after saying you wanted to write something for him in your meeting. He has people tell him that all the time but they don't usually follow through. So, he's very open to doing the role.'

Bingo! That was all I wanted to hear, that there was a chance. I told the agent to let me jump on the phone with Jason so that I could convince him. When Jason called the next day, he was as cool and friendly as ever. He reiterated how much he liked the script but was frankly a bit nervous about doing a straight-up comedy. He also wanted to make sure that I wasn't going to play him as a guy who couldn't actually fight.

'Oh, no, I want you kicking ass in this,' I said emphatically because who *wouldn't* want to have a few Jason Statham fight scenes in their movie? 'It's just that you make some bad decisions because you're so angry that Susan Cooper is getting in your way. And as far as comedy goes, we will have your back with tons of extra jokes. All you have to do is play it dead serious.'

We ended our call and the next thing I heard, Jason was in!

A couple of months before production, I did some read-throughs with the main cast members. This is something I always do during the writing process so that I can see how an actor is going to play the role and then rewrite the part for them to fit their strengths and natural inclinations. I have always been a believer in letting the actor be a part of the process in this way, as opposed to hiring someone and making them stick to the script word for word with no deviation from your original text. Great actors, and especially great comedic actors, are such a wealth of creativity that to cut off their input and ideas is to only to hurt your movie. That day, I did a session with Melissa McCarthy and Rose Byrne that went really well and then after Rose left, Jason came in to go through his scenes.

'I shouldn't try to do anything funny with these, right?' he asked me as he sat at the long table in our conference room.

'Play it exactly the way you would play any of your other movies,' I said.

And so he did.

Melissa and I watched in awe as he brought the character of Rick Ford to life. Every speech he read made us burst out laughing. I truly felt like I was floating in the air I was so happy. Jason Statham was absolutely perfect in the role, so much so that it was the first time I never rewrote an actor's lines in a script. He was nailing every word of it.

When he finished reading the last scene, he looked at me to see what I thought.

'Jason, close the script and don't look at it again until we're on the set shooting each scene,' I said excitedly. 'You crushed it.'

He gave me a look that made me think he might not be sure if I was actually happy or not, since I think he was expecting us to rehearse more. But why would you ever over-rehearse a performance that's perfect?

When Jason came to Budapest and we started to shoot his first scene, which was of Rick Ford having broken into Susan Cooper's Paris hotel room, he already had a hilarious scripted speech to read about all the terrible things that have happened to him on his missions throughout his career. Katie Dippold had written some extremely funny runs for this speech and then we also had another favorite comedy writer on the set with us, Tricia McAlpin. As Jason started filming his speech, it was everything any of us on the crew could do not to burst out laughing and ruin the take. He was in full Statham mode, dramatically lit in the corner of a dark room, dressed in a beautiful Anderson and Sheppard brown suit and a burgundy turtleneck, growling out stories about driving a van off a train and jumping from a building using only a raincoat as a parachute. It was all so absurd and yet because he was playing it so straight, it just got funnier and funnier.

And then Tricia started handing me new jokes.

On my sets, I like to shoot a lot of alternate jokes so that when we start screening cuts of the movie for test audiences, I'll have options if certain jokes don't get the laugh we want. We'll come to set with lists of extra jokes, as well as stacks of Post-It notes that we jot down new jokes on as we think of them in the moment. Once you're on the set and in the moment with the actors and the cameras rolling, you start to get inspired by what's happening in the scene and in how the actors are playing off each other. This is where I find some of the funniest moments come from in movie comedies. It's like when you're with your friends and joking around and one funny comment or story will spur another funny comment or story and it just gets funnier and funnier as you all feed off each other and keep building on the jokes. Well, Tricia was now feeding off of how funny it was when Jason would say something really absurd about some tragedy that happened to him, an over-the-top event that would clearly kill any normal person. Some of the jokes were so ridiculous that I was convinced Jason was going to refuse to say them, which would have been fully within his right to do. Lines about swallowing enough microchips and shitting them back out again to make a computer just seemed like a road too far to ask the world's greatest action star. But if he *would* say them, I knew it would be hilarious.

I was sitting on the floor about three feet away from him next to the camera with this list of insane jokes. I dove in.

'Hey, Jason, can I give you a few alternate jokes?' I asked nervously.

'Yeah, sure, Paul,' he said.

I took a deep breath and read the first joke.

'"There's nothing I can't do",' I read trying not to sound as nervous as I was. '"Walk through fire, water-ski blindfolded, take up piano at a late age."'

He paused a second and looked at me. Here it comes, I thought. I'm about to be taken down by the famous devastating Statham punch. At least I'll have a great story to tell for the rest of my life from my wheelchair.

And then he burst out laughing. Laughter that said he trusted me, and that he was game for anything.

This began a pattern that would continue for the rest of the shoot. I'd feed him a ridiculous line, he'd crack up at it, give it a try, start laughing halfway through his first attempt, try again and then absolutely nail it on his second take with a seriousness and dedication that I've experienced with very few other actors, let alone bona fide movie stars. He waded his way through insane dialogue about appearing in front of Congress disguised convincingly as Barack Obama, reattaching his severed arm with his other good arm, and a long diatribe about trying to figure out what his terrifying nickname would be ('Tell them the Vitamix is coming for them ... no, wait, that's a blender'), to name but a few. (If you want to experience full Statham in this way, look at the reels of alternate takes and jokes that are included on the *Spy* Blu ray or digital extras. You will laugh. I guarantee it.) He also let us put him in a ridiculous wig and 1970s porn star mustache and get in a wrestling dance/fight where he was overpowered by Melissa McCarthy on the disco floor, as well as hang from her breasts and legs while dangling off the bottom of a helicopter. And he was a delight the entire time he was doing all of it.

In those few months I spent working with Jason, I saw even more clearly what makes him such a legendary and adored star. He truly loves what he does. One Sunday afternoon in the middle of the shoot, my wife Laurie and I took Jason to lunch in a beautiful outdoor restaurant up in the hills of Buda. Jason regaled us with stories from his past when he was a hawker on the streets of London. He would sell low-end jewelry in front of Harrods by working the crowd with a funny and fast-talking spiel that pulled people in using a mix of compliments, jokes, promises of bargains and the glow of wish fulfillment. He would work the crowd by singling out potential buyers and play on their desire to have some faux luxury item they didn't know they needed, a cheap necklace or bracelet that he then made sound like the center of the universe. If you watch *Lock, Stock and Two Smoking Barrels*, you can see him doing some of his exact pitch in the opening scene. According to Jason, this is how Guy Ritchie first discovered him, by watching him sell his wares on the high street. Jason acted out his full fast-talking sales pitch for my wife and me, making the cheap jewelry he had gotten from a wholesaler sound expensive and then closing the deal by throwing in a fake bottle of Chanel-inspired perfume, all while bending the wording on his pitch so that everything he was saying couldn't be called a lie or false advertising by any passing police officer – the box looked a lot like Chanel No. 5 but was just different enough and he never would put the words 'Chanel' or 'number 5' in the same sentence. We were enthralled. He clearly loved the performance aspect of that former career. But it was his humor and ability to make the customer feel good, calling the women 'darling' and joking playfully with them in a style usually heard on the stages of the old English music halls that really closed each sale he made. He was a crowd pleaser, a spinner of tales and dreams that you loved to listen to and be entertained by and were willing to reward with your hard-earned money in exchange for whatever it was he was selling. Because he made you feel good about yourself and he entertained the hell out of you while he did it.

That's what he's still doing every time you see him larger than life up on the movie screen. He's pulling you in and selling you something you didn't even know you wanted but that you are so happy to be sold. He's the ultimate salesman, which makes him the ultimate entertainer. He's selling us dream after dream with each of his movies, dreams of what we wish we could do in unjust situations, dreams of taking the power back from those who oppress us, and dreams of who we wish we always had on our side in real life. He's our perfect father figure, our perfect big brother, our ultimate protector. He's what we want all those people who say they have our best interests at heart to be. He is our most trusted friend who will always get us out of a jam and whom we love to be with as he does it.

Jason Statham is the people's movie star. And we the people can never thank him enough for it. That's the power of Jason Statham.

4

'It's that peasant mentality': the cult persona of Jason Statham, Hollywood outsider

Jonathan Mack

As one of Hollywood's most prolific and recognisable action stars, the word 'cult' is not the first one brought to mind when one considers the career of Jason Statham. Certainly, sharing the screen with the likes of Sylvester Stallone, Arnold Schwarzenegger, Vin Diesel and Melissa McCarthy in huge box office successes like *The Expendables 2* (2012), *Furious 7* (2015) and *Spy* (2015) would place Statham firmly in the realm of mainstream Hollywood success. Nevertheless, this chapter will argue that the British actor has successfully constructed his star text as both a mainstream and a cult star.

Statham has built his star persona on roles that align with the working-class, masculine, anti-establishment and urban ideology that was the driving force behind the establishment of 'cult' as a serious object of academic study, and that continues to be an important part of how cult films, filmmakers and stars are read as 'other' from the Hollywood mainstream (Jancovich *et al.* 2003). Alongside these roles Statham has cultivated a particular kind of star text within popular culture in numerous interviews that place him firmly outside the accepted formula of a Hollywood star. Free-flowing expletives and brutal honesty characterise real-life interactions that repeatedly reference

Statham's working-class upbringing and his unconventional route into acting. If one can succinctly summarise cult as being in opposition to, or at least significantly divergent from, a perceived mainstream, Jason Statham fulfils the criteria.

More recently, Statham has cemented this liminal position between mainstream and cult stardom by taking on roles that explicitly acknowledge, recreate and parody his own star persona. This kind of self-reflexivity is a marker of a modern formation of cult (or meta-cult) in which intertextual reference and laying bare the artifice of the construction of film is valued as an oppositional stance to the mainstream, and represents a significant evolution of Statham's star text (Mathijs and Sexton 2011). This evolution parallels the one enjoyed by the *Fast and Furious* series of which he is now a part, shifting from solemn crime drama to excessive action spectacle relying heavily on the star texts of its featured players and engaging in self-parody.

Statham and the 'cult' ideology

When applied to films, cult has historically been approached not as a specific set of criteria by which one can identify cult content, but as an ideology embodied by a broad range of different formal, narrative and reception strategies. Mark Jancovich *et al.* recognise that cult 'is not defined according to some single unifying feature shared by all cult movies, but rather through a "subcultural ideology" in filmmakers, films or audiences seen as existing in opposition to the "mainstream"' (2003: 2). In this context, however, defining the mainstream is equally challenging. Like cult, it is somewhat nebulous and conveys a variety of meanings. Jancovich *et al.* use the definition in *Incredibly Strange Films* (1986), which states that 'the mainstream is imaged as some amalgam of corporate power, lower-middle class conformity and prudishness, academic elitism and political conspiracy' (Vale and Juno 1986, cited in Jancovich *et al.* 2003: 2).

Clearly, this is not a comprehensive summation of the complex, overlapping and sometimes even contradictory aspects of all things considered 'cult'. I. Q. Hunter (2016) refers to an eight-point set of factors set out by *Bright Lights Film Journal* encompassing the establishment of a niche subcultural fan community, poor critical reception, lack of mainstream box office success and the general feel of something that is marginal, suppressed or transgressive. He does note, however, that 'the content of a cult film is left vague beyond its being somehow transgressive or outside the mainstream' (Hunter 2016: 3), but even that is not entirely necessary given the cult status of a film like *Dirty Dancing* (1987).

The fact that many disparate cultural artefacts can be considered cult is recognised by Mathijs and Sexton, who note that while Jancovich *et al.*'s notion of the mainstream may be 'fuzzily defined' it nevertheless 'still functions as a crucial concept among fans who use it to define themselves against more "normal" or "average" film viewers' (Mathijs and Sexton 2011: 3).

As an effective starting point with which to approach the ideology behind these features and strategies, we can say that it is an oppositional stance to, or at least a significant measure of divergence from, this perceived 'centre' that most reliably allows for something to be considered cult. Jancovich *et al.* (2003) see the concept as representing a kind of cultural conflict between class groups, with the lower-middle class thought to largely constitute the 'mainstream' audience othered and challenged, even though cult audiences tend to be from the middle classes themselves.

The differentiation of Statham from the lower-middle class traditionally associated with Jancovich *et al.*'s mainstream could not be more apparent. His establishment as a film actor in Guy Ritchie's gangster comedy dramas *Lock, Stock and Two Smoking Barrels* (1998) and *Snatch* (2000) saw him occupying a clearly defined position in the British working class, and helped create a 'type' that Statham has been maximising ever since (see Richard Dyer's work on *Stars* for further information). Interviewed for an *Esquire* cover story in 2015, Statham speaks of his need to keep working and to keep taking on projects regularly as a reflection of his working-class background: 'It's that peasant mentality,' he says of his desire to 'make hay while the sun shines' (Chiarella 2015).

R. Emmet Sweeney (2008) recognises that not only does Statham's prolific output signal that he is 'a worker', but his roles are also defined by labour.

> They have names evocative of union workers and hockey players: Frank Martin, Terry Leather, Chev Chelios. These are single-minded anti-heroes out to complete a mission. Nothing concerns them but the job, whether it's a 'Bank Job,' an 'Italian

Job' or a 'Transporter' gig. The thrills in a successful Statham film come from this focus – the hurtling narratives rarely pause for backstory, concerned only with bridging the gap between a plan and its execution.

This link to the working class is made explicit in the opening of *Death Race* (2008), which sees Statham's character, a manual labourer, unceremoniously made redundant. A violent conflict ensues between the workers and the police, who arrive on behalf of the company to quash dissent, in a scene reminiscent of news coverage of similar real-world events. His financial struggle to provide for his family is emphasised in this portion of the film, as is the unfeeling nature of the corporate structure above him; but perhaps most interesting is that he goes on to be used as a pawn by a complex, corrupt entertainment organisation. Entertainment itself fills the role of the cold corporate entity and the primary antagonist in the film. This is a detail that resonates perfectly with Statham's consistent appearance as not only from a lower class than his contemporaries, but also outside of and apart from Hollywood itself.

This separation is reinforced by Statham's extratextual star persona. Reviewing the significant number of interviews Statham has given throughout his career, one is struck by the way in which each interviewer seems to revel in the broad cockney accent and dialect the star never attempts to hide, or even soften in service of being more clearly understood. His entire demeanour in pieces like Chris Nashawaty's 2007 interview seems to communicate a discomfort with simply being in places like the Polo Lounge in Beverly Hills. Expressing this, he observes: 'F-in' 'ell, this place is as old as Hollywood gets' in what the journalist describes as 'his rough cockney growl'. Not only does Statham make no attempt to clean-up his language for the interview, but Nashawaty reports the accent as much as the content, complete with the dropped g's and h's so commonly associated, particularly in Statham's home nation of the UK, with being raised in a lower socio-economic class. This is not just colour for the interview or a disarming journalistic detail, it is a key part of Jason Statham's star persona. As the article puts it: 'Needless to say, these are not Statham's people.'

As Stuart Heritage (2013) discovered when he attempted to present the star with a copy of his own calendar, Statham's perspective has remained firmly outside the wealthy and self-congratulatory tone of Hollywood: 'Seven-ninety fucking nine?

Fuck! I should try and claim back the nine pence!' exclaimed the man who had recently starred in *The Expendables 2*, a film that earned a reported $305 million worldwide box office (Mendelson 2016). This apparent contradiction, or at least a conspicuously visible separation between the excesses of the glamorous American film business and Statham's 'down-to-earth' approach to it all, is a key aspect of how he distances himself from the mainstream and therefore a crucial part of his construction as a cult figure.

Another thing to consider when looking at the ideology behind the formation of cult is the organisation along gender lines. As Joanne Hollows (2003) has outlined, this perceived opposition or deviation from the mainstream is actually gendered. She asserts that the emergence of cult audiences in the urban (masculine) space of 'the street' immediately placed the concept in a place considered more male than female. Historically, the sleaziness and dirtiness of the exhibition spaces tended to be celebrated as a key part of the oppositional nature of the subculture. This positioning fundamentally excludes femininity as a concept wrapped-up in the mainstream that cult exists specifically to oppose. As Jancovich notes: 'The Otherness of the lower middle classes has frequently been associated with its feminization and, as a result, it is hardly surprising that cult fandom not only works to affirm bourgeois tastes but is also related to the legitimization of masculine dispositions' (2003: 3).

In addition, films from what has been generally perceived as 'male' genre cinema such as science fiction, fantasy, horror and exploitation movies have historically colonised the concept of cult. While not explicitly excluding female audiences, this genre content can be said to be aimed towards largely male audiences and makes female engagement with cult less likely (Hollows 2003).

If appealing to this sense of masculinity is also a contributing factor in the construction of what it is to be 'cult' then Statham clearly fills this role too. So much of what defined the masculinity of stars like Clint Eastwood, as well as one of Statham's own inspirations Bruce Willis, is present in his own performances. Deborah Ross of *The Spectator* reviewing *Hummingbird* (2013) describes the star as 'a big lump of macho' (2013). Like his predecessors, he is commonly unemotional, monosyllabic, unencumbered by domesticity, frequently a man of action and treats every major, life threatening situation with a sense of detachment.

The fact that he performs the majority of his own stunts also contributes to this performed masculinity and is frequently raised in interviews. Philip G. Atwell, the director of *War* (2007), noted that Statham made a ten-foot jump between two rooftops that were seven stories high above the pavement during filming and remarked, 'I don't think Bruce Willis would do that' (Nashawaty 2007). This comment invites the interpretation of this kind of hands-on approach from Statham, and his willingness to talk about it, as a kind of contest of masculinity. It's a way to prove he is even more masculine than other icons of masculinity like Willis, and that perfectly reflects the kind of masculinity associated with the notion of 'cult' outlined by Hollows. It is a show of bravado, and a performativity of maleness that is replicated by followers of cult cinema demonstrating their encyclopaedic knowledge of particular stars, series or films, or collecting an archive of rare DVDs.

Statham's brief stint as a male model also positions him as a literal icon of masculinity, as an idealised male to be desired and identified with, but he is careful to distance his own modelling from anything that might be considered feminised. '"It's not like I was on the catwalk," he says defensively. "I'm too short and my f-ing nose is halfway across my face. All I had to do was sit in a deck chair"' (Nashawaty 2007). Clearly Statham is eager to reaffirm his own particular brand of masculinity against the more feminised form he associates with the fashion industry and being 'on the catwalk'. As an action star, with his body still conspicuously foregrounded and fetishised to some extent, Statham's physique clearly requires a great deal of work and attention. Steve Rose (2015) notes that the training regimen for the then-forty-eight-year-old is eye-catching in its intensity, with 'rowing machines, circuit training, weights, sprints, rings, trampolines' suggesting a kind of vanity more in keeping with what people might think of as youth and fitness-obsessed Hollywood. Even this is played down by the man himself, however, saying, 'I've had untold years of burning the candle: going out, overeating, over-drinking ... As you get older, you get a bit wiser' (Rose 2015). Statham is reassuring the audience that he's just like them really. He likes to overindulge in food and alcohol, mentioning that he still gets drunk and floats in his pool with his girlfriend (actress and model Rosie Huntington-Whiteley), adding yet further 'manliness' to his already almost comically macho star text. The use of profanity and self-deprecating humour throughout all of these interviews also helps to realign his masculinity with a more traditional, conservative formation of maleness more in keeping with the working class or 'blue collar' persona so crucial to his 'type'.

Statham and cult stardom

All of this demonstrates how Statham's star persona aligns with much of the ideological driving force behind that which has historically been considered 'cult', but what of cult stardom specifically? As pointed out by Matt Hills, star personas are necessarily constructed for audiences, not by them. There is a contradiction at the heart of the notion of being a 'cult star' because while 'cult' suggests a level of audience autonomy, the construction of a star persona suggests a text or a categorisation that is forced upon them. This is not a binary state however, and audiences negotiate with star texts frequently in order to grant cult status to a wide range of stars for a wide range of reasons. Hills recognises that stars can be considered cult stars by starring in 'cult movies', or by being small but consistent components of more mainstream content (Hills 2013).

There is certainly an argument to be made that Statham has starred in a number of cult films. Many of these projects aligned with the ideology of cult described above, with the majority being testosterone-fuelled, macho, action spectacle thrill rides focusing on a lower or working-class anti-hero fighting the odds and a corrupt hierarchy of power. A number of these titles, however, also speak to another potential identifier of cult film, namely being 'bad'. Poor critical response and lacklustre box office returns upon initial release can often lead to the formation of fan bases around certain films or types of film. Marginality, suppression, economics and a 'niche' following constitute four of I. Q. Hunter's eight-point summary of cult factors. This understanding of cult posits that, generally, cults are born out of a failure on some level, be that on economic, cultural or artistic grounds (Hunter 2016: 5). Jeffrey Sconce's examples of 'bad films' encapsulate 'studio-era B-films, low-budget 1950s sci-fi, grindhouse porn and horror, or even wildly excessive contemporary summer blockbusters' (2007: 2) among others, and while the term initially appears to be a simple and pejorative value judgement, it is more reflective of a collective commercial and critical reception to something that does not fit the consensus definition of 'quality' film.

Following his *Lock, Stock* and *Snatch* roles, Statham starred in *Ghosts of Mars* (2001), which is considered to be a failure both economically and critically. In a fascinating review of the film for *Variety*, Robert Koehler likens it to something you would expect to see at a drive-in, immediately aligning it with the 'B-movie'-style 'trash' that Sconce is talking about in his book. Koehler states that the film belongs 'to a bygone filmgoing culture that revelled in cheap – rather than corporate-busting expensive – chills and thrills', and asserts that there is no place for this particular kind of entertainment in the modern multiplex landscape, 'aside from a fluke case like *The Fast and the Furious*' (Koehler 2001). This would prove to be an oddly prescient statement given that more than a decade later Statham would be an established cast member of the *Fast and Furious* series, but it exemplifies the kind of critical dismissal and exclusion that drives the formation of cult films and stars. *Mean Machine* (2001) and *The One* (2001) met with similarly cold reactions, and Statham was even in a straight-to-DVD release with Wesley Snipes, *Chaos* (2005). Other critical disappointments like *Revolver* (2005) and *War* (2007), combined with the niche appeal of the better-received but conspicuously low-budget 'British' nature of *Lock, Stock and two Smoking Barrels* and *Snatch* (certainly for American audiences), meant that Statham's star text had become acutely associated with marginalised and/or 'bad' genre entertainment, the likes of which routinely fill cinemas at cult film festivals worldwide.

Despite the modest successes of films such as *The Transporter* (2002), *Cellular* (2004) and *Crank* (2006), Statham's consistent performance style and character type had firmly established a cult persona as 'the last action star', an ironic and nostalgic narrative only enhanced by the fact that his films had never broken through into significant mainstream box office success. People were interested in him regardless, as evidenced by the uncommon amount of press, features and interviews that followed his anticipated rise to the elite of Hollywood. That struggle became part of his narrative in wider culture and it gained him a significant number of followers. Dre Rivas (2011) decries the apparent unfairness that Statham can repeatedly star in subpar content and still demand a high level of fandom and respect from what he calls 'film buffs', while stars like 'Ashton Kutcher, Katherine Heigl and Cuba Gooding Jr' have become 'punchlines' because of their poor choices (Rivas 2011). It is Statham's cult status that has allowed him to escape their fate, and this perception would only be enhanced as his career continued.

In Mathijs and Sexton's discussion of the phenomenon of 'meta-cult', understood as the way in which use of the term 'cult' has widened in public discourse and been seized on as something that can be achieved, rather than categorised after the fact, they note that part of this phenomenon is 'self-conscious cultism'. They suggest that drawing on cult cinema sources can actually lead to certain filmmakers being considered cult themselves. Tim Burton and Joe Dante are used as examples of how a certain level of knowledge and quotation of cult film in their work has aided the construction of their respective cult personas (Mathijs and Sexton 2011: 236). This kind of activity reflects a level of engagement that mirrors that of cult fans, many of whom place great value on their 'subcultural capital' as Matt Hills describes it, embodied by encyclopaedic knowledge of niche genre films or extensive collections of hard-to-find material (Hills 2013). Demonstrating that they share the same genuine love and knowledge for that material as fans lends a sense of authenticity to a star that is also an important part of constructing and maintaining a cult persona.

This 'self-conscious cultism' is evident throughout Statham's career, particularly after 2008. In that year he appeared in *Death Race*, which was marketed extensively as a remake of the cult classic *Death Race 2000* (1975) produced by iconic cult figure Roger Corman. Corman was also among the production credits of *Death Race*, which heavily indulged its cult, excessively violent, genre film origins, but importantly began a string of films in which Statham would appear to recognise and self-consciously inhabit his established cult persona. *The Mechanic* (2011) is also a remake of a cult film from 1972 that was a box office flop at the time, was critically panned for its unnecessary levels of violence and 'sadism', and was helmed by noted cult director Michael Winner. This alignment with a classic cult film was only part of Statham's continuing cult stardom, however, as his star text was now so established that he, and filmmakers, could use audiences' expectations of it to their advantage.

The Expendables (2010) teams Statham up with Sylvester Stallone, Dolph Lundgren and Bruce Willis, among others, to pay tribute to the action movies of the 1980s. The excessive, graphic violence of the film echoes the kind of cult genre cinema that would have earned widespread critical dismissal and generated popular distaste among the mainstream in that era, but the scale of the budget and the stars involved negated that kind of marginalisation in 2010. Additionally, the premise of the movie relies heavily on the extratextual knowledge of the audience regarding the stars involved. It is the 'knowing' nature of bringing these stars together specifically to celebrate their star personas that constitutes a level of metareference, and confers the authenticity associated with self-conscious cultism. There is a large-scale, large-budget, effects-laden blockbuster on offer for the mainstream, but for audiences who know their film history, *The Expendables* offers a subtextual pleasure beyond the immediate plot and narrative. It offers a game of connecting and reading star texts – a pleasure that particularly appeals to cult audiences eager to demonstrate subcultural capital.

Matt Hills (2013) also refers to the term 'character' as an example of the 'structuration' of cult stardom. Hills notes that William Shatner has embodied Captain Kirk for decades on both film and television, making it difficult to separate the character from the actor, but he has also contributed to that perception by repeatedly engaging with the *Star Trek* fan base in self-reflexive ways by taking roles such as in *Free Enterprise* (1998) and *Fanboys* (2009). By being playful and metareferential with his celebrity persona he has cemented his status as a 'character' in a way that moves beyond simple typecasting, engaging with audience agency and fan-driven stardom as much as his industry-driven casting. Statham is not a 'character' in Hills' definition as he is not eternally bound to one specific on-screen character, but much as Clint Eastwood essentially played the 'Man with No Name' for much of his career, Statham has repeatedly represented a consistent character beyond the name and backstory provided by the script. His ability to play with and interrogate that character has added yet more authenticity to his cult construction.

Statham demonstrated this ability to play with the perception of his star persona in *Spy*, with a comedic role playing an absurdly exaggerated version of many of his previous characters. This performance won Statham considerable praise, particularly from the mainstream critical media that had marginalised him for so long as the tough guy action hero of generally 'bad' movies. A review of *Spy* for *Empire* states that 'Statham, frankly, should only ever play this role for the rest of his life' (Richards 2015). Inflecting all the characteristics of his old-school, action hero cult persona into one that mocked the entire construction of that star text demonstrated that he had significant knowledge of the perception of his own celebrity among a wider audience. This self-awareness/self-reflexivity is a particularly effective means by which stars can find themselves generating or increasing a cult following. It adds to the sense of detachment from Hollywood that Statham has cultivated in his interviews discussed above and demonstrates a 'knowingness' that aligns him with cine-literate audiences who tend to form niche groups based on sharing and demonstrating that knowledge as subcultural capital. Indeed, Jim Whalley (2013) points out that this is a key feature of Bill Murray's cult celebrity, noting that journalistic coverage of Murray often portrays him as possessing greater perspective than other Hollywood stars, setting him apart and adding significantly to his cult persona.

This ability to stand apart from his own established star persona and regard it playfully is only further enhanced by Statham's appearances in the *Fast and Furious* series. Much like himself, the franchise has developed significantly between 2001 and 2018, from a marginalised, macho and solemn but critically dismissed crime drama, to a high-budget, effects-laden, over-the-top spectacle that parodies its own wider perception even as it continues to reinforce it. There is perhaps no current mainstream successful franchise that walks the line between Hollywood spectacle and cult curiosity more than the *Fast and Furious* series, so it is fitting that Statham is now a regular cast member.

The *Fast and Furious* franchise has gained a cult following (in addition to global mainstream commercial success) due to the fact that it is constantly making unusual, unexpected choices, highlighting its own artifice, parodying itself and, perhaps most importantly, inviting audiences to read the franchise extratextually at every opportunity. This was possibly most obvious at the end of *Furious 7*, with the final three minutes saved for a tribute to Paul Walker, who had died in a car accident during filming. The sequence comprises edited highlights of the entire series with a voice-over from Vin Diesel about family being the most important thing, which is a key component to the franchise throughout. Fans and critics alike have recognised that this scene is not about the characters but the actors, who ask the audience to recognise their real-world circumstances and use that extratextual knowledge to contextualise the sequence. The need to engage with the films beyond the level of the text is not unique to this high-profile moment, however. While Statham's first appearance in *Fast and Furious 6* (2013) was merely a cameo, his dominance over the opening of the seventh instalment is a comedy sequence aimed squarely at fans of his existing persona. Over the course of a four-minute continuous take, Statham provides a short burst of exposition about how he is going to settle the score for his comatose brother (played by Luke Evans) and then goes on to lead the camera around what remains of the hospital as he leaves. As the audience views the total destruction of broken windows, cowering staff and patients as well as dead SWAT team members, Statham regards the entire scene with disregard and detachment. The implication is that he has caused all of this destruction while breaking into the secure hospital to visit his brother, and the scene only increases in absurdity. He steals a grenade from one of the dead police officers in the foyer and casually tosses it behind him as he leaves the main entrance, causing the entire front of the building to collapse, all of which he walks away from (towards camera) as if it is not happening. This complete indulgence in the underplayed, hypermasculine tough guy persona, which Statham has built throughout his appearances in a constant succession of stereotypical action movies, invites viewers to engage in the fun of playfully reading Statham's star text as something to be celebrated and gently mocked here.

The franchise has been engaging in this kind of self-reflexivity for a long time, a feature that has allowed it to be embraced by cult audiences as well as mainstream ones. *The Fast and the Furious* (2001) performed well commercially, despite being largely dismissed critically and labelled 'the sort of thing that would rule at drive-ins if they still existed' (McCarthy 2001), but *2 Fast 2 Furious* (2003) lost headliner Vin Diesel. Production of the third film, *The Fast and the Furious: Tokyo Drift* (2006) was plagued by stories reporting that none of the original cast would return. The fact that nobody knew why the stars wouldn't sign-up (although it was assumed to concern contract disputes) helped create an attractive mystique around the release; however, a surprise cameo from Vin Diesel at the film's conclusion was kept secret. This created significant buzz and allowed fans to generate theories about how the characters might be linked. It is significant that the figure linking the old and new casts was Han Lue (Sung Kang), a character imported wholesale from Lin's first feature *Better Luck Tomorrow* (2002). As a low-budget indie hit given limited release, but receiving significant critical praise, a character from *Better Luck Tomorrow* appearing as a key figure in the *Fast and Furious* series is an especially playful piece of intertextuality that further encourages fans to join the dots and exercise specialist film knowledge to get the most out of the experience.

From that point on the series also employed an unusual non-linear narrative in which the next three entries would be set prior to the events of *Tokyo Drift*, allowing Han to return despite his on-screen death. This would become yet another feature of the films for fans to analyse and debate, wondering when the series would return to Tokyo and deal with the events of the film, and is teased multiple times in the dialogue of the following films.

These are not features of an action spectacle aimed solely at a mainstream audience; they are examples of self-conscious cultism, and are part of a strategy that has seen the franchise adopted by specialist fan bases not usually reached by such commercially successful action fare. When Jason Statham fights Dwayne 'The Rock' Johnson in *Furious 7*, Johnson performs his signature manoeuvre from his time wrestling professionally in the WWE (World Wrestling Entertainment). This is not an important part of his character's backstory – it is an invitation to wrestling fans to see The Rock, not Luke Hobbs, performing in a way they know from other media. It is more intertextual metareference encouraging the audience to engage their extratextual knowledge. When we are introduced to Statham's on-screen mother in *The Fate of the Furious* (2017) and it turns out to be Helen Mirren affecting a broad cockney accent and sporting a leopard-print jacket, the comedy does not arise from seeing Deckard Shaw's mother, but from Helen Mirren playing Jason Statham's mum. There can be no better place in which Statham can find himself than this ensemble of contrasting star texts, with each instalment creating new links, connections and references to their wider public personas for fans to enjoy and then share with one another in order to activate all their subcultural capital.

Despite these games being part of an obviously constructed appeal to those with cinematic and wider media knowledge, the explicit laying bare of the artifice of these films imbues them with a sense of authenticity that appeals to niche, subcultural and cult audiences in a way that other successful action franchises lack. This authenticity is also what has cemented Statham's place as one of Hollywood's most successful cult personas. Among those perceived as 'fake' within the Hollywood elite, Statham is more 'real'. He can view himself and his own star persona from afar, poking fun at it from a position of authentic joy and wonder, like the fans who flock to see him. As Tom Chiarella says: 'Everything Statham says stinks of truth [...] Everything declares: He wasn't made in the Hollywood Hills. He came from elsewhere.' As a performer 'he regards things sideways, incredulous at the very prospect of them' (Chiarella 2015). That incredulity at the absurdity of Hollywood connects him to particular audiences just like his working-class masculinity, his association with marginalised and self-consciously cult film, and his ability to inflect and parody himself. 'It's that peasant mentality,' he says of his decision to keep working no matter what the project; but more than that, it is the very core of the authenticity that anchors the cult persona of Jason Statham.

References

Chiarella, T. (2015). 'Jason Statham, for your amusement'. *Esquire*. www.esquire.com/entertainment/movies/interviews/a35122/jason-statham-cover-story-0615/ (26.05.15, accessed 15.01.18).
Dyer, R. (1998). *Stars*. London: BFI Publishing.
Emmet Sweeney, R. (2008). 'Jason Statham, working class (action) hero'. *ifc.com*. www.ifc.com/2008/11/kicking-ass-the-jason-statham (26.11.08, accessed 18.01.18).
Heritage, S. (2013). 'The secret life of Jason Statham'. *Guardian*. www.theguardian.com/film/2013/jun/21/secret-life-jason-statham (21.06.13, accessed 12.12.17).
Hills, M. (2013). 'Cult movies with and without cult stars: differentiating discourses of stardom', in Egan, K. and Thomas, S. (eds). *Cult Film Stardom: Offbeat Attractions and Processes of Cultification*. Basingstoke: Palgrave Macmillan. pp. 21–36.
Hollows, J. (2003). 'The masculinity of cult', in Jancovich, M., Lazaro Reboll, A., Stringer, A. and Willis, A. (eds). *Defining Cult Movies: The Cultural Politics of Oppositional Taste*. Manchester: Manchester University Press. pp. 35–53.
Hunter, I. Q. (2016). *Cult Film as a Guide to Life: Fandom, Adaptation and Identity*. London: Bloomsbury.
Jancovich, M., Lazaro Reboll, A., Stringer, S. and Willis, A. (2003). 'Introduction', in Jancovich, M., Lazaro Reboll, M., Stringer, J. and Willis, A. (eds). *Defining Cult Movies: The Cultural Politics of Oppositional Taste*. Manchester: Manchester University Press. pp. 1–13.

Koehler, R. (2001). 'John Carpenter's ghosts of Mars'. *Variety*. http://variety.com/2001/film/reviews/john-carpenter-s-ghosts-of-mars-1200469404/ (19.08.01, accessed 18.01.18).

Mathijs, E. and Sexton, J. (2011). *Cult Cinema*. Oxford: Wiley-Blackwell.

Mendelson, S. (2016). 'Box Office: "Mechanic: Resurrection" Becomes Jason Statham's Biggest Solo Hit'. *Forbes.com*. www.forbes.com/sites/scottmendelson/2016/11/03/box-office-mechanic-resurrection-becomes-jason-stathams-biggest-solo-hit/#309a2dc71d15 (03.11.16, accessed 18.01.18).

Nashawaty, C. (2007). 'Is Jason Statham the last action star?', *Entertainment Weekly*. http://ew.com/article/2007/08/24/jason-statham-last-action-star/ (24.08.24, accessed 18.01.18).

Richards, O. (2015). 'Spy review', *Empire*. www.empireonline.com/movies/spy-2/review/ (accessed 19.02.18).

Rivas, D. (2011). 'Why does Jason Statham get a pass?' *MTV.com News*. www.mtv.com/news/2767083/why-does-jason-statham-get-a-pass/

Rose, S. (2015). 'Jason Statham: "Do I want to be the next James Bond? Absolutely"'. *Guardian*. www.theguardian.com/film/2015/jun/01/jason-statham-i-want-to-be-the-next-james-bond (01.06.15, accessed 18.07.17).

Ross, D. (2013). 'Film review: I was right: a British thriller starring Jason Statham is to be avoided'. *The Spectator*. www.spectator.co.uk/2013/06/film-review-i-was-right-a-british-thriller-starring-jason-statham-is-to-be-avoided/ (accessed 18.01.18).

Sconce, J. (2007). 'Introduction', in Sconce, J. (ed.). *Sleaze Artists: Cinema at the Margins of Taste, Style and Politics*. London: Duke University Press. pp. 1–18.

Whalley, J. (2013). '"You're Bill groundhog-day-ghostbusting-ass Murray": "Mainstream" success, star agency and cult reinvention', in Egan, K. and Thomas, S. (eds). *Cult Film Stardom: Offbeat Attractions and Processes of Cultification*. Basingstoke: Palgrave Macmillan. pp. 57–72.

5

A balancing act(or): Jason Statham and the ensemble film

Sarah Thomas

Commenting on the late Paul Walker's keenly felt absence in *The Fate of the Furious* (2017), the eighth in the *Fast and Furious* franchise, one reviewer suggested Walker may have been 'the mayonnaise of the *Fast* sandwich all along – not terribly compelling on his own, but a much-needed binder. These films live and die by the balance of the ensemble, and without [him] the equilibrium's been thrown off' (Yoshida 2017). Jason Statham joined the hugely profitable franchise in the previous film, *Furious 7* (2015), as the antagonist intent on destroying the tight-knit group. By *The Fate of the Furious* he was presented as one alternative to the missing Walker, with his character promoted into the heroic ensemble and allowed a redemption arc. Another review called the twist of Statham's inclusion 'F8's smartest move ... [with] his snarky one-liners and aptitude for hand-to-hand combat helping to break up the sometimes exhausting in-car sequences' (Mumford 2017). An important action star in his own right, Statham remains a somewhat unusual performer, something reflected in his widely-observed success in the high-octane franchise where he embellishes but does not overwhelm the established ensemble cast, helping to redress the imbalance left by Walker's death.

As David Greven notes when defining Hollywood's 'double-protagonist film', 'we think of the star in isolation, fighting his way through the complications of plot [and] narratively imposed anxieties' (2009: 23). Statham is, of course, an extraordinary *individual* star, but, from films like *Lock, Stock and Two Smoking Barrels* (1998), *Snatch* (2000), *The Italian Job* (2003), the *Fast and Furious* sequels, the *Expendables* series (2010–14) and many more, one of his strengths as a performer lies in his ability to cohere with larger casts across the ensemble film. Many of his leading roles are sustained by appealing repartee with compelling secondary players, including the *Crank* (2006–2009) and *Transporter* series (2002–2008); and even his comic turn in *Spy* (2015) relies on interplay and contrast with other actors in addition to its own parodic excess. Interactions are as vital a part of the Statham aesthetic as choreographed combat. Through this, Statham is always a precisely balanced actor – literally and figuratively – working to support and enhance those around him. His performances do this without sacrificing his own distinct star identity; he is not the bland-but-functional mayonnaise, but binds the ensemble together with added bite. This chapter will explore Statham's work in the ensemble film, paying attention to performance style, the interplay across group casting, and how this synthesises into a star identity informed by, but deviating from, conventional action star types. In doing so, it also engages with studies of the interrelationship between genre-specific texts and the techniques of screen performance (see Cornea 2010: 7).

Hierarchies and types in the male action film

Partly due to his proliferation in ensemble films, unlike other action icons, Statham's screen identity is often not the singularly extraordinary 'best of the best' or 'lone wolf' figure, but more akin to being '*one of the* best of the best'. Occasionally, it does not even appear to register strongly enough to warrant close attention, with other individuals drawing a fuller gaze. *Time*'s original review of *The Expendables* heralds 'if you collected movie action figures, you'd find almost the complete set' (Corliss: 2010), but namedrops the absent Jean-Claude Van Damme and Steven Seagal rather than acknowledge Statham. *Variety*'s review of his breakthrough film, *Lock, Stock and Two Smoking Barrels* – a film that opens with a show-stopping speech from the actor – notes only that 'Of the central quarter, [Jason]

Flemyng makes the most impact' (Elley 1998). As I will explore, this may be down to the complex space and deliberately cohesive function that Statham occupies in groups and star hierarchies more than underwhelming personality. Simple frameworks and axioms erase what Statham brings rather than explain them as such in existing discourse; for example, as analyses of the musclebound action star, Statham does not quite fit the mould being offered. Therefore, in an example like Ellexis Boyle and Sean Brayton's (2012: 479) reading of *The Expendables*, which relies on defining the cast through action types of 'former wrestlers, prize fighters, and professional athletes', there is little sustained analysis of Statham as an individual. Instead at various moments he is conflated with what they deem the 'inauthentic celebrity presence' of Sylvester Stallone (despite not aligning with the central examination of Stallone's ageing body), with Jet Li as 'martial artist' (despite working beyond these genre and stylistic distinctions), and excluded from the other 'professional athletes' Terry Crews and Randy Couture (despite a career as a competitive diver) and from Mickey Rourke's 'character actor' (despite being cast in these types of roles, especially in his British films).

Boyle and Brayton partly draw from Yvonne Tasker's (1993) taxonomy of action stars and modes of masculinity, notably the 'Tough Guy' and the 'Wise Guy', where emblematic tough guys tend to be strong, silent and usually solitary (Stallone, Schwarzenegger, Norris, Van Damme), with the wise guys constructed through voice and humour as much as physique (Willis and Russell). Tasker outlines the potential for fluidity between types, especially as careers extend, actors grow older and more experienced in screen performance. From the outset, though, Statham's work crosses boundaries between the two, and he does not occupy the conventional 'buddy' role or appear much in Greven's suggested genre of double-protagonist films. So, for instance, when Statham acts alongside Stallone in *The Expendables*, his performance and character function is not the same as Kurt Russell's wise guy contrast to Stallone in *Tango and Cash* (Tasker 1993: 88). But as an extensive performer across multiple-protagonist genre cinema, typage should play an important role in Statham's stardom. Films like *The Expendables* have significant continuity with the platoon film, a genre partly defined by the checklist of 'the hero, the group of mixed ethnic types, the objective they must accomplish, their weapons and uniforms' (Basinger 2003: 15). He is also associated with the heist film (*Snatch*, *The Italian Job*, *The Bank Job* (2008) and even the *Fast and Furious* films), a genre again well-defined through recognisable character roles of leader, mentor, and individually skilled team members (see Lee 2014). Team leader, token Brit, wheelman, matey sidekick – whichever 'bruvver or other' Statham plays, the variety in his casting means he remains unfettered by supporting status or character type; performance and stardom extend beyond conventions of basic ensemble types, and into a more refined character acting that shifts register as required by each individual film.

Christine Geraghty has observed the interplay of stars, types and performance styles in ensembles where she foregrounds the necessity of hierarchy. Using Al Pacino and Robert De Niro in *Heat*, she argues that 'ensemble playing position[s] the star as 'one of the boys' [and is] paralleled by a strong sense of performance as competition' (Geraghty 2000: 105) where character conflict is conveyed through acting one-upmanship. Within this framework, the individual star still reigns supreme (even when there are two of them). However, Statham's performances tend to be harmonious and balanced rather than competitive or conflicted, even if his characters are not. Here, Ernest Mathijs' observations about acting in the ensemble film are valuable. He suggests that performance in ensemble casts stress a sense of collectiveness and community rather than competition, even within overt divisions of acting labour among diverse types. Ensemble acting is constructed by performative devices drawing from formalism, body typage, negotiating other performers' screen styles, and an awareness of popular culture identities and discourses off-screen. Mathijs terms this process 'referential acting', where 'the meaning of an activity is only achieved by dint of its reference to another act' (Mathijs 2011: 91). The actor's task includes 'creating a sense of belonging through rituals of impersonation, role-play and mimicry, and by involving the audience in the play' (Mathijs 2011: 96); the formalism, typage and referential nature aligns diverse characters within screen communities and welcomes the viewer into that coherent and balanced world.

This sense of *belonging* can be observed in Statham's acting in the ensemble film. His performances work as significant nexus across points of reference, representation, interpretation and co-ordination, around which other performers are balanced in the group's overall role playing, character construction and generic affect. In this landscape Statham adapts to the contexts of casting and group dynamics across different films, demonstrably embodying a 'referential acting' style. Unlike conventional players in the action ensemble film – a format that tends to rely on the constancy of casting/character hierarchies – who occupy more fixed casting statuses of (and acting styles associated with) 'star/lead', 'character actor/villain or sidekick', 'supporting actor/team member', Statham's performances negotiate the requirements of virtually all types of roles, characters, spaces, functions and even modes of delivery. From group leader (*The Bank Job*) to second-tier player (*The Expendables* trilogy) or disposable member (*Ghosts of Mars*); from big talker (*Snatch*) to low-key stalker (*The Mechanic*) to cartoonish (*Crank* and *Spy*); from his own charismatic star vehicles (*Death Race* and *The Transporter* films) to underpinning other big-name stars (Stallone, Mark Wahlberg, Dwayne Johnson, Melissa McCarthy), there is an observable mutability that has enabled a wide-ranging film career and distinguishes him from his peers. His acting foregoes the excessive knowingness of forces of nature like Johnson, Schwarzenegger or Van Damme, or the emotional action melodrama of Stallone and Willis. Alternatively, he does not use the underplayed minimalism of Daniel Craig or Matt Damon to reflect a hero's search for meaningful identity. The preciseness of his physicality aligns him with Jackie Chan's light touch, but their comic personas vary immensely. Charismatic as he may be, Statham's acting is usually in a low-key register (although he is also comfortable in a higher register, as in *Crank*), highly contained, responsive in nature, and therefore easily adaptable to different scenarios. As a star performer, Statham manages an effective reconciliation of seemingly incompatible elements: the lone wolf, the sympathetic sidekick, the unwavering hero, the playful character actor, the physical and the verbose, the comic and the dark, the spectacle and the supporting frame.

Cockpit conversations: negotiating stardom in *The Expendables* ensemble

At the heart of the three *Expendables* movies lies a fascination with the spectacle and hierarchy of star performance. Second-billed Statham appears in all as Lee Christmas, knife expert and right-hand man to Sylvester Stallone's Barney Ross. Each film increases the ensemble of star personalities, drawing on established action stars from the 1980s and 1990s (to name only a few, Bruce Willis, Jet Li, Chuck Norris, Wesley Snipes) with some additions from sports-action star crossovers (Terry Crews, Ronda Rousey) and younger Hollywood stars (Liam Hemsworth, Kellan Lutz). As the trilogy progresses, more space is devoted to the interactions between recognisable star icons, informed by playful intertextual references designed for a genre-aware audience: from reuniting the 'Planet Hollywood' trio of Stallone, Willis and Schwarzenegger, to Chuck Norris's lone wolf cameo in *The Expendables 2*, to *The Expendables 3*'s expansive casting which made space for Snipes, Harrison Ford and Mel Gibson, character actors Robert Davi and Kelsey Grammar, and an uproarious comic turn from Antonio Banderas. Typical of the general rules of the ensemble film, in every film each star is given their own performative set piece. For Statham, this includes a showcase for his hand-to-hand skills in a fight on a basketball court between him and an abusive boyfriend in *The Expendables*, and in *The Expendables 2* a knife/martial arts fight staged a remote Bulgarian village, where he dons a monk's cowl and delivers the line 'I now pronounce you ... man and knife'.

But *Expendables 3* makes no space to showcase Statham's spectacular fighting prowess; instead it foregrounds him through an alternative sphere that expands upon his non-fighting scenes in the first two films. Throughout the trilogy, Statham's presence signals equilibrium and stability. This is partly created in dialogue with Stallone and is certainly revealed in the final sequence of *The Expendables* where the two celebrate the narrative's restoring of order by sitting side by side, drinking beer and bumping fists, staged symmetrically and filmed in a mid-shot. This cohesive motif of character, narrative, performative action and formal style ends all three films, and in each there is affectionate banter between Ross and Christmas that Stallone and Statham perform with naturalistic charm and pacing, where the underplayed acting removes what could be interpreted as competitive bravado inherent in the script. This pleasing visual balance between the two stars is also found in the start of the fight scene in the village bar in *The Expendables 2* where they face off against a larger foe.

In the sequels, Stallone's concluding interactions with Statham contrast with preceding moments where he plays off the grander star identities of Willis, Schwarzenegger and Ford and draws more overtly on intertextual reference and ostentatious performance; for example, in *The Expendables 2*, where Stallone delivers the head of their 1990s action cinema competitor Van Damme to Willis and Schwarzenegger ('A little extreme. But nice') and the prototypical lone wolf Chuck Norris admits, 'It's sometimes fun to run with the pack'. In these moments, Stallone acts with broad strokes that emphasise delivery of obviously scripted, highly knowing jokes, with the other stars mirroring his overt intonation and gesture. Here, Geraghty's 'one-upmanship' of star performance is clear: they are performing against each other as distinct and fully formed star identities as much as characters. However, such structuring of delivery and rhythm is mostly absent between Statham and Stallone (even when the script suggests competitive dialogue). As such, Statham increasingly functions as a means of stabilising the films – and the larger-than-life Stallone – in a sense of realism and authenticity away from the array of intertextualities and generic identities of the postmodern ensemble.

This is especially observable in the sequences shared by the two in the cockpit of *The Expendables*' airplane. The tiny set consistently indicates status and hierarchy throughout the films; none of the older 'B-list' or below actors (Lungren, Couture, Crews, even Li) are allowed access to a space defined as belonging equally to Statham and Stallone. As Boyle and Brayton explore, there is a racial aspect to the group/star hierarchies, with white men privileged as central characters (2012: 476). It is a site around which the 'A-list stars' constantly negotiate access, although none succeed in embodying it in the way Statham and Stallone command it. In Bruce Willis's first scene in *The Expendables*, in an aesthetic that mirrors their characters' strained relationship, he and Stallone meet in the plane just beyond the boundary of the cockpit. The scene frames each actor in close-ups and cross-cuts between these separate filmic spaces, with the actors using aggressive, sharp and formalistic delivery of combative dialogue. In *The Expendables 3* Schwarzenegger and Banderas sit in the co-pilot's seat next to Stallone (Statham's usual position), but only temporarily: Banderas is ordered out before take-off at the reappearance of the original team and Schwarzenegger speaks no lines during his short sequence. In contrast, Stallone and Statham share the space more equally, with the sequences usually filmed in symmetrical mid-shots of both men (like the endings of the films) or through over-the-shoulder shots suggesting that both figures are interconnected, even when needling each other. This visual symmetry is challenged in sequences where they travel with women in cars (Giselle Itié in *The Expendables* and Yu Nan in *The Expendables 2*); sitting in the middle of the front seat, the women disrupt the established equilibrium. In general, the visual staging of the ensemble film articulates the cohesiveness of the group and distinct character relations. *The Expendables* trilogy is no exception, and it is notable how the spaces of Statham and Stallone are managed and how they compare to the formal treatment of the wider ensemble, often being utilised at the expense of the more balanced full group shot, as demonstrated in each film's conclusion.

Movement limited by the confines of the cockpit, the two actors rely on voice, with back-and-forth exchange forming an intrinsic feature of their relationship. Jeremy Strong (2013: 70, 74–76) notes that dialogue is often the realisation of the ensemble film whereby speech differentiates characters and represents individual contributions to the team. As alternatives to Statham, Schwarzenegger is too silent – or elsewhere, too reliant on lines referencing his earlier films; Banderas's chatter is too overwhelming; and Willis's speech too antagonistic in tone. Instead Statham and Stallone's softened, low-pitched voices constantly bind together into a harmonious rhythmic exchange. Their overlapping speech flows together smoothly and melodiously, rather than discordantly. Overlapping dialogue, as François Thomas observes, becomes a 'highly, permanently regulated aesthetic technique' with a variety of character functions – from articulating realism, power struggles or cohesion (2013: 131). Outside his interactions with Statham (and throughout his career) Stallone's delivery of banter can be overstated and reliant on punctuating his intonation with large gestures that de-naturalise his characters' supposedly easy-going teasing; here restricted setting limits gesture and Statham's more nuanced vocal control brings Stallone's register down from a *presentational* acting style into a *naturalistic* one, creating a balanced sound that articulates the authentic cohesion of the ensemble group.

In these cockpit conversations, Statham's performance help ground the films amid the excess of self-reflexive stardom by acting as a fulcrum around the greater spectacle. Both the *rhythm* of speech and concepts of *authenticity* are foregrounded in his interactions with Wesley Snipes (Doc) in the latter's extended introduction in *The Expendables 3*. Snipes's on- and off-screen histories have been referenced in exchange with

Dolph Lungren and Randy Couture at the plane's rear, with a nod to being incarcerated for 'tax evasion' and Snipes's typically overstated and forceful acting overwhelming the other personalities. Moving to the doorway that splits cockpit and cabin, Doc goads Christmas over the authenticity of his name, the tattoo signifying his Expendables credentials, and his skills with a knife; all of which the viewer knows to be well proven. Stallone's Ross encourages Doc to 'thank the boys' for rescuing him, and turning back, Snipes stomps, stutters and overplays the 'thanks'; Stallone and Statham's dialogue jokingly comments on its lack of sincerity and that Doc is 'finding his rhythm'. Snipes's delivery embraces the script's competitive posturing ('I'm the knife before Christmas'), dominating the soundscape and visuals and creating a suitably bombastic performative spectacle.

Structurally though, its hyperbolic disruption is tempered by the 'everyday-ness' of Statham's performance. As Snipes speaks, Statham tuts, raises his eyebrows and rolls his eyes, bringing the energy back to something manageable. From here, the overlapping fraternal interplay between Statham and Stallone overtakes Snipes's dominance, bringing order to the film's opening sequence. Statham's calm underplaying works with and around the excessiveness of the other cast members and star types. Each action star, by dint of reflexivity, is an emblem of the trilogy's authentic genre identity, but in a different way Statham too represents a dramatic and textual space of authenticity and 'normality'. Through him, new players are introduced and then contained, allowing the film to negotiate its array of icons in a meaningful way, and despite not being showcased in a physical fight, the film still makes use of his particular skills. As contained in and embodied by Statham's performance in *The Expendables* trilogy, the ensemble, not the individual prevails.

Monologues and managing chaos: opening the ensemble film

Although not one of action cinema's wise guys per se, Statham remains one of the genre's most prolific talkers, and along with the martial arts kick, one of his signature star motifs is a wry monologue. *Lock, Stock and Two Smoking Barrels*, *Snatch* and *Furious 7* all open with the sound of Statham's voice, and other films including *London* (2005), *Revolver* (2005) and *Spy* showcase these skills. As a screen performer, Statham demonstrates an acute awareness of how film uses the sonic qualities of the voice; how preciseness of intonation, delivery, pitch and the materiality afforded by close microphone recording can function as characterisation and overall filmic effect. Close miking suits Statham as it allows for important elements of his voice that disappear when the microphone is further away to be picked up; particularly the way it is concurrently high and low pitched, with qualities that are light and scratchy *and* deep and soft. That mixture of brightness and resonance, a growl that can escape a droning tone (unlike say, Vin Diesel) creates the 'sound of Statham' crucial to his star image. While *The Expendables* trilogy uses Statham as a means of promoting collective identity, monologues represent (along with stardom) another paradox of the ensemble film, whereby the individual momentarily takes precedence over the group, only to be reconciled back within it once the speech is over.

Statham's monologues fall into two categories: speeches delivered within the diegesis contextualised by the responses of surrounding characters, like *Lock, Stock...* and *Furious 7*; and voice-over narration heard only by the audience, as in *Snatch*. While the former gives the impression of being delivered 'live' on set and the latter being reliant on studio recording and close miking, contemporary film-making tends to use additional dialogue recording (ADR) in both, improving the overall quality of the recorded sound, although each type retains a different textual quality appropriate to the setting of the delivery. So, the opening of *Lock, Stock and Two Smoking Barrels*, where Statham works through his market-stall shtick, has an immediacy and energy to it, with a thin, reedy quality to the timbre of his voice, a result of being more distanced from the microphone (given the relatively low budget of the film, it is possible that alternative dispute resolution (ADR) was not used for this sequence). The thinness of Statham's voice also comes from his slightly different accent in this, his first film, where a Derbyshire accent (where Statham was raised) can be heard in the pronunciation of certain words, something absent from later films as his London accent becomes prominent. By the time of *Snatch*, the qualities of the timbre have become more guttural, rich and deep, along with the more sustained cockney inflection. Through close proximity to the microphone, his voice's lower tone and a script that reflects on character background, Statham's introductory narration works counter to the earlier film, striving to create intimacy with the audience and distance from the action.

Snatch places Statham centre stage within the ensemble much more than *Lock, Stock and Two Smoking Barrels*, despite his attention-grabbing opening. In *Lock, Stock…*, director Guy Ritchie uses the actor's ability to deliver quick-fire patter, his comfort with vernacular language, and ease of physical and verbal interplay to authenticate the film's tone through basic believability of character identity and interaction. This function served and Statham's presence becomes less significant as the film progresses. By *Snatch*, his skills are more acutely weaved across the whole film, and his opening monologue sets the scene through the act of storytelling. *Snatch*'s use of Statham's voice-over is typical of wider analyses of this technique that aligns the motif of storytelling with character authority as temporal and spatial distance between image and voice creates a sense of composure and control (Garwood 2015: 105). This time, Statham's speech works to anchor the film's narrative around his character, Turkish, as he outlines his background to the viewer. As such, individual identity is foregrounded (Turkish and his partner Tommy) and narrative threads are set up (the talk of diamonds, which sets up the next sequence, a bombastic jewel heist in Antwerp), rather than using it to just sonically embody atmosphere. Statham's delivery is calm and soothing. He does not over-enunciate, so the effect brings the audience into an intimate, not overly reflexive space. The microphone picks up his voice's simultaneous lower, growling vibrations as well as its sharper, higher register, so it becomes a richly textured sound.

These qualities are mirrored in Statham's physicality on-screen, in softly lit close-ups, his movements are limited to signifiers of interior monologue and realistic directional gesture that matches the topics and timings of the voice-over: for example, when he describes Tommy, Statham looks towards him (by contrast, Stephen Graham plays Tommy with quick, fidgety, unfocused gestures). It is a moment of resonance, not dissonance, and once more, Statham (and Turkish) occupies a position of stability that extends across the narrative, visual and aural planes, working to organise the chaotic pleasures of the ensemble film that quickly follow. Statham's performance throughout the film follows the same self-contained managed style introduced here, foregoing excessive elements for low-key delivery and a physicality that emphasises stillness, usually standing with straight posture and his hands in his coat pockets. The excess of the story, the film style and the performances of the diverse cast revolve around the nexus of Statham's 'straight man' performance, which aligns with the overall function of his character. Unlike *Lock, Stock ...*, he works not as performative spectacle, but as the ensemble's evenly balanced core.

That the monologue helps define Statham's star persona is illustrated by *Furious 7*'s decision to mark his arrival into the franchise with this very motif in its opening scene. It also marks continuity with the previous film as his character, Deckard Shaw, speaks over the prone body of his brother Owen Shaw (Luke Evans), the villain from *Fast and Furious 6*, and swears to 'settle your one last score'. This sequence begins a complex negotiation around Statham and plays with stardom, expectation and genre, not least because there is a longer-term franchise game being played that aims to re-orientate Statham's character from this film's loner antagonist into *The Fate of the Furious*'s [anti] hero team player. Interestingly, reports as early as 2011 outlined Statham being in preliminary talks to appear in *Fast and Furious 6* and one or two sequels (Bettinger 2011).

In *Furious 7*'s opening, the duality of Deckard's status is set up formally and performatively. Statham's monologue straddles textural planes; it *is* a 'live' speech but uses devices of interior monologue. The first lines are shot in a close-up of Statham facing away from the camera, looking out of a window across London. Formal convention suggests this to be a private moment of innermost reflection. His delivery is exceptionally close-miked and the low aural qualities are commonly associated with the non-diegetic voice-over. The script has an existential angle – 'They say if you want to glimpse the future, just look behind you. I used to think that was bollocks. But now I realise, you can't outrun the past' – supported by Statham's wistful, underplayed intonation, briefly interrupted by a harsh stressing of 'bollocks' before the aggression is subsumed into the softness. On the last words, he turns and moves to his brother's bed, tracked by the camera and opening out the cinematic space. Now revealed to be a one-sided conversation, his voice remains close-miked and maintains the sense of intimacy and deep reflection, at odds with the visuals. Generically, everything connotes the landscape of film noir, with a self-destructive figure unable to fight the heavy hand of fate, only to comment upon it. In thinking about genre and performance, Richard De Cordova suggests: 'The voice-over in film noir works to problematize the body by introducing a variety of disjunctions between the bodily image and the voice' (1995: 134). In its introduction of Statham, *Furious 7* uses the monologue to promote certain genre expectations around film noir rather than action cinema (which, generically, is more likely to foreground the body as opening 'statement'). This results in dissonance not coherence; that what we see is not consistent with the absolute truth of the character.

As the scene progresses, generic tropes of action cinema come to the fore, setting up Statham as action star-spectacle (and Deckard as villain). Physicality and energy take precedence and the 'internal' sphere is ruptured through the reveal of medical staff hiding in the corner of the frame. Exiting the space, Deckard barks loudly at them over his shoulder: 'Take care of my brother. If anything happens to him, I'll come back looking for you.' The beat of the rap music on the soundtrack and the Steadicam that tracks Statham's swaggering movement dominate. The noirish immobility is obliterated by momentum and scale: he moves through the wreck of the hospital, punctuates action with pithy lines ('Hold this', pushing a grenade into a SWAT team member), and – as his credit comes up on-screen and he faces down an explosion only by putting sunglasses on – acts every inch the authentic action star. However, the noirish dissonance has already taken seed, complicating not his action-star status, but his action-villain status. Before the viewer sees Statham-the-villain, we first see the reluctant fighter; character before spectacle, and motivation before action. More commonly the villain is announced by psychologically unencumbered spectacular violence, only to later reveal motivation, speaking directly to the hero rather than interior contemplation. In opening with a monologue from Statham and playing with genre boundaries, the film gives unprivileged access and understanding to the character, which foreshadows and ultimately justifies his later, unlikely, cohesion into the 'good guys' in *The Fate of the Furious*.

Conclusion: reconciling the 'I' in 'team'.

Paul McDonald (2012) suggests that the basic contradiction of film star acting is the tension between 'story and show', with film performance situated between the two. To this tension between character and star can be added the demands of genre specificity. The ensemble film creates a further paradox around the place and function of spectacular individual identity within a team-playing aesthetic and narrative.

Jason Statham's star acting in ensemble films engages with these central paradoxes, and in these genre films, his work (along with other formal devices and extratextual readings) helps reconcile the individual's function within a group of stars, actors and characters. Significantly, this is achieved without losing his own distinct star identity; he is always showcased in some capacity whether the performance emphasises stunt work, speech or character-driven narrative motivation. Through his referential acting, the 'Statham show' serves, not overwhelms, the story and the group dynamic; grounding star hierarchies and excessive performances, enabling intimate connections between the audience and the core screen group, and setting up the believability of 'bad guy' absolution. These rely upon an exchange between the spectacular and the unspectacular, and Statham's ensemble value is to be both 'present' and 'absent' without losing sense of self, becoming blandly banal, or excessively disruptive to the cohesion required in the genre. Even his show-stopping (or show-beginning) monologues address the paradox of drawing out the individual beyond the group, although they work differently across distinctive films.

Statham's 'balancing act' has an economic upside to it; ensemble films are increasingly valuable in the global marketplace, especially franchise films that rely on repetition, expansion and textual reflexivity where large casts accommodate international stars. *The Fate of the Furious* broke international box office records on its first weekend, eventually making over $1billion in global returns. Statham's flexibility of employment, referential acting and skills at negotiating star hierarchies in the diverse action ensemble film are useful attributes to have in the contemporary film industry.

References

Basinger, J. (2003). *The World War II Combat Film: Anatomy of a Genre*. Middletown, CT: Wesleyan University Press.

Bettinger, B. (2011). 'Could Jason Statham Join the *Fast and Furious* cast to shoot *Fast 6* and *Fast 7* back to back in Europe'? *Collider.com*. collider.com/jason-statham-fast-and-furious-6-7/ (accessed 1 April 2018).

Boyle, E. and Brayton, S. (2012). 'Ageing masculinities and "muscle work" in Hollywood action film: an analysis of *The Expendables*'. *Men and Masculinities*, 15(5), 468–485.

Corliss, R. (2010). 'The Expendables: sly and the family clones'. Time. content.time.com/time/arts/article/0,8599,2010151,00.html (13.08.10, accessed 27.03.18).
Cornea, C. (2010). 'Editor's introduction', in Cornea, C. (ed.). Genre and Performance in Film and Television. Manchester: Manchester University Press. pp. 1–17.
De Cordova, R. (1995). 'Genre and performance: an overview', in Grant, B. K. (ed.). Film Genre Reader II. Austin, TX: University of Texas Press. pp. 129–139.
Elley, D. (1998). 'Lock, Stock and Two Smoking Barrels', Variety. http://variety.com/1998/film/reviews/lock-stock-and-two-smoking-barrels-1200454610/ (24.08.98, accessed 27.03.18).
Garwood, I. (2015). The Sense of Film Narration. Edinburgh: Edinburgh University Press.
Geraghty, C. (2000). 'Re-examining stardom: questions of texts, bodies and performance', reprinted in Redmond, S. and Holmes, S. (eds). 2003. Stardom and Celebrity: A Reader, Los Angeles and London: SAGE. pp. 98–110.
Greven, D. (2009). 'Contemporary Hollywood masculinity and the double-protagonist film'. Cinema Journal, 48(4), 22–43.
Lee, D. (2014). The Heist Film: Stealing with Style. London and New York: Wallflower Press.
Mathijs, E. (2011). 'Referential acting and the ensemble cast', Screen, 52(1), 89–96.
McDonald, P. (2012). 'Story and show: the basic contradiction in film star acting', in Taylor, A. (ed.). Theorizing Film Acting, New York and London: Routledge. pp. 169–183.
Mumford, G. (2017). 'The Fate of the Furious review', Guardian. www.theguardian.com/film/2017/apr/10/the-fate-of-the-furious-review-fast-furious-8-vin-diesel-dwayne-johnson-helen-mirren (10.04.17, accessed 27.03.18).
Strong, J. (2013). 'Talking teams: dialogue and the team film formula', in Jaeckle, J. (ed.). Film Dialogue. London and New York: Wallflower Press. pp. 70–84.
Tasker, Y. (1993) Spectacular Bodies: Gender, Genre and the Action Cinema. London: Routledge.
Thomas, F. (2013). 'Orson Welles' trademark: overlapping film dialogue', in Jaeckle, J. (ed.). Film Dialogue, London and New York: Wallflower Press. pp. 126–139.
Yoshida, E. (2017). 'The Fate of the Furious is weighed down by its own muscle'. Vulture. www.vulture.com/2017/04/the-fate-of-the-furious-movie-review.html (12.04.17, accessed 27.03.18).

Figure 1 *The Transporter* (Corey Yuen: 2002) EuropaCorp, TF1 Films Production, Current Entertainment, Canal+

Figure 2 *The Transporter* (Corey Yuen: 2002) EuropaCorp, TF1 Films Production, Current Entertainment, Canal+

Figure 3 *The Transporter* (Corey Yuen: 2002) EuropaCorp, TF1 Films Production, Current Entertainment, Canal+

Figure 4 *Transporter 2* (Louis Leterrier: 2005) EuropaCorp

Figure 5 *Transporter 2* (Louis Leterrier: 2005) EuropaCorp

Figure 6 *Transporter 2* (Louis Leterrier: 2005) EuropaCorp

Figure 7 *Transporter 3* (Olivier Megaton: 2008) EuropaCorp, TF1 Films Production, Grive Productions, Apipoulai Entertainment, Canal+, CineCinema

Figure 8 *Transporter 3* (Olivier Megaton: 2008) EuropaCorp, TF1 Films Production, Grive Productions, Apipoulai Entertainment, Canal+, CineCinema

Figure 9 *Transporter 3* (Olivier Megaton: 2008) EuropaCorp, TF1 Films Production, Grive Productions, Apipoulai Entertainment, Canal+, CineCinema

Figure 10 *Crank* (Neveldine/Taylor: 2006) Lakeshore Entertainment, @radical.media

Figure 11 *Crank* (Neveldine/Taylor: 2006) Lakeshore Entertainment, @radical.media

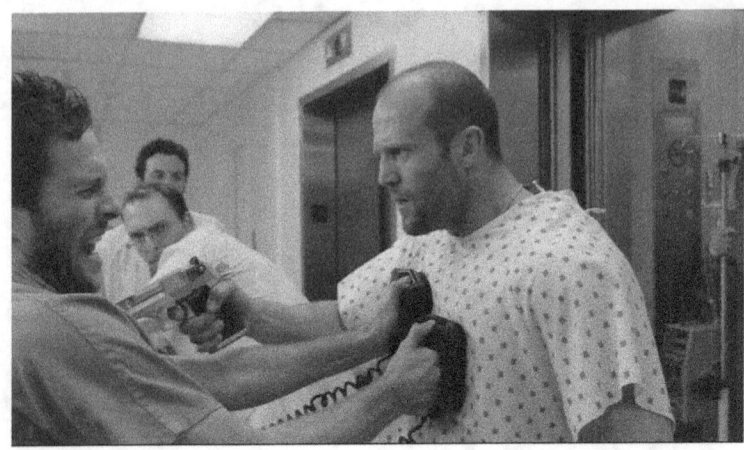

Figure 12 *Crank* (Neveldine/Taylor: 2006) Lakeshore Entertainment, @radical.media

Figure 13 *Crank* (Neveldine/Taylor: 2006) Lakeshore Entertainment, @radical.media

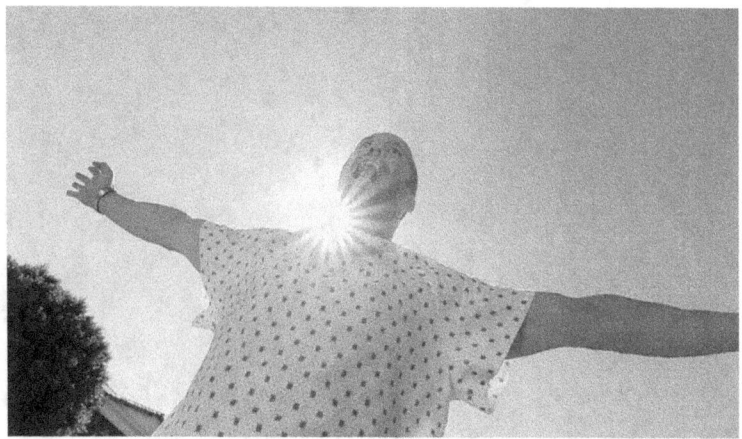

Figure 14 *Crank* (Neveldine/Taylor: 2006) Lakeshore Entertainment, @radical.media

Figure 15 *Crank* (Neveldine/Taylor: 2006) Lakeshore Entertainment, @radical.media

Figure 16 *Crank* (Neveldine/Taylor: 2006) Lakeshore Entertainment, @radical.media

Figure 17 *Crank* (Neveldine/Taylor: 2006) Lakeshore Entertainment, @radical.media

Figure 18 *Crank* (Neveldine/Taylor: 2006) Lakeshore Entertainment, @radical.media

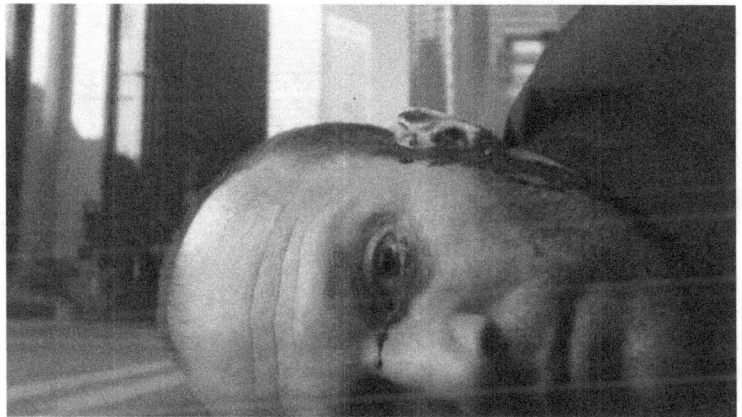

Figure 19 *Crank: High Voltage* (Neveldine/Taylor: 2009) Lakeshore Entertainment, @radical.media

Figure 20 *Crank: High Voltage* (Neveldine/Taylor: 2009) Lakeshore Entertainment, @radical.media

Figure 21 *Crank: High Voltage* (Neveldine/Taylor: 2009) Lakeshore Entertainment, @radical.media

Figure 22 *Crank: High Voltage* (Neveldine/Taylor: 2009) Lakeshore Entertainment, @radical.media

Figure 23 *Crank: High Voltage* (Neveldine/Taylor: 2009) Lakeshore Entertainment, @radical.media

Figure 24 *Crank: High Voltage* (Neveldine/Taylor: 2009) Lakeshore Entertainment, @radical.media

Figure 25 *In the Name of the King: A Dungeon Siege Tale* (Uwe Boll: 2007) Boll KG Productions, Herold Productions, Brightlight Pictures

Part II
Statham and genre case studies

6

Blagging it both ways: *The Bank Job* (2008) and the British heist movie

James Chapman

The Bank Job (2008) – a crime/action thriller based loosely on the Baker Street bank robbery of September 1971, written by Dick Clement and Ian La Frenais, and directed by Roger Donaldson for Lionsgate Films UK – is perhaps best described as a middling popular success for its star Jason Statham. Released in the United Kingdom on 28 February, it took £951,013 in its opening week and was the number one film at the box office in Britain: the distributor regarded this as a 'surprisingly successful launch' despite it not breaking the £1 million mark (Mitchell 2008). It ended the year with a gross of £4.5 million which placed it fifty-eighth in the annual list of top box office attractions but a long way behind the top three films *Mamma Mia!* (£69.2 million), *Quantum of Solace* (£51.1 million) and *The Dark Knight* (£48.9 million). In North America, where it was released a week later on 7 March, *The Bank Job* was shown on 1,613 screens and grossed $5,935,256 on its opening weekend: this placed it fourth behind two other new releases, *10,000 BC* ($35,867,488) and *College Road Trip* ($13,601,419), and the continuing *Vantage Point* ($5,985,212), all of which played on more screens. Its total 'domestic' gross of $30,060,660 placed it just inside the annual top hundred at number ninety-eight. Again, it was a long way behind the super-blockbusters which topped the American box office in 2008 – *The Dark Knight* ($533,345,358), *Iron Man* ($318,412,101) and *Indiana Jones and the Kingdom of the Crystal Skull* ($317,101,119) – but it was consistent with the performance of the year's two other Statham starring vehicles, *Death Race* ($36,316,032) and *Transporter 3* ($31,715,062). *The Bank Job*'s North American receipts accounted for 46.4 per cent of its total worldwide gross of $64,822,796. Other than the United Kingdom, the most lucrative overseas markets were France ($4,849,100), Australia ($4,282,460), Russia ($2,857,373), South Korea ($2,643,105), Mexico ($1,806,999), Germany ($1,561,401) and Brazil ($1,109,932). Overall this represented an above average though far from spectacular success for a British independent film: much less than *Slumdog Millionaire* ($377,910,544 worldwide) or *Atonement* (2007) ($129,266,012), but rather more than *The Boy in the Striped Pyjamas* ($40,416,567), *Miss Pettigrew Lives for a Day* ($16,724,933) or *Brideshead Revisited* ($13,451,186) (all box office figures are taken from www.boxofficemojo.com; all films bar *Atonement* were released in 2008).

Box office data provides at best crude quantitative evidence of popular reception: the critical response to *The Bank Job* is more illuminating in terms of qualitative evidence. It would be fair to say that the reviews of *The Bank Job* were of the sort typically described as mixed. In Britain, for example, Philip French, the long-serving film critic of *The Observer*, described it as being 'scripted with a light touch' and 'directed with considerable verve ... The film races along with the speed of a bullet train ... and is a great deal of ugly, subversive fun' (French 2008). Tim Robey in *The Daily Telegraph* thought it a cut above other Statham pictures: 'Statham makes a bid for a certain kind of respectability in *The Bank Job*, a gritty, British caper ... [A] messy but watchable yarn boasting borderline-absurd levels of 1970s bling and Statham in turtlenecks' (Robey 2008). Derek Adams (2008) in *Time Out* found that 'it all looks authentically old-fashioned, and there are a few nuggets of amusing dialogue amid the occasional violence, sexual debauchery, political corruption and overall hedonistic atmosphere'. However, for Paul Arent (2008), writing for the BBC's film website, '*The Bank Job* doesn't really deliver the thrills' and was 'strangely erratic, aiming for the breezy high jinks of Ealing comedy in the first half, then collapsing into dead-eyed sadism, then back to cheeky cockney chappies for a reasonably rousing climax'. Chris

Hewitt in *Empire* thought it a 'lumbering thriller which feels like it belongs on the telly ... Statham – so good at punching things and growling threats – is stranded with a role that requires him to do little of either' (Hewitt 2007). Kevin Maher (2008) in *The Times* thought it 'is formulaic in all the wrong ways ... [The] realism here doesn't bear much scrutiny, unless of course the London of 1971 was populated exclusively by decent criminals, bent coppers, topless barmaids, and sinister Whitehall toffs in S&M knocking shops'.

American reviews of *The Bank Job* were a similar mixed bag. For Manohla Dargis in the *New York Times* it was a 'wham-bam caper flick' notable for a muscular performance from its star: 'Mr Statham, a B-movie action pinup (*The Transporter*), pumps like a pistol across the screen and fills out his natty leather coat, both of which he does with palpable brute force' (Dargis 2008). The reviewer for *Entertainment Weekly*, preferred its gritty British realism over the glossy style of the *Ocean's Eleven* films: 'One of the pleasures of *The Bank Job* is that it returns us to the days when robbing a bank was a gritty, hole-in-the-wall affair ... Watching *The Bank Job*, you buy the heist, and you also buy the entertaining layer cake of British society' (Gleiberman 2008). For Jim Emerson, Roger Ebert's successor at the *Chicago Sun-Times*, however, it was no more than

> [a] serviceable B-grade British heist movie ... Once it triggers memories of movies as diverse as *The Asphalt Jungle*, *Rififi*, *Le Cercle Rouge*, *The Italian Job*, *Reservoir Dogs*, *Ocean's Eleven*, *Inside Man* – and how could it not? – you may realize that you're not having quite as much fun from watching this picture as you did watching those. (2008)

Leslie Felperin's *Variety* review (2008) felt that the 'pic feels downright old-fashioned – not in an arch-pastiche way, but not in a really good way' and averred that 'the filmmaking lacks flair and looks as though it were done a bit on the cheap'. In contrast – and to take an example from one of the other markets in which it performed well at the box office – Paul Byrnes of the *Sydney Morning Herald* echoed Gleiberman in preferring it to Hollywood franchise films such as *Mission: Impossible* and *Ocean's Eleven* with their 'pretty' stars Tom Cruise and George Clooney:

> *The Bank Job*, on the other hand, being basically British, has hardly any handsome chaps, but it has the delightful cheekbones of Saffron Burrows, the rough-hewn East End charm of Jason

Statham and the advantage of being sort of true. It also has a British sense of humour, which beats Tom Cruise hanging upside down in a harness any day. (2008)

As mixed as the reviews were, however, two particular themes emerge consistently from the reception discourse of *The Bank Job* which provide a useful critical framework for a discussion of the film. One was its Britishness, the other its relationship to the history of what has been termed the 'heist movie'. The heist movie is a subcategory of the crime film which typically dramatises the planning, execution and aftermath of a robbery by a small group of criminals: its conventions include the recruitment of the gang, surveillance of the target, the preparation and rehearsal of the crime, carrying out the robbery (often with the need for some improvisation to overcome an unforeseen hitch), and the aftermath during which the scheme unravels and the gang are (usually) caught by the police or killed while attempting to escape. It could be argued that the heist movie emerged quite early in the history of cinema in films such as Edwin S. Porter's *The Great Train Robbery* (1903) and – to take a British example – William Haggar's *Daring Daylight Burglary* (1903), though it was during the post-Second World War period that the genre really took shape. The archetypal heist films are John Huston's *The Asphalt Jungle* (1950) and Jules Dassin's French classic *Rififi* (1955) – a tale of a diamond robbery gone wrong featuring a celebrated long 'silent' sequence depicting the robbery itself – while other major examples from Hollywood include Richard Fleischer's *Violent Saturday* (1955), Stanley Kubrick's *The Killing* (1956), Lewis Milestone's *Ocean's Eleven* (1960), Walter Hill's *The Getaway* (1973), Sidney Lumet's *Dog Day Afternoon* (1975), Joseph Sargent's *The Taking of Pelham 123* (1974), William Friedkin's *The Brinks Job* (1978), Quentin Tarantino's *Reservoir Dogs* (1992) and Steven Soderbergh's remake of *Ocean's Eleven* (2001) and its sequels. The heist formula can also be found in other genres, including the Western (*The War Wagon*, 1967) and war film (*Kelly's Heroes*, 1970). And the heist movie became a staple of other national cinemas where the action movie has been prevalent: *Reservoir Dogs* is held to have been partly based on a popular Hong Kong action film, *City on Fire* (1987), while the heist picture also became a staple of Hindi ('Bollywood') cinema in the early twenty-first century, exemplified by *Aankhan* (2002), *Dhoom* (2004) and its sequels, *Cash* (2007), *Layer* (2012) and *Happy New Year* (2014).

The Bank Job sits within a history of British heist movies that has its own particular cultural and ideological contexts. Broadly speaking most British heist movies can be placed within one of two distinct lineages or taxonomies. On the one hand there have been British films in the style of American noir thrillers such as *The Asphalt Jungle* and *The Killing*. *Payroll* (1961) – scripted by George Baxt from a novel by Derek Bickerton and directed by Sidney Hayers for Anglo-Amalgamated Film Distributors – is perhaps the nearest equivalent (though it is rather anaemic in comparison to the American films): the film's most distinctive quality is not the somewhat hackneyed plot – an armoured van robbery that goes wrong – but the fact that it was shot on location in Newcastle, which invests the film with something of the 'northern realism' of contemporaneous British new wave films such as *Room at the Top* (1959), *Saturday Night and Sunday Morning* (1960) and *A Taste of Honey* (1961). *Robbery* (1967) – directed by Peter Yates and scripted by Yates and George Markstein for Oakhurst Productions – was a fictionalised account of the Great Train Robbery of 1963. It anticipates *The Bank Job* insofar as it is based on a real event and adheres quite closely to the known facts while changing the characters' names and the eventual outcomes. Paul Clifton (Stanley Baker) masterminds the robbery of the Glasgow to London postal night express by rigging up a false red signal and then hiding at a disused airfield while the police search for the gang. *Robbery* is at pains to present its crooks as old-fashioned 'lags' rather than ruthless career criminals: hence Clifton is insistent that they will not carry 'shooters' ('No guns! I want no victims, no accidents. They don't carry guns, we don't need them.') Yates's direction of the opening car chase – the gang rob a diamond courier to raise funds for the big job – provided his ticket to Hollywood to direct the Steve McQueen film *Bullitt* (1968). Robert Murphy avers that *Robbery* exemplifies the 'vacuous internationalism [that] seemed to seep into the British crime film' from the mid-1960s (Murphy 1997: 217). However, it seems more redolent of the drab realism that re-emerged in British cinema towards the end of the decade: Douglas Slocombe's grainy colour cinematography and the use of 'ordinary' locations such as Leyton Orient Football Club differentiate the film from the glossy 'Swinging London' films of the mid-1960s.

On the other hand, there has been a tradition of what might be termed 'caper' movies that have adopted a lighter and even comedic mode. This tradition extends back to *The Lavender Hill Mob* (1951) – written by T. E. B. Clarke and directed by Charles Crichton for Ealing Studios – in which a mild-mannered bank clerk (a masterful performance by Alec Guinness) hatches a gold bullion robbery. One of the reasons for the prominence of the more-comedic variants of the heist movie was undoubtedly the policy of the British Board of Film Censors (BBFC) which for many years maintained a ban both on 'true crime' subjects and on what it termed '"crook" films in which sympathy is enlisted for the criminals' (Robertson 1985: 182). *The Lavender Hill Mob* is entirely free from objection on these grounds: it is essentially a wish-fulfilment fantasy for the 'little man' in which 'the meek are allowed to inherit the earth by means of a massive crime that hurts and offends no-one' (Barr 1977: 117).

In Britain the comedy-drama heist movie persisted – and was often more popular than the more realistic mode – beyond the relaxation of censorship in the 1960s. It is exemplified by films such as *The League of Gentlemen* (1960), *The Italian Job* (1969) and *The First Great Train Robbery* (1979), to which one might add the comedies *The Big Job* (1965) and *The Great St Trinian's Train Robbery* (1966). *The League of Gentlemen* – scripted by Bryan Forbes from a novel by John Boland and directed by Basil Dearden for Allied Film Makers – features a group of cashiered ex-army officers who use their military skills to plan and execute a bank robbery. ('I do hope he hasn't the National Provincial in mind – they're being awfully decent to me at the moment,' remarks one of the gang, which might be read as a tongue-in-cheek reference to the fact that the National Provincial Bank provided the financing for the production company.)

The high-water mark of the heist comedy-drama is *The Italian Job* – scripted by Troy Kennedy Martin and directed by Peter Collinson for Paramount Pictures – in which a British gang brings off an audacious bullion robbery in Turin under the noses of the Italian Mafia. *The Italian Job* has achieved cult status by dint of its quotable lines ('You're only supposed to blow the bloody doors off!') and its spectacular driving stunts. Yet it is also a highly ideologically charged film. Steve Chibnall suggests that 'the criminal underworld represents the Eurosceptic flip side of Britain, the vein of patriotic isolationism that runs deep beneath the surface of an island race' (Chibnall 2005: 149). Paramount's remake of *The Italian Job* (2003) detached the film from its British roots and turned it into a slick Americanised caper in the style of *Ocean's Eleven* though the Mini Coopers remained: Jason Statham was cast to type as the gang's 'wheelman' known as Handsome Rob.

A recurring feature of the history of the heist movie in British cinema – including both its realist and its comedy-drama variants – is that the major examples of the genre have tended to coincide with periods of social and political upheaval. *The Lavender Hill Mob*, for example, was produced during the last months of the post-war Labour government: it marks the transition from the post-war culture of austerity to the newly emergent affluent consumer culture of the 1950s. The Ealing comedies of the late 1940s such as *Passport to Pimlico* and *Whisky Galore!* were celebrations of community spirit: in contrast, *The Lavender Hill Mob* is very much about the individual and the self. *The League of Gentlemen* is a Janus-faced film that sits on the cusp of what, following Arthur Marwick, we may term the 'cultural revolution' of the 1960s (Marwick 1984). If, on one level, the film harks back to the British war films of the previous decade such as *The Colditz Story* and *The Dam Busters* with their emphasis on male camaraderie and teamwork, on another level it points to the obsolescence of those values ('I served my country well as a regular soldier and was suddenly rewarded after 25 years by being declared redundant') (Elliott 2014: 62). *The Italian Job* refers to Britain's worsening trade deficit in the late 1960s (Noël Coward's Mr Bridger – an underworld godfather who orchestrates his criminal empire from inside a prison cell – agrees to back the robbery 'to help this country with its balance of payments') and to the increasing American presence in the British film production industry ('I can always take it to the Americans. They're people who recognise young talent and give it a chance'). By the end of the 1960s the National Film Finance Corporation estimated that around 85 per cent of British features were financed in whole or in part by Hollywood studios (Murphy 1992: 267).

The Bank Job occupies a particularly distinctive place in the history of the British heist movie in so far as it draws upon elements from the different traditions within the genre. On one level it resembles a film such as *Robbery* in that it was based – if somewhat loosely – on an actual event. On the night of 11–12 September 1971 a gang of robbers broke into the vault of the Baker Street/Marylebone Road branch of Lloyds Bank in

London: they tunnelled in from a leather goods shop called Le Sac which they had rented two doors away. The gang was overheard by a radio ham, who picked up the walkie-talkie communication between the tunnellers and their lookout. However, the police were initially unable to identify which bank was being robbed, and the gang got away with a cash haul reported variously as between £500,000 and £3 million as well as valuables from safety deposit boxes. The robbery made headline news but after several days, newspapers stopped reporting it: this led to speculation that the government had issued a 'D Notice' to suppress the story on the grounds of national security. A conspiracy theory later emerged that the robbery had been set up by the Security Service (MI5) in order to retrieve sexually compromising photographs of the Queen's sister Princess Margaret which had been kept in a safety deposit box by the militant Black Panther leader known as 'Michael X' (Michael de Freitas) (Daily Mail 2007). A possibly more plausible – if rather less salacious – explanation for suppressing the story is that it revealed evidence of police incompetence and corruption. Indeed, Channel 5 featured the Baker Street robbery in its series *Britain's Biggest Bank Jobs* (23 November 2015), alleging a 'cloud of secrecy' including police corruption. In the film, the character of Lew Vogel (David Suchet), a Soho underworld boss who keeps a ledger of payments to corrupt police officers, was based partly on the pornographer James Humphreys whose relationships with members of the Metropolitan Police's Flying Squad caused a corruption scandal when they were exposed by the press in 1972.

The production discourse of *The Bank Job* sought to position it as the 'untold story' of the Baker Street robbery. According to co-producer Charles Roven: 'This is an amazing, untold story of murder, sex and corruption. It's going to excite and entertain audiences everywhere, but it will also give them plenty to think about' (Thorpe 2007). The coverage of the production in the press included references to a 'Deep Throat' informant who had inside knowledge of the robbery: this was later revealed to be journalist George McIndoe who claimed to have met two of the robbers – four men had been convicted at the Old Bailey in January 1973 – and who is credited as one of three executive producers of the film (Jones 2008). McIndoe had long-harboured the ambition to make a film about the incident and as early as the 1970s had touted it as a possible vehicle for Sean

Connery and Michael Caine, who later appeared together in John Huston's *The Man Who Would Be King* (1975).

Yet the 'untold story' aspect of the film does not seem to have informed the reception discourse of *The Bank Job* very strongly. One reason might be that the Baker Street robbery, while a cause célèbre in its day, has not exerted the same grip on the popular imagination as more notorious crimes such as the Great Train Robbery. One reviewer, for instance, referred to 'the slightly famous Baker Street heist of 1971' (Byrnes 2008). Another might be that in promoting the conspiracy theory narrative, *The Bank Job* possibly seemed to be opting for the least plausible version of the story. The film does not mention Princess Margaret by name, though there is little doubt regarding the identity of the 'certain royal personage' identified in the photographs: 'Holy shit, you know who that is!' exclaims Terry Leather (Statham) when he sees the evidence for himself, while Lord Mountbatten (Christopher Owen) observes with a wry smile that 'she is a scallywag!' Yet ultimately the film seems to step back from asserting its own credentials as 'truth' or 'fact' with an end title which acknowledges its own fictionality while at the same time providing an ironic twist on the standard legal disclaimer: 'The names of many of the people identified in this film have been changed to protect the guilty.'

This is not to say that *The Bank Job* is entirely inauthentic. Its relationship to the historical facts might be compared to *The Great Escape* (1963): John Sturges's film of Paul Brickhill's book, scripted by James Clavell, actually presents a fairly accurate account of the planning of the mass escape from Stalag Luft III in 1944 until the point where the escapers are outside the prisoner-of-war camp whereupon it becomes a work of pure fiction with its celebrated motorcycle chase and other invented incidents. Similarly, the details of the robbery in *The Bank Job* – including tunnelling under the Chicken Inn restaurant using a thermal lance and the radio ham who overhears and records their communications – are reasonably accurate, whereas the events of the second half of the film where Terry plays MI5 off against underworld boss Vogel are very much the invention of the scriptwriters. Dick Clement and Ian La Frenais had a long-established writing partnership: they specialised in situation comedies, notably *The Likely Lads* and *Porridge*, but they had also written several British films, including the spy comedy *Otley* (1968), the war adventure *Hannibal Brooks* (1968) and the gangster film *Villain* (1971). The latter, a fictionalised biopic of notorious East End gangster Reginald Kray starring Richard Burton, has some parallels with *The Bank Job*.

It might be argued that *The Bank Job* exhibits a form of cultural authenticity rather than strict historical accuracy. Several reviewers commented favourably upon its imagining of the London of the early 1970s: it evokes the period after the 'swinging sixties' but before the severe economic downturn occasioned by the oil crisis of 1973–1974. For Geoffrey Macnab in *Sight and Sound*:

> Whatever its flaws, Roger Donaldson's crime drama does a sterling job of recreating the London of the early 1970s. From the T-Rex music (which we hear over the credits) to the haircuts, costumes, cars and even the slang, Donaldson and his team have gone to exhaustive efforts to do justice to their period. Nor is there anything mocking or knowingly ironic in their revisiting of the era: the British society they portray is instead corrupt from the top down, and all the characters – whether the Royal Family (at risk of becoming embroiled in a sex scandal), the secret services (public schoolboys busy orchestrating bank robberies), the porn barons (paying off corrupt cops), the gangsters, the brothel madame or even Jason Statham's everyman hero Terry – are bending the rules. (Macnab 2008: 55)

To this extent *The Bank Job* might also be understood within a vogue for 1970s nostalgia in British popular culture in the 2000s that also included the BBC's police series *Life on Mars*: both feature a 'sounds of the seventies' soundtrack – *The Bank Job* includes tracks by The Kinks and Wilson Pickett as well as T-Rex – while actor Daniel Mays, who plays gang member Dave, appeared in the final season of *Life on Mars*'s sequel *Ashes to Ashes*.

As well as being inspired by real events, *The Bank Job* would also seem to have taken other heist movies as reference points. There are broad parallels to *The Lavender Hill Mob* (the amateur crooks who succeed in bringing off the robbery despite some comic bungling) and *The Italian Job* (the likeable cockney rogue who manages to stay one step ahead of the police and the mob). Statham's presence inevitably mandates comparisons to his film debut in Guy Ritchie's *Lock, Stock and Two Smoking Barrels* (1998), the film which kick started a cycle of postmodern, genre-aware British crime movies to which *The Bank Job* partly belongs. The opening sequences of *The Bank Job* employ the device of non-linear narration and flashbacks familiar from films such as

Reservoir Dogs and *Ocean's Eleven*: this is an economical means of setting up the conspiracy elements of the film – Terry is lured into carrying out the job by his old flame Martine Love (Saffron Burrows) after she is picked up at Heathrow Airport carrying drugs and brokers a deal with government 'spook' Tim Everett (Richard Lintern), who also happens to be one of her boyfriends, to retrieve the photographs – though its inclusion at the beginning of the film denies the possibility of the 'twist' ending of films like *Ocean's Eleven*. *The Bank Job* also recalls both *The Italian Job* and *Lock, Stock and Two Smoking Barrels* in its mobilisation of football metaphors: there are references to 'looking for the big score' and, at one point, Terry suggests that 'it's time we stepped up to the First Division'. The robbery in *The Italian Job* takes place under cover of an international match between England and Italy, while *Lock, Stock and Two Smoking Barrels* famously featured ex-football 'hardman' Vinnie Jones as Big Chris.

There is a sense in which *The Bank Job* represents a point of convergence between the two lineages of the British heist movie. The first half of the film adopts the light-hearted tone of films such as *The League of Gentlemen* and *The Italian Job*: the gang themselves are characterised as amateurs and prove to be comically inept at times. One particular exchange over the radio – 'No names, Eddie', 'Sorry, Dave' – is in the tradition of the famous 'What is your name?', 'Don't tell him, Pike' moment of the classic British sitcom *Dad's Army*. However, the tone of the film changes in the second half: it becomes much darker and more violent in content. Vogel kidnaps one of the gang members, Dave, whom he recognises from a porn film that Vogel has financed. The torture of Dave with a blowtorch and his subsequent murder recalls the torture of the captured cop by Mr Blonde (Michael Madsen) in *Reservoir Dogs*. Other victims are gang member 'the Major' (James Faulkner), who is stabbed to death, and Gale Benson (Hattie Morahan), murdered by Michael X (Peter de Jersey) when he discovers she is spying on him for the security services. Moments such as these sit uneasily with the lighter tone of the first half of the film, and it would probably be fair to say that *The Bank Job* is less successful in merging comedy and violence than, say, *Lock, Stock and Two Smoking Barrels*. This probably helps to explain its mixed reception by critics: *The Bank Job* seems uncertain as to what kind of heist movie it wants to be.

This uncertainty also extends to Statham's role in the film. While *The Bank Job* was clearly designed as a star vehicle, it seems unsure how to use him to best effect. On the one hand the narrative offers little scope for Statham's skills in choreographing action sequences – he has only one (relatively low-key) punch-up towards the end of the film – or for the sort of stunt driving that characterises the *Transporter* series. On the other hand, *The Bank Job* promotes Statham to the leadership role having played team members in previous crime and heist films such as *Lock, Stock and Two Smoking Barrels* and *The Italian Job*. In planning the robbery and staying one step ahead of both the police and the gangsters, Statham's character Terry Leather has to demonstrate brain rather than brawn. In this context Tim Robey's comment that *The Bank Job* marked 'a bid for a certain kind of respectability' is particularly apt. There is a sense in which Statham is the early twenty-first century version of Michael Caine: his cockney persona roots his star image in a distinctively British cultural and social idiom that serves to differentiate him not only from other contemporary British actors more associated with 'heritage' roles such as Hugh Grant, Rupert Everett or Colin Firth, but also from Hollywood action stars such as Bruce Willis, Vin Diesel or Dwayne Johnson. Indeed, Statham's role in *The Bank Job* is very similar to Michael Caine's in the original *The Italian Job*: the main difference is that rather than ending on a (literal) cliff-hanger, *The Bank Job* reunites Terry with his family and allows them to enjoy the fruits of his ill-gotten gains.

In conclusion, *The Bank Job* was something of a transitional film for Jason Statham. On the one hand, it harks back to the independent British-made films such as *Lock, Stock and Two Smoking Barrels* and *Snatch* (2000) in which Statham first made his name. On the other hand, it was very consciously devised as a starring vehicle for Statham rather than as another ensemble drama. Excluding the three *Transporter* films (2002, 2005, 2008), *The Bank Job* was Statham's fourth top-billed feature, following *Revolver* (2005), *Chaos* (2005) and *Crank* (2006). It was made at a time when his star was very much in the ascendant but before he had quite achieved the superstar status that came with his role in *The Expendables* (2010) and its sequels. While *The Bank Job* would not be Statham's last British film – it was followed by *Blitz* (2011), *Killer Elite* (2011) and *Hummingbird* (2013) – it was in Hollywood that his future lay. In this sense *The Bank Job* belongs to the end of the period of Statham's career when he was caught between Britain and Hollywood and was still blagging it both ways.

References

Adams, D. (2008). 'The Bank Job'. *Time Out*. www.timeout.com/london/film/the-bank job (26.02.07, accessed 16.02.18).

Arent, P. (2008). 'The Bank Job'. *BBC Movies*. www.bbc.co.uk/films.2008/02/25/the_bank_job_2008_review.shtml (27.02.08, accessed 26.02.18).

Barr, C. (1977). *Ealing Studios*. London: Cameron & Tayleur/David & Charles.

Byrnes, P. (2008). 'The Bank Job'. *Sydney Morning Herald*. www.smh.au/news/film reviews/the-bank-job/2008/07/25/1216492719757.html (25.07.08, accessed 16.02.2018).

Chibnall, S. (2005). 'The Italian Job', in Brian McFarlane (ed.). *The Cinema of Britain and Ireland*. London: Wallflower Press. pp. 145–153.

Daily Mail (2007). 'How MI5 raided a bank to get pictures of Princess Margaret'. www.dailymail.co.uk/news/article-456479/How-MI5-raided-bank-pictures-Princess Margaret.html (21.05.07, accessed on 16.02.18).

Dargis, M. (2008). 'Tunneling thieves strike lode of loot (and valuable smut)'. www.nytimes.com/2008/03/07/movies/07bank.html (07.03.08, accessed 22.04.18).

Elliott, P. (2014). *Studying the British Crime Film*. Leighton Buzzard: Auteur Publishing.

Emerson, J. (2008). 'The Bank Job'. *RogerEbert.com*. www.rogerebert.com/reviews/the-bank-job-2008 (06.03.08, accessed 16.02.2018).

Felperin, L. (2008). 'The Bank Job'. *Variety*. variety.com/2008/film/markets-festivals/the-bank-job-1200536237/ (28.02.08, accessed 16.02.2018).

French, P. (2008). 'The Bank Job'. *The Observer*. www.theguardian.com/film/2008/mar/02/thriller.drama (02.03.08, accessed 16.02.2018).

Gleiberman, O. (2008). 'The Bank Job'. *Entertainment Weekly*. ew.com/article/2008/03/06/bank-job/ (06.03.18, accessed 16.02.2018).

Hewitt, C. (2007). 'The Bank Job'. *Empire*. https://empireonline.com/movies/bank-job/review/ (18.11.07, accessed 16.02.2018).

Jones, J. R. (2008). 'What's the real story behind *The Bank Job*?', *Chicago Reader*. www.chicagoreader.com/Bleader/archives/2008/03/07/ (07.03.08, accessed 16.02.18).

Macnab, G. (2008). 'The Bank Job'. *Sight and Sound*. New Series 18(3), March 2008.

Maher, K. (2008). 'It's a goal for Ferrell, a towering player'. *The Times*. 28 February 2008. pp. 15.

Marwick, A. (1984). '*Room at the Top*, *Saturday Night and Sunday Morning*, and the "Cultural revolution" in Britain'. *Journal of Contemporary History*, 19(1), 127–152; 19(8), 1069–1083.

Mitchell, W. (2008). 'Lionsgate UK: ready to roar'. *Screen Daily.* www.screendaily.com/lionsgate-ukready-to-roar/4040462.article (29.08.08, accessed 23.04.18).
Murphy, R. (1992). *Sixties British Cinema.* London: British Film Institute.
Robertson, J. C. (1985). *The British Board of Film Censors: Film Censorship in Britain, 1896–1950.* London: Croom Helm.
Robey, T. (2008). 'Film reviews: *The Bank Job, Untraceable* and more'. *The Telegraph.* www.telegraph.co.uk/culture/film/filmreviews/3671483/ (29.02.08, accessed 16.02.18).
Thorpe, V. (2007). 'Untold story of Baker Street bank robbery'. *Guardian.* www.theguardian.com/uk/2007/mar/11/film (11.03.07, accessed 16.02.2018).

7

Jason Statham in *Spy*: subverting genre and gender

Clare Smith

> I drove a car off the top of a freeway onto a train while on fire. Not the car. 'I' was on fire.
>
> Rick Ford, *Spy*

This is one of the tamer tales Rick Ford (Jason Statham) tells of his exploits as a CIA agent in the film *Spy* (2015). The line epitomises the comedy inherent in the character of Ford. As a performer Statham is renowned for his prowess in action roles. In *Spy* it is his comedic skills that are on display. It is also fairly tame by the standard of Jason Statham's on-screen actions. This line combines scenes in *Crank: High Voltage* (2009) when Chev Chelios (Statham) carries on fighting in a mass brawl while he is on fire and *Transporter 3* (2008: Megaton) when Frank/Statham drives a car onto a moving train. This established screen persona is central to the comedy and action of *Spy* and the performance of Statham within the film subverts expectations of genre and gender within action films. This chapter will examine how Statham, one of the most successful of contemporary action stars engages with comedy and how this change in metier subverts genre and gender in the film.

Spy stars Melissa McCarthy as desk-bound CIA agent Susan Cooper who is the eyes, ears and brains behind James

Bond-like agent Bradley Fine (Jude Law). Secretly in love with Fine, Susan runs his field activities which encompasses everything from informing him of the location of assorted villains to packing his allergy tablets for his travels. When Fine is apparently killed by villainess Rayna Boyanov, Susan offers to go into the field to track her down and find a stolen nuclear bomb in her possession. The mission is undertaken by Cooper, as Fine's counterpart Rick Ford has had his cover blown and cannot go back into the field. Rick resigns from the CIA and goes rogue, attempting to track down Rayna and the bomb himself. This is very much in keeping with the EON-produced James Bond series, most notably *Licence to Kill* (1989: John Glen) when Bond moves away from Her Majesty's Secret Service to act as a lone agent on a personal vendetta. While most Bondian exploits have elements of comedy, *Spy*'s comedy and subversion of the spy genre takes over when the overweight, early-middle-aged female agent Susan, who has no experience out in the field, succeeds in her mission. In contrast the muscled, experienced, male agent Rick Ford is comically inept, and needs to be saved by Cooper at every turn. His ineptness makes every dangerous situation he is in much worse.

The two lead male roles in the film are based on famous screen male action heroes. Jude Law as Bradley Fine has classic good looks, wears a tuxedo, has an elegant fighting style, and employs suave one-liners and quips to smooth over the precarious state of affairs he often finds himself embroiled in. He is the traditional filmic James Bond. However, as Ford, Statham is technically the newer edgier male action hero, arguably one removed from the 'older' Bond and linked more to the post-millennial one of Daniel Craig: he is working class, much more prone to a form of street violence, less dependent on gadgets, with more emphasis placed on increasingly impossible stunts performed with an insouciance that underplays the seriousness of what is happening on-screen. Rick Ford is the summation of all the roles Jason Statham has played on-screen to this part of his career. This approach should be applauded, for the postmodern meta-casting of Statham playing a comedic role with a straight face seems to subvert his entire film career. Russell Meuf (2017) described him as playing 'a caricature of his action-film persona'. However, if the role was merely a caricature the comedy would quickly become a one-joke performance and not sustain the humour for the length of the film.

Statham's performance in *Spy* hinges upon the concept that the audience expect a specific star to play a specific role. By using the theoretical structure set forward by Richard Dyer concerning audience identification of stars, this chapter will examine the screen persona developed by Statham in some of his film roles before *Spy* that the film then subverts. By focusing on *Spy*, and with reference to Statham's work across various film franchises this chapter will focus on the actor across these films and how his role as Rick Ford subverts 'type', genre and gender.

Richard Dyer (1998) argues that both the genre of a film and the image of an individual star can combine to create and provide a form of audience expectation whereby the star/character and genre conventions become formulaic in terms of both ideological and physical traits. Dyer sets out a number of elements that can be used to signify the 'type' of character in a film. As part of what he calls audience foreknowledge Dyer identifies star-genre expectation, whereby audiences expect John Wayne to play a particular kind of character. What then does an audience know of Statham and the action films he has appeared in? Looking at the film franchises mentioned earlier, while they do have different narratives, they have a number of similarities concerning the characters played by Statham.

In both *The Transporter* and *The Expendables* films Statham's character is an ex-British Special Forces operative. In the tradition of action films, each one has a set of intricate fight scenes, through which Statham's character moves. Statham is an actor who performs his own stunt work. The fight scenes in these films often see Statham in combat against a number of enemies, and he often utilises everyday objects as weapons with increasing degrees of impossibility. For example, in *Transporter 2*, Statham's character Frank uses a fire hose against a gang of armed men, and in *Crank* his character Chev Chelios throws a champagne bottle at a man armed with a gun, which is then dropped causing it to fire and shoot off his own fingers.

Apart from Chev Chelios, unrepentant assassin for drug dealers, there is an inherent goodness in Statham's characters even when his profession is based on illegal activity. In the *Transporter* series Frank is employed as a driver-for-hire. In the first film he saves a young Asian woman from being kidnapped; in the third instalment he averts political corruption. In the second, his most caring side is revealed: he is a driver to a young boy whose parents are experiencing marital problems. When the mother arrives at his home drunk and making sexual advances to Frank, even though he is attracted to her, he rejects her. This morality in Frank's character gives the audience an expectation that while Statham will play a character who will be violent, he does have a moral sense of right and wrong.

Dyer (1998: 122) argues that, the character's name both particularises her/him and also suggests personality traits. Dyer uses the example of Blanche DuBois from *A Streetcar Named Desire* (1951), a name that has connotations of French sophistication and Southern/French ancestry. The characters of Statham always have simple, often monosyllabic names: Chev, Frank, Lee. This may seem an insignificant detail but it places these characters within the simple man-of-action demographic of characters such as James Bond, Jason Bourne and John McClane. It is with the villains that exotic-sounding names rest: Ernst Stavros Blowfeld, Hannibal Lecter, Anton Chigurh. Therefore, in the case of Rick Ford, both his forename and surname echo the trait of the simple man of action.

Appearance is also a signifier of character, and for a male action hero this is related to his musculature and its display on-screen. In all of the *Transporter* films Statham appears topless at least once. In *The Transporter*, a fight sequence culminates in Frank fighting a gang of men while topless and covered in engine oil. In this five-minute sequence, Statham loses his jacket, shirt and tie, yet beats all the fully clothed men by utilising the garage equipment around him, coupled with his own unique fighting style. In terms of his muscular physique Statham still remains firmly within the action genre; but compared to Sylvester Stallone and Arnold Schwarzenegger, his stature is smaller, and this sees him as one of a new breed of action heroes who have moved away from the body builder musculature of past action heroes. As Yvonne Tasker (1993: 179) stated, the stars of 'action movies work hard, and often at the expense of narrative development, to contrive situations for the display of the male body'. In this genre the display of the male body is acceptable when it is in motion: that is, when it is running, jumping, fighting, and *not* as a passive spectacle. The male body is there to be admired and stared at.

The final component of Dyer's list to be considered is that of speech. Dyer (1998: 26) writes that personality traits are used to indicate a character and his/her social outlook. The majority of the characters played by Statham across his work are laconic to say the least. In *The Transporter* the rules that Frank has in place for his business dealings – 'no names' and 'the deal is the deal' – are designed to shut down communication.

Statham epitomises the strong man of few words in the majority of his films. Unless he is in a relationship (either familial or through friendship), his characters only interact verbally *when required to* and out of necessity, rather than out of social politeness and etiquette. For example, in *The Expendables*, Lacy – the woman Lee Christmas (Statham) has been dating – complains that he has not told her what he does for a living. In *Transporter 3*, Frank's dialogue with Valentina suggests that talking about his feelings is not something he is comfortable with and is initially hesitant to do. When Frank does verbalise his feelings for Valentina, it is a sign of character and plot development in terms of their relationship. These films are far more action based than dialogue led, but even a little dialogue can still be revealing in regard to character. When Statham does speak it is often to offer quips, give out scant information, or to use profanities. This juxtaposition of silence and swearing is the modern dialogue for Statham's male action hero.

Having now used Dyer's formal elements in identifying the formation of a character (audience expectation, appearance, name and speech), this chapter will now turn its attention to how they/Statham are used in *Spy* to comic effect. By contending that what *Spy* does, and what makes the performance of Statham such a success, some of these elements will invert certain aspects of his performance, thus in turn serving to allow the audience the experience of familiarity that is then invoked for comedic effect.

Speech is an interesting element in *Spy* as it is partly maintained in terms of swearing: Rick Ford gives Chev Chelios a run for his money in terms of bad language. As Ford, Statham is playing a comedy role that encompasses both physical and verbal comedy, whereby the physicality of the comedy in terms of timing, choreographing and interacting with other actors has similarities to action sequences. It is the extended verbal comedy dialogue that is a new departure for Statham. It is also a new experience for his audience who are not used to hearing him speak so much on-screen. Gone is the laconic man of action to be replaced with a character who is comically loquacious, especially when the subject he endlessly pontificates upon to Susan is his own remarkable career and increasingly improbable stunts. As Ford says, 'I make a habit of doing things people say I can't do. Walk through fire, water ski blindfolded, take up piano at a late age'.

The dialogue Statham is given is a major element of the comedy in the film. It identifies the intellect of his character. When he is removed from active duty his solution is to volunteer to go into the 'Face Off' machine and get a new appearance. It takes his boss a minute to convince him that the machine is not real. That Rick is willing to believe that the CIA has a machine from a John Woo film *Face Off* (1997), that transformed John Travolta's character into Nicholas Cage's and vice versa, clearly demonstrates Rick's lack of intelligence for a member of the intelligence community. This is what makes Ford funny: the juxtaposition of his important position with his stupidity creates laughter through its very incongruity.

More comedy is found in the boasts of his exploits that Rick uses to try to convince Susan that he is the superior agent. The comedy is twofold. First, that the ludicrous nature of what Rick claims to have done ('I've jumped from a high-rise building using only a raincoat as a parachute and broke both legs upon landing; I still had to pretend I was in a fucking Cirque du Soleil show!' and 'Nothing kills me. I'm immune to 179 different types of poison. I know because I ingested them all at once when I was deep undercover in an underground poison-ingesting crime ring') remains funny because of its absurdity and defiance of what is actually possible for a human being to do and survive. Second, that the humorous elements are derived through processes of audience recognition. These quotes are actually not that far removed from what the audience has seen Statham do on-screen. In *Transporter 2* Frank chases a bus using a jet ski, both on water and on the road, and unsurprisingly he catches up with it and boards it. In *Crank* and *Crank: High Voltage* Chev survives a poison that should have killed him, keeping himself alive by administering electric shocks to keep his heart beating including being given shock-paddle treatment ('Juice me!' he shouts to the hospital technician).

As the audience laughs at Rick and his ridiculous boasts, the audience are also arguably laughing at themselves for going to see and enjoy the films they have watched where Statham's characters undertake preposterous stunts. This tongue-firmly-planted-in-cheek approach clearly recognises Statham as an action hero, but the incongruous way that this has been overturned in *Spy* ensures laughter.

The second element of audience recognition that *Spy* turns to comedic purposes in terms of Statham is his abilities as an action hero in relation to the meting out of screen violence. Elaborately choreographed fight sequences remain at the heart of most of Statham's movies. Their beauty of construction often come to dominate the films' spectacular approaches to on-screen body representation and are performed and arranged with balletic grace and agility. For example, in *Transporter 2*, a fight scene with the villainess Kate Nauta sees both her and Frank fly around her palatial residence balancing on drapes and ornamental chains. In his role as Lee Christmas in *The Expendables* Statham shares screen time with iconic male action stars of past action cinema films: Sylvester Stallone, Arnold Schwazenegger, Jet Li, Bruce Willis, Jean-Claude Van Damme – and he has earned his place among this pantheon. *Spy* subverts this aspect of audience expectation by depicting Rick as clumsy and having to be rescued by Susan. A recurring trope in action films is when the male hero fights a group of heavily armed men, of course emerging triumphantly as the victor. Towards the end of *Spy* Susan and Bradley (who wasn't dead after all) are being held a gun point by a group of eight men. The door is flung open and Rick bursts in gun in hand. Rather than blazing away at the assailants, he gets his coat caught on the door handle, trips and knocks himself out. When Susan says, with a slight air of desperation, that 'he means well', the humour is there to enjoy: Rick is useless. That Statham's physical comedy performance at this point, coupled with an air of patient pity from Susan towards Rick, makes the laughter all the more apparent. The reason it is funny is that Statham is quite clearly adept at performing physical comedy with aplomb, and that from an audience's viewpoint it is completely unexpected. Rather than seeing Rick sweep in to rescue Susan, he falls flat on his back. As a juxtaposition to Bradley's suave and sophisticated Bondian spy, where his attire reflects his cool, measured and controlled outlook, Rick's raincoat and cloth cap become the antithesis of everything that the glamorous world of the James Bond franchise and Bradley evoke. Clothes do seem to make the man. If this is the case, then Rick produces laughter not just through his utter incompetence but through the very ordinariness of his clothing when seen against the glamorous world of cinematic spy films.

That is not to say that Bradley can escape this incongruity. He relies on Susan, and it is the ineffectiveness of Rick and

Bradley that places the onus on Susan to be the hero of the action film. While many of the post-millennial female action heroes are found in franchise movies in the Marvel Cinematic Universe and similar, *Spy* offers a genuinely engaging and strong element of the comedy from Melissa McCarthy usurping both Law and Statham as the film's action hero. Melissa McCarthy is viewed as a plus-size, early-middle-aged woman. Female action heroes on-screen are becoming more prevalent across disparate genres from superhero narratives, young adult genre and science fiction. What these genres maintain is a specific body type, aspirational and within the accepted female body as object of desire range. Three of the female stars who have taken on iconic action roles – Gal Gadot as Wonder Woman, Scarlett Johansson as Black Widow and Jennifer Lawrence as Katniss Everdeen – have also fronted campaigns for high-end fashion brands. These women fit the look of the screen heroine – strength with beauty. In this way McCarthy does not fit the usual casting of the female action hero. Interestingly, her character Susan says that she does not have the confidence to take on an action woman's role, telling her friend Nancy that her mother advised her to blend in and let other people win. This makes her the opposite of the competitive alpha male spies. When Susan creates an alter ego of Amber Valentine, after discussing whether this is actually her porn name or her spy name, she adopts attributes that the audience have previously come to recognise as belonging to the male role, specifically that of Rick/Statham. In this way, then, Susan becomes Rick and Bradley.

There are two main elements to this assumption of the male screen identity; language and action. In the first part of the film Susan is modest, unassuming and wants to avoid conflict. When Fine asks her to fire his gardener, Susan agrees but then cannot bring herself to do it. She opts to cut the grass herself to avoid upsetting either Fine or the gardener. After spending time with Ford and being out of the office Susan/Amber becomes much more verbally aggressive. She insults Rayna's hair and outfits, and she becomes a 'prolific curser' (Meuf, 2017: 59). Both Rick and Susan (as Amber) are rebuked by their female superiors for their use of aggressive and bad language. Susan's bad language and violence is combined in a threat to one of Rayna's bodyguards that could very easily have been a line given to Statham in any of his films. Susan holds up her fists:

> You want me to have Cagney and fucking Lacey explain it to you? Cagney's coming down your fucking throat. Lacey, she's gonna come up your ass. I'm gonna meet them in the fucking middle and play your heart like a fucking accordion. I'm gonna pump that shit until it pops, you Swedish bitch!

which sounds more like a line *Crank*'s Chev Chelios than the assumed-language from a desk-agent of the CIA.

While Susan does not carry out this action she does knock a man unconscious by throwing a mobile phone at this head, much in the way that Statham has in other films used the elements around him to beat his assailants. In the film's finale, Susan fully channels her inner-Statham. When Rick is knocked out and Susan and Bradley are surrounded by eight armed men, it is Susan who beats them up in the ensuing fight. The choreographing of the scene is perfectly attuned to a scene that Statham would play, whereby a single combatant beats multiple assailants. Ever resourceful, Susan throws her empty gun at a thug's head to knock him out and then proceeds with hand-to-hand combat with him, which she wins. All the while, Rick lies unconscious on the floor.

As the villain makes his escape in his helicopter, Rick and Susan both chase him. Susan reaches the helicopter first and grabs on. Rick arrives in time to grab onto Susan, but due to his positioning, he holds onto her breasts. As Susan shouts that she will report him to Human Resources, Rick falls from the helicopter into a lake, which he later mistakes for the sea. After a fight onboard the helicopter, Susan throws out the villain, lands the helicopter and rescues the nuclear bomb. In the course of the action genre's usual traits, the predictable ending of either Rick or Bradley saving the day is overturned. Susan remains the hero and a hero in the traditional mode of representation in the genre (and, to that extent, Statham's characters throughout the majority of his career). Susan is a female action hero but she has learnt her iconography in terms of audience recognition from a male action hero – Statham.

This merging and subverting of gender is present throughout the film but remains most potent in the movie's final sequence. The camera pans slowly around a hotel bedroom. On the floor are empty champagne bottles and discarded clothes. As the camera pans to the bed, it focuses on Susan and her dawning realisation that she is not alone in bed. Rick snores and mutters the word 'bosoms' in his sleep. In the majority of comedies this would be the moment for Rick to wake up and be horrified that he is in bed with Susan. Instead, the tables are turned and it is Susan that is horrified and screams. Rick tells her to stop screaming as she 'loved it' and he hugs her: he loved it just as much. While the audience may be expecting Susan to be apologetic, in *Spy* the embarrassment is for Susan as she is in bed with the incompetent Rick.

Interestingly, it this focus on women that makes *Spy* all the more unusual within Statham's body of work. Rather than the mostly male-dominated *Expendables* and *Fast and Furious* franchises, where Statham sits alongside his male counterparts, for *Spy* Statham takes a backseat to the majority of the female-centric plot escapades. As with the majority of his films, and especially others within the action genre, the female appears either as a villain or love interest (and often the 'prize') for the male hero. However, in *Spy* it is not just the sustained presence of Melissa McCarthy that changes the audience experience of Statham's role as Rick Ford, it is the expectation of McCarthy's performance and the juxtaposition of the male/female body as spectacle that certainly alters those expectations.

This mélange of audience expectations being met alongside tropes of the genre being inverted and male/female roles being reassigned produces an audience experience bordering on the uncanny. What the film *Spy*, and especially the performances of Statham and McCarthy, does is to turn the uncanny away from its usual horror usage to comedic effect. In lesser hands the film could have easily become a novelty performance from McCarthy and a caricature from Statham. One of the reasons for this uncanny comedy is that part of the audience foreknowledge for both of these stars is concerned with the concepts of authenticity versus performance and body as spectacle.

Male action stars are assumed and desired to have authenticity within their performance. This can range from the body building background of Arnold Schwarzenegger, the martial arts abilities of Bruce Lee or the wrestling experience of Dwayne 'The Rock' Johnson. Performance in terms of the male action star must not veer too close to artifice; the audience want to believe that the abilities that these actors are imbued with are real, as contradictory as that may first appear when considering the art of acting on film. In the case of Statham, he was already known for performing his own stunts and for training in kickboxing and mixed martial arts. In a *Vanity Fair* interview

Statham was scathing about actors who 'act' their stunts rather than doing them:

> Then you have some guy standing in front of a fucking green screen screwing his face up pretending like he's doing the stunt. To me, it's like a farce. I have a real frustration with that because I know these coordinators. I train with them all the time and they are incredibly talented. (Miller 2013)

In essence what Statham is criticising is actors acting as action heroes. The performance that Statham gives in *Spy* is an inversion of this: he is an action hero acting as if he is not. This uncanny presentation is comedic rather than unnerving because the audience understand that it is this element of Statham's screen persona that is a performance, and in his next role he will return to his 'authentic performance' as an action hero.

This can be compared to the audience understanding of Melissa McCarthy's performance as the Statham-inspired Amber Valentine. In her film roles McCarthy has created a certain persona. Anne Helen Petersen (2017: 28) described McCarthy's on-screen roles as a combination of her body and her characters perceived Otherness: 'Her comedic personas revel in the unruliness of the fat body; her most popular characters are some intersections of low class, sexually dominant, profane and generally negligent of their place in the societal hierarchy.' In his examination of the films of Melissa McCarthy, Russell Meuf highlighted the difference between McCarthy's on-screen performances and the reality of her personality that is presented in media interviews. He wrote that 'most of McCarthy's coverage in popular magazines insist that she is a friendly, lovable, Midwestern Mom rather than someone like the raucous characters she portrays onscreen' (Meuf 2017: 58). In terms of McCarthy's role as Susan Cooper she is close to her 'real' self, friendly and disguised as Midwestern characters. However, when McCarthy takes on her Amber Valentine persona she moves back towards the foul-mouthed, unruly, raucous character that she is synonymous with on-screen. This acts as a mirror to Statham's usual on-screen roles. Therefore, McCarthy's performance and artifice are multilayered in the film as she embodies both the unruly woman and the male action hero. For an audience to recognise the self-conscious performance by McCarthy serves to remind that Statham in this role is also performing in a way that is not usual for him on-screen.

By considering the body of Jason Statham in *Spy* in conjunction with that of Melissa McCarthy, the body forms the role of spectacle. In an action movie this is usually fulfilled by the male being looked at as a subject of adoration (for example, Frank Martin's frequent bouts of near-nude fighting), while the female's body becomes objectified on-screen. In *Spy* while Statham remains fully clothed his body remains the area of spectacle for the audience. This is achieved in two ways: first, by his costume; second, by discussion of his anatomy.

In terms of costume, Statham's past occupation as a catwalk and catalogue model is touched upon during the narrative. When meeting Susan in a cafe in Paris Rick carries a Louis Vuitton backpack and wears a Burberry mac and a contextually trendy tweed flat cap. The way that the camera follows him through the crowd is reminiscent of a high-end fashion advert, replete with close-ups of the material set against the backdrop of Paris itself. In the scene where Rick trips and falls as he tries to beat up the villains, it is his coat that causes him to be knocked out. The costumes may not be appropriate wear for a (traditionally cinematic) spy in the James Bond mould, but they showcase the physique and appeal of Statham as a mode of spectacle in themselves. The fact that they form his protective shield, but one that eventually proves useless, emphasises not just his failings as a genuinely tough guy in *Spy* but also Statham's postmodern and bricolage approach to referencing his past as a fashion model. It is *this* incongruity that provokes laughter here. Statham was known as a fashion model. Rick wears high-end fashion; the fashions end up undoing Rick, therefore Statham. Laughter is generated.

While Statham stays fully clothed during the narrative (unlike many of his other film roles), his body is still a source of spectacle as it, or at least a part of it, is discussed. When the phone of a dead criminal is examined it is found to contain images of his erect penis that he had taken. One of the female analysts at the CIA looks at the photographs and comments that Ford's is bigger. This references back to *Crank: High Voltage* where Chev is having his organs harvested and next in line after his heart is his penis. This focus on costume and physical attributes is usually reserved for the female star but in *Spy* the role of spectacle is transferred on to Rick/Statham. The reason for the shift in focus is that the audience recognition of McCarthy does not include viewing her as an object of female desire in the traditional filmic mode. Her presentation relies on the use of her body for comedy not erotic spectacle. This difference in the reception of the bodies of Statham and McCarthy can be viewed in their relationships to high fashion. Statham was a model, part of the couture cultural world of display, whereas McCarthy has been shunned by this world. Meuf (2017: 39) records, 'McCarthy revealed in 2014 that several prominent fashion designers refused to make a plus-sized Oscar dress for her when she was nominated'. As Statham has conformed to the physicality of the action hero, he is able to assume the role of spectacle. Even when in the film Statham's character is an inept action hero, he still looks the part and is therefore acceptable as a figure of male display.

Spy remains a unique film in Statham's cinematic career. The comedy is possible because of the screen identity that the actor has honed over many films and many fights, car chases and impossible stunts. The character of Rick Ford can only subvert audience expectations of gender and genre because Jason Statham has upheld expectations in previous roles. At the time of writing, Statham's next film role is as Jonas Taylor in *The Meg* (2018), which will see him battle against a seventy-five-foot-long prehistoric shark, thus planting the actor firmly back within the action genre. With rumours of a sequel to *Spy* being touted at the time this chapter was written, it is not impossible that one of Rick Ford's next boasts to Susan will include wrestling a giant shark into submission as part of a secret fish-fighting club. The possibilities for Rick Ford's character remain endlessly fascinating. While it may be unusual for an action star to be able to pull off a comedy role with such success, Statham achieves this through the inversion of both his own star identification and the expectations of gender within the action film genre. Statham appears to now straddle both the action and comedy genres with some form of ease. With *Spy 2* on the cards, one can only wait to see what awaits Rick Ford. In a 2016 interview with *Empire*, Paul Feig said that, 'Susan Cooper is one of my favourite characters I've ever come up with. But Rick Ford is possibly the one I'll take to the grave with me. Will he get any more self-aware in the sequel? No, God no. He'll get less self-aware'.

The lack of self-awareness (from Rick Ford's perspective) and the parody of the male action star (from Statham and Feig's) are important components of just what makes *Spy* and Statham's performance so appealing to audiences. This appeal, combined with the self-awareness of Statham makes the role not only engaging, attractive and likeable, but also interesting and successful. With his gift for comedy plainly in evidence – even his role as Chev Chelios contains moments of hilarity – it will be interesting to see just where future roles lie for the actor.

References

Dyer, R. (1998). *Stars*. London: BFI Publishing.
Meuf, R. (2017). *Rebellious Bodies Stardom, Citizenship, and the New Body Politics*. Houston, TX: University of Texas Press, 2017.
Miller, J. (2013) 'Jason Statham says stuntmen deserve Oscars if 'poncy' actors faking it get them.' *Vanity Fair*. www.vanityfair.com/hollywood/2013/11/jason-statham-stunt-oscars (19.11.13, accessed 07.03.2019).
Petersen, H. A. (2017). *Too Fat Too Slutty Too Loud the Rise and Reign of the Unruly Woman*. London: Simon & Schuster. pp. 28.
Tasker, Y. (1993). *Spectacular Bodies: Gender, Genre and the Action Cinema*. London: Routledge.

8

Arthouse Statham

Martin Carter

In 1923, the pioneer film theorist Riciotto Canudo declared cinema to be the 'seventh art' (Canudo 1926: 29) alongside architecture, sculpture, painting, music, dance and literature. Even so, difficulty has sometimes been found in recognising artistic expression within such a commercial and industrial medium. This has certainly hampered cinema in being taken seriously as an art form on a par with the more recognised, or perhaps more respectable arts. In an effort to counter this perception, two distinct forms of cinema have been developed; commercially driven movies made for mass consumption in order to make a financial profit; and artistically inspired films made for more discerning audiences by directors who garner acclaim for having an individual vision and signature to their work. This attempt to separate high and lowbrow cinema – although fraught with contradiction and unfounded assumptions about their target demographics – has established itself and there is a clear difference between big-budget Hollywood blockbusters shown in multiplex cinemas for mass audiences and independent, foreign language and avant-garde films which are the province of smaller independent cinemas visited by a select and informed audience. If we accept this generalisation as a given – mainstream versus arthouse – it would be obvious to categorise Jason Statham as a movie star with a clearly defined persona, and one who works strictly within the boundaries of commercial mainstream cinema.

There is much to support this claim; he works primarily within franchises that rarely require him to move outside of a tight-lipped hardman stereotype. To date, his punishing work schedule – he has appeared in nearly fifty films since 1998 – has seen him take on such roles as: driver and martial arts expert Frank Martin in three *Transporter* films made between 2002 and 2008; hitman Chev Chelios in the pair of *Crank* movies (2006 and 2009); knife expert Lee Christmas in *The Expendables* trilogy (2010–2014); hitman Arthur Bishop in *The Mechanic* (2011) and *Mechanic: Resurrection* (2016); and the expansion of his uncredited role as Deckard Shaw in *Fast and Furious 6* (2013) into a key character within that franchise in episodes 7 and 8. All have cemented his screen image with the cinema-going public to the extent that Statham can humorously subvert it in more comedic films like *Spy* (2015), where, as tough-but-dim secret agent Rick Ford, he shows he is unafraid to make fun of himself. As well as his recurring roles within these film franchises, almost all of Statham's other films employ his tough guy character to great, if not always imaginative, effect. So set is the actor's screen persona that John Patterson (2012) declared Statham's movies 'scarcely discernible either tonally or kinetically' and that within his body of work 'he repeats himself more than Ozu and Eric Rohmer combined'. Put more bluntly by Len Brown in his hagiographic biography of Statham, he is 'the greatest action-adventure hero of his generation' (Brown 2011: 220). All of which somewhat begs the question, is there anything more to Jason Statham?

The answer is far less clear-cut than might be expected. A close examination of Statham's extensive body of work actually reveals several instances where he has been given the opportunity to both broaden his acting range and develop crossover appeal to a different audience. His filmography includes three serious attempts to break out of the mould that success has created for him and show that, when given the opportunity, he is capable of far more as a performer. The three films – *London* (2005), *13* (2010) and *Hummingbird* (2013) – all met with varying critical receptions; all of them were commercially unsuccessful (two of them gaining little or no theatrical release in many territories) and are an idiosyncratic trio of films that would be unfamiliar to most viewers, while possibly being dismissed by hardcore Statham fans. Interrogating each film, all produced at different points in Statham's career, illustrates his progress from a supporting actor to a recognised movie star while hinting at a performative range that is belied by his more stock-in-trade roles.

The first film to consider is Hunter Richard's *London*, a claustrophobic chamber piece that takes its name not from the city that Statham is often assumed to come from – Statham is originally from the Midlands town of Shirebrook in Derbyshire – but from one of the film's leading characters. The film fits into the category of arthouse cinema for a number of reasons: it can be classed as an 'indie' having been produced by a group of independent production companies such as Destination Films and LHR Productions – a company set up by Richards himself and with only this film to its credit. As an 'indie' film it need not follow the prescribed mainstream narrative model of clearly defined characters, a three-act structure and a closed ending. Instead its characters are difficult to empathise with; two-thirds of the film takes place in a single room and the film's conclusion leaves little resolved.

London is the story of Syd (Chris Evans), young, rich and in despair over his failed relationship with the beautiful model, London (Jessica Biel). It concentrates almost all of its action in a plush New York loft apartment that is hosting London's farewell party before she starts a new life on the West Coast. Fired up on alcohol, drugs and self-pity, Syd decides to gate-crash the party along with Bateman (Jason Statham), a Wall Street broker and sometime drug dealer he has casually met in a bar. Bateman cuts a somewhat enigmatic figure, describing himself to Syd as being 'not a dealer ... I'm a buyer'; his British accent hints at him being a wide-boy broker, probably having moved from London to make more money on the New York Stock Exchange. Having got into the party, Syd and Bateman retreat to the penthouse apartment's enormous bathroom (a space that curiously only a few other guests ever need to use) where, as the evening progresses, they consume vast quantities of drugs and liquor while opening up to each other and confessing their innermost fears and desires. This is common template for a low-budget independent film: few locations, a limited number of characters and the action almost entirely dialogue-driven. In the absence of any physical action sequences, Richards stages a number of frank discussions between Syd and Bateman on their failures and obsessions; Syd is insanely jealous of anyone London might have ever met and has a severe case of penis envy, while Bateman confesses to being impotent and only able achieve an erection through expensive BDSM sessions. Various characters wander in during the hour or so that the pair spend in the bathroom, some merely taking narcotics or alcohol, others to move the plot onto the rather anti-climactic denouement between Syd and London. Thus, Statham is, for the first time, put into a situation where his performance skills must be tested instead of his physical athleticism.

All three of the leading actors are on the cusp of finding Hollywood success; Evans has yet to become a mainstay of the Marvel Comic Universe as Captain America and, although having appeared as Johnny Storm in *Fantastic Four* (2005), is not a major star; similarly, although Jessica Biel had featured in remakes and sequels such as *The Texas Chainsaw Massacre* (2003) and *Blade: Trinity* (2004) she was yet to become a star attraction. Statham had also yet to establish himself in Hollywood at this point. Statham, although having starred in a number of British and European productions, had been restricted to supporting roles in his few Hollywood films. By coincidence, all three actors had worked together before in the previous year's *Cellular*, a Larry Cohen-penned thriller in which Statham had played the villain of the piece. Therefore, *London*, with its cast of attractive up-and-coming actors (none of whom would have been expensive to employ), is a modest indie film aspiring and hoping to find an audience and gain wider distribution.

Alongside the casting, the film has a number of stylistic tropes associated with an indie film that is hoping to get itself noticed. The long central section in the bathroom feels like a piece of filmed theatre (although it is broken up with several short flashback sequences); there are hints at high culture with the pair snorting cocaine from a Van Gogh painting that they have taken from the bathroom wall; and there are self-conscious scenes such as Syd and London's final moments at the airport, shot in a continuous static three-minute take that zooms in and out in order to keep the pair in medium shot. Richards obviously hoped *London* would be a calling card for him to go on to bigger and better things; it aspires to be an edgy film that would appeal to a hipster audience through its ambiguous title and a frank script dealing with difficult adult themes.

However, *London* failed to provide acclaim for anybody concerned with it. Reviews for the film were overwhelmingly negative. Roger Ebert gave *London* a one-star rating and succinctly described the film as 'Ugly. Bad,' only managing some faint praise for the performances: 'Chris Evans and Jason Statham have verbal facility and energy, which enables them to propel this dreck from one end of 92 minutes to the other ... I have seen all of these actors on better days in better movies' (Ebert 2006). Although the role of Bateman provided Statham with a number of grandstanding acting set pieces, he is unable to exploit the potential of these scenes; Richards' limitations as both a writer and director do not allow him to convince as the troubled Bateman. The fact that Richards has not made another feature is a stark reflection of the film's weaknesses. If better executed, the film could have been a low-budget indie 'sleeper' that, by building up a reputation on other platforms, might have found a cult following.

Statham's next venture in arthouse cinema had a far stronger pedigree; *13* (2010) was a Hollywood remake of Géla Babluani's *Tzameti* (2005) helmed by the original director himself. Babluani's film first made its mark at the 2005 Venice Film Festival where he picked up two awards for his directorial skills. The film then went on to be the sensation of the 2006 Sundance Film Festival winning the Grand Jury Prize in the World Cinema Dramatic category. Babluani, a Georgian-born filmmaker based in France, produced a taut thriller on a tiny budget that both gripped and shocked festival audiences and seemed to announce the arrival of a major new talent. *Tzameti*, the Georgian word for thirteen, refers to the number given to a young immigrant labourer, Sebastien (played by Georges Babluani, Géla's brother), in a secret contest where rich gamblers bet on who will survive a circular game of Russian roulette. Babluani's film is an exercise in controlled horror as it slowly reveals this appalling contest being played by the desperate and the poor for the pleasure and profit of rich men. Austerely shot in black and white and revealing its information sparingly, the horrific revelation of what the game is, delivers a genuine shock moment. The film then proceeds to show how this ghastly knockout competition builds up to a climatic faceoff between the two surviving contestants with millions of euros gambled on the outcome.

The film was enthusiastically received by many critics: Peter Bradshaw (2006) of the *Guardian* greeted the film with a four-star review stating that Babluani 'makes a stunning debut with what might yet become a classic', while *Empire* magazine's David Parkinson was even more effusive calling the film an 'astonishingly accomplished debut feature that combines Hitchcockian suspense with a showdown whose unflinching attitude to violence will pin you to the seat' (2006). Although a film that would specifically appeal to arthouse audiences, its thriller aspects had potential crossover appeal and Babluani's debut created enough attention for Hollywood to offer the now-familiar scenario of producing a remake with the original director at the helm.

But such things also present dangers: *The Vanishing* (1988) by George Sluizer was originally a film that avoided melodrama and sensation and was successful on the arthouse circuit. The film's 1993 remake, helmed by the same director, included an all-star cast (Jeff Bridges, Kiefer Sutherland, Nancy Travis and Sandra Bullock) and a happy ending: the film was a box office and critical disaster.

Although technically still an independent film, *13* was given the budget and a cast to significantly upgrade the lo-fi production values of the original film along with a screenwriter, Greg Pruss, to translate the film into a more Hollywood-friendly vehicle. The cast was headed by young British actor Sam Riley and featured an impressive supporting cast that included Mickey Rourke, Curtis '50 Cent' Jackson, Ray Winstone, Michael Shannon and Ben Gazzara, with Statham in a small but key role. However, this cast of such relatively well-known actors would prove problematic as major changes to the original script were made in order to provide far more backstory for several of the contestants, unlike *Tzameti* which provided next to no background for any of the game's participants. Thus, *13* spends considerable screen time fleshing out unnecessary detail that ultimately adds little to the narrative and dilutes the atmosphere of the film, all in order to give the cast's biggest names a flashback and at least one scene in which to develop their character. Ryan Gilbey (2006), in his *Sight and Sound* review of *Tzameti*, pointed out the original was 'distinguished by one undervalued quality – leanness', something the remake does not have. *Tzameti* built up tension by not revealing exactly what was going on until the last possible moment, making the awful revelation of the contest so much more powerful. From the very start, *13* begins explaining everything and then carries on doing so for the next ninety minutes, dissipating the original film's mystery and suspense. Most disastrously, *13* reveals its trump card – what the game actually is – in the very first scene. Whereas *Tzameti* drew critical admiration for how it kept one guessing about what was actually going on, the opening shot of *13* shows Riley and Winston pointing revolvers at each other's heads followed by the title card 'Four Days Earlier'. The game is, quite literally, immediately given away.

Eschewing the original's monochrome visuals, *13* adopts grainy colour cinematography that recalls the look of a 1970s thriller such as Peter Yates's *The Friends of Eddie Coyle* (1973). Although, this aesthetic choice loses the austere bleakness of the original's black and white cinematography, the look of *13* creates an immediate nostalgia and association with that cycle of crime thrillers and police procedurals. In a further attempt to create an ambiguous time frame, the film's costume design also harks back to the 1970s, most obviously with Statham's character, Jasper, who wears a pork-pie hat and an overcoat that immediately recalls Gene Hackman's Popeye Doyle in William Friedkin's *The French Connection* (1971).

Statham and Winston as the 'Number 6 Brothers' (contest veterans looking to clean-up at this competition) do actually benefit from being given more screen time. Jasper is the fixer, the money man who sets up deals and increases the stake of their bets as the number of contestants grows ever smaller after each round. His brother, Ronald (Winstone), is seriously ill and kept in an expensive sanatorium, visited only by Jasper when there is a contest for him to compete in. The film never explains how these two unabashed cockney characters came to be in up-state New York but the two actors work well together and have enough chutzpah to carry it off. One of the film's best scenes is before the final round of the tournament where Ronald reveals his long-suppressed anger at how Jasper has exploited him for years giving the film its one genuinely affecting moment. The scene hints at there being far more going on between the two than what we have been shown and discover that although Ronald seemed to be barely holding it together, he is far more aware than even Jasper realises; whereas Jasper, the consummate wheeler-dealer is revealed to be something of a straw man.

The film would have benefited from more moments like this but the expository material dramatically slows the pace of the film and the Russian roulette sequences are lazily staged and lack the impact of *Tzameti*'s viscerally explosive shoot-outs. The measured pacing of *Tzameti* was obviously deemed to be too slow for multiplex audiences and *13* had to be both explained and sped up with added incident and exposition. Babluani does manage to retain his bleak finish where Jasper, after the death of Ronald at Vince's hand in the game's final round, meets with his brother's killer on a train. Jasper shoots Vince, and escapes with what he believes is a bag full of money. However, the film's final shot of Jasper running away down a tunnel into the light exactly highlights the misjudged narrative construction of this remake. *Tzameti* ends with a shot of Sebastien mortally wounded and staring out of the train window – the film has been centred around him and his journey to this final tragic moment; *13*, however, leaves us with Statham's Jasper escaping, as if he was the film's protagonist. The film ignores Vince in his final moments and skews the structure of the film. This perfectly illustrates how *13*, with its insistence on giving each of its name cast expository backgrounds, loses its focus on narrative and character in its translation. Statham's Jasper is just one of far too many people that we get to know but actually do not *need* to know a lot about. Reflecting this narrative confusion, the film's marketing presents a false impression of what an audience should expect; Statham's presence in the film is heavily featured in its trailer portraying Jasper as a gun-toting hitman, giving the impression it will be an action-driven movie aimed at Statham's core audience.

Babluani's remake found distribution difficult to secure and sat around for more than eighteen months before being given cursory one-week theatrical engagements in single venues in New York and Los Angeles in October 2011. Thereafter it disappeared into the anonymity of home video – a place where such *film maudits* can find re-evaluation and redemption after failing to find an audience theatrically. No such fate awaited *13*; the apocryphal bad luck associated with that number applied itself to the film. What few reviews there are found no saving graces in it. Stephen Holden's review in *The New York Times* dismissed *13* as 'sweaty, chest-heaving, macho nonsense' (Holden 2011) and *The Village Voice*'s Michael Atkinson picked up on the film's drabness with his comment that it 'looks and sounds like something Charles Bronson paid the bills with in 1979' (Atkinson 2011). Babluani's Hollywood career was stillborn and Statham, who was establishing himself in Hollywood as a bona fide action star, retreated back into more familiar but lucrative territory with *Crank: High Voltage*, *The Expendables* and *The Mechanic*.

After mixed results from appearing in a low-budget independent film and working with a highly regarded European *auteur*, Statham's third venture outside of mainstream cinema would prove more fruitful. Steven Knight's *Hummingbird* (2013) is by far the most successful of Statham's attempts to extend his range as an actor. Set in contemporary London, Statham is on his home turf and in a film that cannily exploits his mainstream persona while also subverting it in a number of intriguing ways. Statham plays Joey, an alcoholic living rough on the streets of London, haunted by his past as a member of the Special Forces in Afghanistan. Through a series of fractured flashbacks Joey's past is revealed: he is a deserter who has committed war crimes in Helmand Province. Sleeping rough in London's Soho and suffering from PTSD, he lives under constant threat from a pair of thugs who terrorise the homeless. After one particular attack Joey retaliates and is chased until he literally falls on his feet as he tumbles into a deserted, but decidedly upmarket, warehouse apartment.

Conveniently, the owner is away for six months and, remarkably, the designer clothes in his wardrobe are a perfect fit for Joey. This has all the ingredients of a rather unremarkable and predictable narrative. However, the film's first-time director, Steven Knight, a screenwriter with a proven track record having written such acclaimed screenplays as *Dirty Pretty Things* (2002) and *Eastern Promises* (2007) – both films that can lay claim to have arthouse credentials – takes this initially banal premise and turns it into a redemptive fable. Joey, in this smart bachelor pad, has six months before the flat's owner returns to get himself clean and sober, and make amends for the mistakes of his previous life. (In the US the film was released under the title of *Redemption*, which is not only lacking in subtlety but obscures the film's depth and the complexity of its themes.) In order to make the film work, Knight is completely dependent on Statham's ability to deliver a nuanced performance to convince not only as a tough guy but also as a psychologically damaged and extremely vulnerable man. In interviews Knight claims that it was David Fincher who recommended Statham to him for the role, recalling that Fincher remarked that Statham 'said the only person he would cast in this role would be Jason Statham. I thought "He knows what he's talking about."' (Knight, quoted in Jaggernauth 2013). Statham immediately accepted the role.

Settling into the material comfort of the luxury apartment, Joey embarks on his physical and moral transformation played out in a succession of scenes that both exploit and subvert Statham's star persona. Joey washes off the dirt of the street in a cathartic hot shower that evidences the wounds he has gathered both on active service and living rough; and, in the most transformative act, his long, lank and greasy comb-over is shorn off until Statham's familiar shaven head is restored. Joey kicks the booze and takes advantage of the wardrobe full of smart designer wear to become Joey Jones. However, in the process of drying out, alcoholic withdrawal initiates flashbacks to Afghanistan where he carried out the summary execution of an innocent Afghan civilian after his armoured vehicle was attacked and fellow soldiers killed. The memories of that event haunt his waking and sleeping life, manifesting themselves as hallucinations of a swarm of hummingbirds that give the film its title (the drones through which we see much of the Afghan sequences are called 'hummingbirds'). We discover that the yuppie penthouse apartment belongs to gay fashion photographer, Damon, whose work decorates the walls of his flat – high contrast monochrome photographs of oiled muscular male bodies, which gives the film a twist of homoeroticism. Knight takes this even further when Joey has to pretend to be one of Damon's boyfriends after neighbours become suspicious of his presence in the flat. As part of his rehabilitation, Joey takes a job as a dishwasher in a restaurant in Soho's Chinatown. His employers recognise his potential when he is called upon to calm down a group of drunken football fans who are remonstrating about the bill for their meal. Knight's patient build-up to this moment now rewards the audience with its first action set piece. Joey politely asks the belligerent fans to leave, and once outside, faces off with the five of them. The verbal aggression increases until one lunges at Joey and he engages his Special Forces training to have them all floored in seconds. It is a short but sharp piece of action that, due to the film being set in a far more realistic milieu than Statham's Hollywood action movies, delivers far more effect. The other highlight of the scene (and of the entire film) is its use of authentic London locations; Soho's Chinatown and Covent Garden Market are used extensively throughout the film. Chris Menges' cinematography gives the film both an aura of realism and a sheen of neo-noir glamour, and rarely has London recently been so beautifully and knowingly lensed. After the brief but brutal fight Joey is recruited by a Chinese Triad boss as a driver and enforcer, a job which will lead him to the darkest depths of London's criminal netherworld.

Joey's odyssey is paralleled with a number of redemptive subplots: seeking out his estranged wife and daughter in order to absolve his guilt for having abandoned them; searching for his friend Isabel, another down and out with whom he used to share a cardboard box; hunting for a sadistic city banker who abuses and murders prostitutes; being involved with the trafficking of illegal immigrants; and an eventually romantic relationship that he strikes up with Cristina, a nun running a refuge for the homeless in Covent Garden. This overcrowded plot is often in danger of collapsing under its own weight and not all of these narrative threads are fully developed or resolved. However, what these plotlines do provide is a range of situations through which Statham must convincingly navigate through performance. The love affair with Cristina is perhaps the most problematic element of the plot but the scenes of Joey's attempt to reconnect with his daughter provide an excellent example of a less-is-more approach to avoid any mawkishness. In their only scene together, Joey delivers a bag of money that he has accumulated through his work for the Triads to his wife's flat and has a brief but tender moment with his daughter before setting off back into the night to resolve the more violent aspects of his life.

While it could be argued that the film does have an overly schematic narrative structure to depict Joey's struggles with love, family and violence, Knight has deliberately crafted *Hummingbird* as an urban fairy tale, an elegant fable and, therefore, such a structure works to Statham's advantage. The film eventually comes full circle with Joey, having performed everything he needed to be absolved for his perceived sins, being tracked by CCTV cameras as the police close in on him – directly echoing how we are introduced to him in Afghanistan at the beginning of the film with footage from a Hummingbird drone. Again, this circular structure adds to the film adopting the form of a fable, albeit one played out in a hyperrealist depiction of modern London.

The film garnered a number of thoughtful reviews that recognised the performance of its star. Trevor Johnson seemed to hit the notes of the film precisely: in *Sight and Sound* he wrote that Knight had 'manage[d] to cajole Statham into a performance that's his closest yet to a fully realised characterisation rather than the tight-lipped, tighter coiled persona on display in pretty much every other assignment' (Johnson 2013). The film's success lies in its skill in employing Statham's screen image and then presenting it in situations that work against expectations. Rising to the challenge of playing a complex and flawed man, Statham presents a full gamut of emotions and acquits himself with aplomb throughout.

Taking these three films together as being examples of 'arthouse' cinema, it is evident that although Jason Statham has yet to fully extend his screen persona, a film like *Hummingbird* strongly hints at future possibilities. He is in a similar position to other actors such as Matthias Schonaerts, who in Alice Winocour's *Disorder* (2015) undermined his tough guy image by playing an Iraqi War veteran suffering with PTSD and was hired as the bodyguard for the family of an arms dealer. Like Statham, Schonaerts can do much by doing very little, and his screen presence has been used to great effect in this and several other arthouse films.

More speculatively, after twenty years, one wonders if Statham might just tire of the lucrative but repetitive franchises that require so little from him as a performer. Sylvester Stallone was so exhausted with his increasingly formulaic run of action movies that he made *Cop Land* in 1997, giving a subtle performance as an overweight deadbeat cop which reinvigorated his career. For Statham, there are several possible avenues he might explore: one potentially fascinating collaboration might be with Midlands-based British director Shane Meadows who grew up in Uttoxeter, not far from Statham's hometown of Shirebrook. One does not have to try hard to see Statham fitting into the cast of one of Meadows' social realist films about working-class life. Even more fertile ground might be for the actor to exploit his potential as a gay icon and portray a more sexually ambiguous character in a dramatic role.

To conclude this examination of some of the lesser known and more esoteric works in Statham's filmography, the final word goes to Steven Knight (Mortimer 2013) as he explains Statham's persona and how he believes his work will be seen in the future:

> It seems to me that actors like (Statham) are too often pigeonholed and patronised while they are doing their stuff, and then they're rehabilitated and turned into cult figures 20 years later ... and I think ... [he] is one of those people who, in 20 years' time, those films he's already made ... will be seen as classics of their type.

References

Atkinson, M. (2011). 'Tzameti'. *Village Voice* (25.10.11).
Bradshaw, P. (2006). 'Tzameti'. *Guardian* (14.01.06).
Brown, L. (2011). *Jason Statham: Taking Stock*. London: Orion.
Canudo, E. (1926). 'Reflections sur le septieme art'. *L'Usine aux Cinema* (1926).
Ebert, R. (2006). 'London'. *Chicago Sun-Times* (02.02.06).
Falk, Q. (2018). 'Desperately seeking Statham', BAFTA Guru. http://guru.bafta.org/desperately-seeking-statham-steven-knight-interview (accessed 26.02.2018).
Gilbey, R. (2006). 'Tzameti'. *Sight and Sound*, 16(1), 78–9 (01.06).
Holden, S. (2011). 'Get rich (if you're lucky), or die trying'. *New York Times* (27.11.11).
Jaggernauth, K. (2013). 'Director Steven Knight says David Fincher suggested Jason Statham for "Redemption"'. *IndieWire*. www.indiewire.com/2013/06/director-steven-knight-says-david-fincher-suggested-jason-statham-for-redemption-96865/ (18.6.13, accessed 10.3.19).
Johnson, T. (2013). 'Hummingbird'. *Sight and Sound*, 23(6), 98–99 (June 2013).
Mortimer, B. (2013). '*Hummingbird* director Steven Knight on debuts, gangland London, and casting advice from David Fincher' on heyuguys.com. www.heyuguys.com/hummingbird-director-steven-knight-interview/ (accessed 06.03.18).
Parkinson, D. (2006). 'Tzameti review'. *Empire* (01.04.06, accessed 25.2.19).
Patterson, J. (2012). 'Jason Statham, he's an unprepousterous action hero'. *Guardian* (28.04.12, accessed 19.2.19).

Figure 26 *In the Name of the King: A Dungeon Siege Tale* (Uwe Boll: 2007) Boll KG Productions, Herold Productions, Brightlight Pictures

Figure 27 *The Bank Job* (Roger Donaldson: 2008) Mosaic Media Group, Relativity Media LLC, Skyline (Baker St) Productions

Figure 28 *The Bank Job* (Roger Donaldson: 2008) Mosaic Media Group, Relativity Media LLC, Skyline (Baker St) Productions

Figure 29 *The Bank Job* (Roger Donaldson: 2008) Mosaic Media Group, Relativity Media LLC, Skyline (Baker St) Productions

Figure 30 *Death Race* (Paul W. S. Anderson: 2008) Relativity Media, Cruise/Wagner Productions

Figure 31 *Death Race* (Paul W. S. Anderson: 2008) Relativity Media, Cruise/Wagner Productions

Figure 32 *Blitz* (Elliott Lester: 2011) Davis Films, Lipsync Productions

Figure 33 *Blitz* (Elliott Lester: 2011) Davis Films, Lipsync Productions

Figure 34 *Killer Elite* (Gary McKendry: 2011) Omnilab Media, Ambience Entertainment, Current Entertainment, Sighvatsson Films, Film Victoria, Wales Creative IP Fund, Agora Films, International Traders, Mascot Pictures Wales

Figure 35 *Killer Elite* (Gary McKendry: 2011) Omnilab Media, Ambience Entertainment, Current Entertainment, Sighvatsson Films, Film Victoria, Wales Creative IP Fund, Agora Films, International Traders, Mascot Pictures Wales

Figure 36 *The Mechanic* (Simon West: 2011) Millennium Films

Figure 37 *The Mechanic* (Simon West: 2011) Millennium Films

Figure 38 *The Mechanic* (Simon West: 2011) Millennium Films

Figure 39 *Hummingbird* (Steven Knight: 2013) IM Global, Shoebox Films

Figure 40 *Hummingbird* (Steven Knight: 2013) IM Global, Shoebox Films

Figure 41 *Hummingbird* (Steven Knight: 2013) IM Global, Shoebox Films

Figure 42 *Parker* (Taylor Hackford: 2013) Incentive Filmed Entertainment, Sierra Pictures, Sidney Kimmel Entertainment

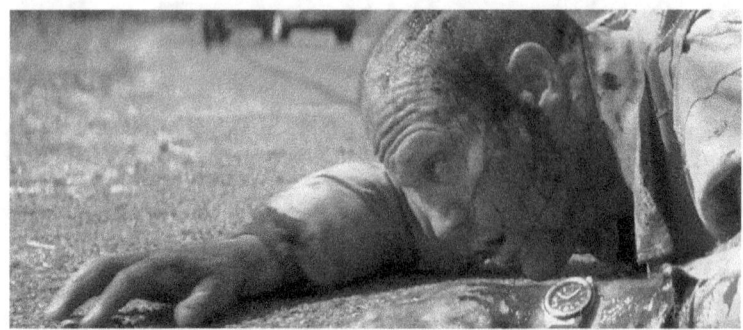

Figure 43 *Parker* (Taylor Hackford: 2013) Incentive Filmed Entertainment, Sierra Pictures, Sidney Kimmel Entertainment

Figure 44 *Parker* (Taylor Hackford: 2013) Incentive Filmed Entertainment, Sierra Pictures, Sidney Kimmel Entertainment

Figure 45 *Spy* (Paul Feig: 2015) Chernin Entertainment, Feigco Entertainment, TSG Entertainment

Figure 46 *Spy* (Paul Feig: 2015) Chernin Entertainment, Feigco Entertainment, TSG Entertainment

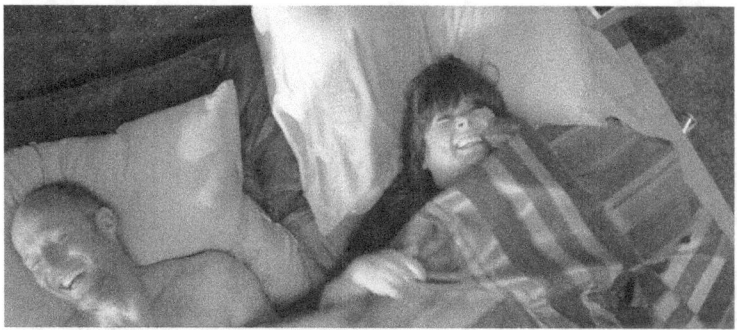

Figure 47 *Spy* (Paul Feig: 2015) Chernin Entertainment, Feigco Entertainment, TSG Entertainment

Figure 48 *The Meg* (Jon Turteltaub: 2018) Warner Bros. Pictures, Gravity Pictures, Flagship Entertainment, Apelles Entertainment, Di Bonaventura Pictures, Maeday Productions

Figure 49 *The Meg* (Jon Turteltaub: 2018) Warner Bros. Pictures, Gravity Pictures, Flagship Entertainment, Apelles Entertainment, Di Bonaventura Pictures, Maeday Productions

Figure 50 *The Meg* (Jon Turteltaub: 2018) Warner Bros. Pictures, Gravity Pictures, Flagship Entertainment, Apelles Entertainment, Di Bonaventura Pictures, Maeday Productions

Part III
Rebranding Statham

9

Transporting Jason Statham: national identity in *The Transporter* trilogy

Jennie Lewis-Vidler

Until Frank Martin, Jason Statham's celluloid identity lingered within the comfort of a distinct 'Britishness', from his mock-cockney and mononymous characters in Guy Ritchie's *Lock Stock and Two Smoking Barrels* (1998) and *Snatch* (2000) coupled with his performance as 'Monk' in Barry Skolnick's *Mean Machine* (2001). However, it would be fair to say that producer Luc Besson's Transporter trilogy (2002, 2005 and 2008) tangibly broadened Statham's range of roles and offered a tantalising glimpse into the examination of the interaction of a British star in a 'transnational' identity. This chapter will examine Statham's work within the codes these transnational action movies display, supporting their Hollywood blockbuster status.

First, in terms of this discussion, what is meant by a 'transnational' identity needs to be defined. Traditionally, the word indicates an extension of identity across national boundaries (Mitchell as cited in Anderson *et al.* 2003: 74). Additionally, it is also worth noting that 'transnationalism' is a social construct. Certainly, identity, or more specifically national identity, has varied dramatically over time; borders change, nationalities adapt and the definition of what constitutes a nationality and how society assign people to one country or another changes. Yet, 'transnationalist' is a perfect title to assign to Martin as it describes his fictional identity accurately. It is also worth noting that there are no political or economic factors to consider when analysing Statham's portrayal of Frank Martin's national identity throughout the films. Therefore, transnationalism for this discussion will focus purely on a cultural perspective.

Research into transnationalism highlights that nationality is the primary example of a border (Niekrenz *et al.* 2016: 126). To that end, how Statham depicts Martin's nationality will have a focus throughout the chapter. In truth, Besson went to great lengths to conceal Martin's nationality: Statham's accent was displaced to a mid-Atlantic dialect, a generic cross-national name and Martin's military career within an intergovernmental NATO Special Forces unit all helped to confuse his character's true identity. Furthermore, it is clear that his distinctiveness across the trilogy is one of an 'outsider'. Indeed, even Inspector Tarconi (François Berléand) asserted in *The Transporter* that Martin had a 'good sense of humour for a foreigner'. This placed Martin's transnational identity at the forefront of the audiences' minds. To that end, analysing the portrayal of Statham's character is crucial to understanding his role as Martin. Also, the prefix 'trans' automatically indicates movement and change. Especially in terms of the mobility of Statham's character which is stressed throughout the film: from the titles of the movies clearly representing mobility, to Martin's occupation as a driver-for-hire, as well as the physical action expressed in all three films, all place the 'transportability' of the character's identity firmly front and centre in the audiences' mind. Therefore, Martin's multifaceted definition of the prefix is clear, which leaves the complexities of the word 'national'. This discussion does not require a traditional translation.

There are many elements to the *Transporter* films that could be analysed to outline Statham's transformation into a transnationally charismatic commodity. Nevertheless, this chapter will focus on how his masculinity transformed his persona. Or more specifically, how the movies portrayed his 'Hollywood masculinity' by using a blue-print that had been in motion pictures for decades to establish hegemonic masculinity; without it, the trilogy would not have been such an international success. Pre-*Transporter*, Statham's accomplished career and displays of masculinity continuously remained 'traditional' or 'British' in each role. The audience could easily understand his fictional characters where he maintained and consistently formed a 'manly' depiction of an idealised macho identity – both for a positive or negative architype, for example, the Scottish prisoner with a taste for aggressive goal-keeping (*Mean Machine* 2001). Yet, as Martin, the viewers could conceptualise Statham's masculine presence and he was propelled globally into a new era of class, style and *je ne sais quoi*. Even throughout the violent fight scenes, Martin is a far cry from 'The Monk'. Both of these characters provide an interesting platform for discussion of the display of 'proper' manliness. Indeed, masculinity enacted through violence adjusts and manifests itself as physical aggression. Furthermore, it is also deemed 'unmasculine' or 'ungentlemanly' to display unnecessary physical force. This is where Statham's two characters differ: Monk's viciousness was unrelenting and uncontrolled, whereas Frank portrayed a moral code of self-defence and heroism. Therefore, how does Statham's role as Frank Martin convey a masculinity? Is there a one-type-fits-all masculine depiction that represents all men globally?

This chapter will emphasise three elements of Statham's masculine expression of a transnational identity, within the codes of the Hollywood films and through the character of Martin. Masculinity remains a form of global identity, but it does have different cultural connotations within every country. However, traditional notions of 'Hollywood masculinity' are recognised to have three elements, all of which are crucial to the international success of the *Transporter* trilogy. First, it will assess how Statham utilises his body throughout the movies. His action and movement remain a constant focus within the franchise and how he exploits his body in scenes, specifically the fighting sections, highlights his transnational identity. Second, this discussion will analyse the heroic nature of Statham's character, and in particular, how Besson represented his international military career to enhance Statham's depiction of Martin's transnational body. The final stages of this chapter will investigate the codes of the film, both the technical and the symbolic, which convey transnationalism. It will consider the technical props, for example, the cars, as well as importance of the films' locations in generating transnational appeal. The purpose of the themes is to give a clear and concise picture of Statham's transnationality and his wider persona.

Transnationalising a British body

Contemporary masculine stereotypes are persistently represented globally in films through the use of men's bodies. What constitutes manliness, particularly in the western world, can be generically promoted to a worldwide market. What is perceived as 'masculine' universally is subjective, although Muth and Cash have suggested men's body images may be understood as a multidimensional construct that represents how individuals 'think, feel and behave' (Muth and Cash 1997: 1438 as cited in Morrison and Halton 2009). Moreover, 'manliness' as a construct, as Brod and Kaufman (1994: 120) have highlighted further, 'is not the manifestation of an inner essence; it is socially constructed. Manhood does not bubble up to consciousness from our biological makeup; it is created in culture'. With the understanding that masculinity is a social concept, Statham's heightened manliness with the use of his body intensifies both Statham and Martin's transnational character. Still, it is a leap to assert that Statham's performance asserts a specific transnational manliness without further definition and examples of how this profile is orchestrated.

After the first scene of *Transporter* the spectators are in no doubt of Martin's masculinity. From his cool and calm attitude in juxtaposition with fellow male 'client' passengers, to his clean-shaven, 'suited and booted' attire, the audience can only admire his manliness. This portrayal is further heightened by a skilful car chase racing through narrow alleyways and precision manoeuvres as he expertly misses pedestrians and other vehicles, while his customers are left in a constant state of anxiety, leaving one male traveller unable to control his bodily functions, unceremoniously vomiting out of an open window.

All aspects of this initial scene assert Frank Martin's personality and his stereotypical 'manhood' that appeals to many men; men who want to be Statham, men who admire his driving talents, as well as his well-mannered passive-aggressive tact; his masculinity as an ideal is constantly suggested. Still, this example does not explain how Statham utilises his body to portray transnational manliness. Even though Statham is fully clothed in this scene, he was transformed into a Gallic masculine icon. It was not his concentration while negotiating the narrow side streets that depicted his 'Gallicness'. Rather, it was his attire. Ultimately, then, it was his body image that cemented the change. The outfit was not accidental and was selected by Besson to mimic the iconic French actor, Alain Delon, and his performance of Jef Costello in Jean-Pierre Melville's 1960s hitman movie *Le Samouraï* (1971). In this classic French New Wave *tour de force*, the captivating presentation of Delon's performance as the hitman loner provided Statham with a perfect blue-print as to how to represent his new 'European' charisma and cement his transnational identity, and a comparison between Costello and Martin will be offered later in this chapter.

The imitation of Costello's outfit progressed Statham's identity not only into 'Gallicness' but, furthermore, into a transnational and international status. The clothing has its own personality that has been created by Hollywood and its reputation does not recognise national borders. The dark suit, white shirt and black tie archetypal uniform has been used in countless Hollywood blockbusters to address a certain type of masculinity, with modern and notable examples including Hugo Weaving/ Agent Smith in *The Matrix* (1999), Quentin Tarentino's violent 'Mister' crew in *Reservoir Dogs* (1992) and Vincent Vega (John Travolta) and Jules Winnfield (Samuel. L. Jackson) in *Pulp Fiction* (1994). Within these films, all of the characters demonstrated an inherently aggressive persona. As discussed, even though Statham conveys a cool, calm and collected persona, he also has a physically forceful presence. For instance, in *Transporter 3* (2008), when a villain had the audacity to touch 'the suit', Martin stressed 'I'll give you five seconds to remove your hand', which led into a complexly choreographed hand-to-hand combat scene where, against seemingly insurmountable odds, he defeats several men.

Besson's intention was to create a new style of European action film, one that would shake Hollywood. For that, he needed an image that epitomised Hollywood's stylishness, expressed a European edge, but would still convey aggressive masculinity when challenged. The iconic British spy, James Bond seemed to capture the overall 'look' for Frank Martin, but rather than map Martin's persona onto the contextual Bond-persona of the more-gentle Pierce Brosnan, Besson turned to Agent Smith (*The Matrix*, 1999) who demonstrated the durability of the dark suit with the same fighting style as Martin's. The classic image, captured through Statham and his role as Martin contributed to what Kath Woodward described as a 'manhood formula' (2006: 12). Woodward asserted that violence, in particular fierce sports such as boxing, produced a particular code of heterosexual masculinity (2006: 12). This became a code that was understood by men, which in turn created a statement of hegemonic masculinity that could be understood worldwide. Therefore, Statham's interaction with the suit and its code advanced his transnational identity. Statham absorbed both a well-known classic Gallic film identity and incorporated it with the definitive Hollywood characteristic, the use of a dark suit, white shirt and tie, to transport his own British identity into one that is transnational. As argued, Statham's costume had the previous reputation of being worn by violent and aggressive characters. Therefore, it is important to discuss how Statham's physical aggression also contributed to his transnationalism.

There have been generations of actors who have performed violence in the name of entertainment. Also, groups of audience members that have watched that violence; Roman amphitheatres were filled with citizens who watched gladiators perform until their or their challenger's death. The staged and choreographed fighting of movie actors provides a similar, but non-life-threatening form of entertainment, with a fictional element of violence or death that is still enjoyed by the viewers. Steven Neale has asserted that 'male genres and films constantly involve sadomasochistic themes, scenes and fantasies or that male heroes can at times be marked as the object of an erotic gaze' (Neale 1993: 281). The transnational heroic identity of Statham will be analysed in more detail later in the chapter. Now, Neale's assertion can be used to further evaluate Statham's masculinity. The discussion for this section will highlight how Statham used his body physically to demonstrate his transnational manliness.

There can be no doubt of Jason Statham's physical prowess in any of the *Transporter* films, but his ability is not what is being discussed. Statham's brand of combat and style of fighting established a major element in his international, and thus transnational, identity. Similar to the earlier discussion, it was crucial that Besson and Statham chose the right combative mode to market to an international audience. This strand of fighting was elaborately orchestrated and choreographed, and the combination of *Krav Maga* and mixed martial arts perfectly demonstrated Statham's fighting ability. The significance of these two fighting styles is crucial to understanding his transnationality. *Krav Maga*, Hebrew for 'contact combat', as Todd Samuel Presner suggested, 'is a system of self-defence developed for the Israel Defence Forces (IDF) in the 1940s' (2007: xix). Although this does emphasise Martin's military career, analysis on *Krav Maga* and what other fighting styles it incorporates also stresses how Statham transformed his identity. This particular technical form of violent acting became an extension of who he was. Statham's fluidity through the *Transporter* franchise's fighting scenes was sophisticated and elegant.

Comparatively, prior to 2002 his representation of violence was ungentlemanly and awkward. For example, when embodying Mr B in *Turn It Up* (2000) and as the MVA agent in *The One* (2001) his performances were clumsy. Training for this confrontational style of acting required dedication. Indeed, Statham trained for hours every day in order to perform the action sequences, and his commitment resulted in a depiction of Martin's elegant brawls. However, the relevance that *Krav Maga* encompasses boxing, wrestling Aikido, Judo and Karate is important as this validates Statham's transnational masculinity. All of these sports are acknowledged worldwide. Significantly, choosing a fighting style that encompasses all these elements, elements that Statham expertly mastered, asserts his interaction with other cultures and enriches his transnational body. While not wishing to deny that Statham's fitness or elegance was not already established – after all his membership of the British National Diving team in 1992 had already asserted his abilities – it was not until his role as Frank Martin that the international audience got to appreciate Statham's capacity to perform such physicality that embodied global fighting styles.

All three *Transporter* films converted Statham's national identity. It is clear that he demonstrated a transfer of his performing identity into a personality that incorporated a transnational character. Statham used his body, both in the representation of his clothing and in acting a specific type of violence. Significantly, he dedicated an abundance of time to train for this role, in order to symbolise his and his character's masculine transnational identity. As Neale (1993: 279) has asserted 'constant work is needed to channel and regulate identification in relation to sexual division, in relation to the orders of gender, sexuality and social identity'. Neale's suggestion leads conveniently on to the next section of analysis – how the heroic identity of Martin represented Jason Statham's conversion form a British star to transnational body.

Transporting transnational heroism

What constitutes heroism, as with masculinity, is subjective. Yet, there are elements that are perceived globally to be contributing factors: a military career, for example, which then ultimately proceeds towards acts of self-sacrifice. Every nation considers soldiers to be heroes because they defend their countries and protect citizens. It is the belief that: 'the occupation of the soldier demands high levels of physical strength, endurance and discipline, as well as the capacity to withstand unpleasant, dangerous, oftentimes lethal working conditions, all of this being characteristic of a certain kind of discursively-produced masculinity' (Godfrey et al. 2012: 546).

The two attributes of a military career and self-sacrifice are generally recognised worldwide as characteristics of 'heroism' due to global hegemony of Hollywood's version of masculine heroism; both qualities were features of Frank Martin. Therefore, it is not a huge leap to assert that Martin's heroic identity aided Statham's conversion into a transnational movie star. Although the discussion could be further enhanced by the suggestion that Statham's fictional *Transporter* heroism, expressed a specific masculine transnational identity. Undeniably, the use of the film's other characters, specifically female characters, aided Statham to embody a patriarchal self-sacrificial identity, similar to the fictional knight in shining armour; a myth that every nation recognises. However, while most military heroes defend their nation for patriotic motives, this was not the case for Martin. Nevertheless, this aspect contributed to the transnational identity and needs to be analysed. Therefore, the two elements of Martin's military career and self-sacrificial identity will be evaluated to understand the perceived masculine heroic transnational identity of Statham.

However, Statham's character as the reluctant hero was orchestrated to portray a champion. This part of his character helped Statham venture into a transnational identity. One major element that advanced the change was Frank Martin's military career. The audience discovered his previous occupation in *The Transporter* through the eyes of Lai (Shu Qi), when she looked around Martin's house and located a box containing medals and old photographs. The find informed the audience that Martin was an ex-member of NATO's Special Forces. Not only does this automatically make Martin 'fit for purpose' to protect Lai (as well as Jack Billings and Valentina), it also highlighted his disciplined character. Godfrey *et al.* (2012: 548) have suggested that military men ultimately have 'disciplined bodies'. This in turn suggests that a 'military body is, first and foremost, a masculine body even when it is female' (Godfrey *et al.* 2012: 553 and 558). It is significant to the transnational argument that Frank was a member of the NATO Special Forces. Undeniably, this made him the ultimate 'western' hero, for he was not just a patriotic solider that only served one nation (not that we are privy to his nationality, therefore, he is patriotic to all), he served the western world in middle-eastern countries. This non-nationality and the protection against malevolent forces is conveyed through all of the *Transporter* trilogy.

This is a similar pattern to previous Hollywood movies, notably *Rambo* (1982). Indeed, Rambo's military career and its psychological impact on him, as well as the presentation that he was the ultimate hero – the strong silent type who used skilled and violent action to accomplish the mission – yet here it seemed to make Martin *dissimilar* to Rambo. Martin did not serve just one nation and consequently his role was to protect the globe, much like James Bond has done. In *Transporter 2* Martin saved not only a child from biological warfare, but the world. Likewise, in *Transporter 3* he protected a Ukrainian woman while saving the planet from toxic waste. The plots of the series presented the western world's most feared enemies: adversaries with selfish financial desires, biological and chemical warfare, not to mention kidnapping. The combination of these points combined with Martin's military career in NATO and his habit of defending the western world against its anxieties all contributed to the shaping of Statham's transnational persona.

This heroic character can be further extended to demonstrate his 'transnational masculinity'. The homosocial genre of the franchise ultimately appealed to men and thus reinforced a conservative Hollywood hegemonic masculinity by the heroic nature of its lead star. Sharon Bird (1996: 121) has stated that 'homosocial interaction contributes to the maintenance of hegemonic masculine norms'. Certainly, movie stars are valorised and put on cultural pedestals, they are the modern gladiators: the last heroes (Craig 1992: 174). Therefore, Martin's fearlessness has promoted Statham's global superstardom and endorsed his transnationalism. Yet, this in turn leads on to an additional quality of heroism – self-sacrifice. Although Martin complied with his own rules, whenever he relaxed them it would be for the women. As with Jef Costello in *Le Samouraï* (1971), it is no accident that all his difficulties are started by women (Neale 1993: 280). Conclusively, the outcome of Statham's interaction with the leading female actors constructs an additional element of self-sacrifice.

In abundance, there is one quality in all of the *Transporter* trilogy films that stands out: self-sacrifice. There are two separate strands to Martin's subtle martyrdom and both are valued in Hollywood's version of masculinity – paternalism and male patriarchy. In order to become a hero, there has to be an element of self-sacrifice, but how Statham portrayed Martin's martyred personality was how he became a heroic superstar. In the franchise Martin is continuously the reluctant hero, who is only fighting to defend himself and his companions. The film's approach to violence is vague and, as with other films of its genre, the violence is validated as a crucial component to the character's self-defence. Still, what is important to this section is the type of heroism that was depicted.

In *The Transporter* and *Transporter 3*, Martin finds himself a custodian of unwitting women – women that have been forced into their predicaments but need protecting nonetheless. In *Transporter 2*, Frank's heroism saves Audrey Billings (Amber Valleta) but also her son Jack (Hunter Clary). In the case of Frank Martin/Statham, all of his leading women remain pivotal, but not for the roles that they play or the positions they occupy within the narrative. Rather, it is for the role that they allow Statham to play. As Laura Mulvey cited in her discussion with Budd Boetticher, 'She is the one, or rather the love or fear she inspires in the hero, or else the concern he feels for her, who makes him act the way he does. In herself the woman has not the slightest importance' (Mulvey 1999: 837).

This indicates that the female lead roles are there only to support Statham's innate heroism, though some scenes are a little far from heroic. For instance, when he caught his runaway cargo, Lao in *The Transporter*, and threw her over his shoulder gagged and bound. There are also several fighting scenes where we are offered the spectacle of Statham's body, unmarked and half-naked as a form of erotic display (Neale 1993: 285). To illustrate, in *Transporter 3*, Valentina looks on at a topless Martin as he combats a group of adversaries. This formula and type of masculinity where the male lead has such a dominantly patriarchal role, combined with Frank's reluctant heroism, popularly equate to a healthy heterosexual masculine male role model (Messner and Sabo 1990: 149).

This prevalent Hollywood hierarchical manliness is understood worldwide and has been portrayed in movies decades over. Susan Jeffords (1993: 245) asserted that 'the male body – principally the white male body – became increasingly a vehicle of display – of musculature, of beauty, of physical feats, and of gritty toughness'. For an example, the discussion can return to Jef Costello and the relationship with the two leading female actors in *Le Samouraï* (1971). Both Jane Lagrange (Nathalie Delon) and the pianist (Cathy Rosier) were placed in the narrative to support Costello, even providing a false alibi for the night he performed a contracted killing. Likewise, Besson's other popular movie series *Taken* (2008, 2012, 2014) uses Bryan Mills' (Liam Neeson) reliance on his CIA training skills to rescue his daughter.

Clearly, the method of patriarchal and paternalistic masculinity is why Statham's identity developed into a transnational identity through the character of Frank Martin. Every woman and man understood the Hollywood patriarchal theme of 'man saves woman' and it did not need to be culturally translated, it was automatically understood. Indeed, Hollywood had globally cemented these values and reproduced their version of 'masculinity' for decades. Mulvey has suggested that by a constant recreation of a type of manliness the spectator identifies with the on-screen male (Laura Mulvey in David Green 2009: 27). Besson reproduced blockbuster Hollywood movies that pushed the classic 'damsel in distress' or masculinity as fathering theme. To that end, Statham's transnational success is rooted in the hegemony of western patriarchal values. Moreover, in order to become an international star, it seems that Statham had to conform to some very conservative male attributes.

A combination of Martin's military career, the benefits of it, and with elements of self-sacrifice, provided an identity that Statham could interpret into the heroic character in all of the *Transporter* movies. Due to Hollywood's prescribed masculinity, these qualities did not require any cultural translation, as the heterosexual masculinity was understood and the formula of 'me Tarzan, you Jane' that has been suggested throughout the movies, became universally understood. To that end, Statham's Hollywood heroic identity of Martin supported his transformation from mock-cockney into a transnational star. Also, to aid Statham's conversion the technical and symbolic codes of the *Transporter* trilogy had to represent the transnational identities of the characters and movies themselves. Consequently, the next section will discuss how this was accomplished.

Cosmopolitan coding of Statham

The technical and symbolic codes of the *Transporter* series greatly aided Statham's transnational identity. There are many technical and symbolic codes that could potentially be discussed to support the argument. However, there are two technical and symbolic codes that will highlight why this particular trilogy adapted Jason Statham's identity. The technical analysis will evaluate how the use of the cars and filming locations significantly supported Statham's new transnational identity. The symbolic exploration will assess how the actor's facial expressions, as well as how the use of the other characters assisted his transnationality. The combination of all the codes significantly influenced the transition of Statham's identity.

The technical codes of the *Transporter* franchise are fundamentally identical. Undeniably, this was the reason why all the films were such a global success. Tom Bond (2017), when discussing the success of *The Fate of the Furious* (2017) movie, another of Statham's franchises, asserted that 'fast cars and Hollywood have always been a crucial part of American identity' and that 'cars are the means with which the central heroes pursue the American dream'. Therefore, Bond's comment suggests that Hollywood has a direct-line into many Americans' identity with which cars they endorse in the films. Moreover, due to the global success of the *Transporter* series, this discussion will propose that it took Statham's identity beyond America; it catapulted it across the world. To that end, although both the make of cars and the locations where the films were set changed through the course of the series, this is what ensured Statham's transnationality. Of course, cars were fundamental in the films due to the nature of Frank Martin's occupation. Nevertheless, the importance of which cars were used and how he drove them indicated the transnational distinctiveness. Statham drove BMWs, Mercedes and Audis throughout the trilogy, all symbolising status, each made by multinational companies and all essential in conveying the message of luxury and, therefore, that the right car elevates your persona. Furthermore, how the cars were used was vital and, although Bond's article was about *The Fate of the Furious*, his observation accurately assesses the *Transporter* movies. For example, he stated 'the old cliché about flashy cars being an extension of the male ego is truer than ever in this universe' (Bond 2017). This was the appeal of the films and this was how Statham became the transnational star we know today. With the use of cars to represent a very male world, for instance, epitomised by the fact that women are predominately the passengers (even when tied up in the boot of the car), Frank's male counterparts were constantly reminded to respect the 'rules' of the car and subconsciously admire the driving skills of Martin/Statham. As Bond continued to note, the cars and the man driving 'notably represent a very male version' of the quest (2017). This in turn leads on to where the cars are being driven, or where they are being driven to, and how that further highlights Statham's transnationality.

The movie locations were paramount in turning Statham into a global sensation. Gone were the streets of London, with scenes set in dark British pubs, dingy flats and the 'wrong-coloured' caravans (aka Turkish's office). Now Statham/Martin traversed (literally) across the world in expensive and luxurious status symbol cars. His fictional character lived and travelled through stunning parts of the world: from the South of France, to Miami and then across Europe. This movement contributed to the audiences' perception that Statham was a man of the world. For him there were no national borders. When combined with the earlier discussion of Martin's unknown nationality, both factors helped transform Statham from national into transnational star. When seeing a star behind the wheel of an expensive car, the audience's experience is based on the pleasure of seeing the actor 'exist' in or through cityscapes and landscapes (Neale 1993: 281).

Although there is no doubt in the viewers minds that Martin remains a fictional character, the popularity of the films and the hegemonic masculinity-based storylines could not help but rub off onto Statham. He was 'born again'. No longer did he remain the cockney stereotype. Rather, through Martin he was an international superstar, and one that moved from country to country and continent to continent with ease. Not only was this helped by the cars themselves, but also the locations he drove through: exotic, hot, beautiful. These locations seem to cement Martin as a globetrotter, much in the same way as James Bond has always been; but, just as importantly, they helped to create the idea that Statham is now a man of the world. This was also aided, especially in the *Transporter* trilogy with the help of an international cast that cemented Statham's persona as working outside of the United Kingdom.

The symbolic codes performed in films are crucial to the success of any movie. In particular, how the actors portray their characters' identity through facial expressions and how the cast members work together to support an individual performer's character, are codes which make movies a commercial success. Therefore, when discussing the codes required to analyse Statham's identity, both the expressions he presented, as well as the other identities of international cast members, aided his new transnational distinctiveness.

As previously examined, Besson based the character of Frank Martin on Jef Costello and this in turn supported Statham's identity alteration. Alain Delon's 'Frenchness' influenced Statham's character and ended his cockney typecasting. Although Jef Costello played a crucial part in shaping Martin, Besson's aim was to create a Hollywood action film star with a very European perception. Importantly, Martin's accent is hard to place. Even though the film is in English, Statham's dialect was a combination of transatlantic-Dutch-cockney and this also displaced his nationality. Even though this was a contributing factor to transforming Statham's identity, it only partially supported his transnationality. But, by combining his accent with recognisable facial expressions from distinguished characters in Hollywood action movies completed the makeover. For example, several blockbuster movies that also enjoyed a long-lived franchise by following the same heterosexual masculine formula. Film franchises like *Die Hard* (1988, 1990, 1995, 2007 and 2013) with the all-American Bruce Willis as resilient John McClane, or the *Bourne* (2002, 2004, 2007, 2012 and 2016) series of blockbusters with Matt Damon as CIA assassin Jason Bourne, and (dare I say it) Daniel Craig in *Casino Royal* (2006) and his portrayal of the British spy James Bond, have heroes that expressed their character's 'tough grit' through similar facial expressions. All of the actors use the same gestures and look to convey their seriousness and emotional distance. Furthermore, the emphasis in creating a form of enigmatic gaze appears to create an idea that their occupations and responsibilities are of great importance. All of the characters represent a visually appealing strong masculinity. Neale has suggested that 'we see male bodies stylised and fragmented by close-ups, but our look is not direct, it is heavily mediated by the looks of the characters involved' (2007: 1993). This is true for all of the action heroes discussed. This look helped carve out Statham's transnational identity and created a new twenty-first century action hero.

Additionally, Statham's co-stars completed the success of the *Transporter* franchise. Indeed, Martin's relationship with his friend Inspector Tarconi (François Berléand), as well as his interactions with Hong Kong, American and other European actors all contributed to Statham's new identity. Through his interaction with other non-British performers, Statham crossed and transformed boundary lines, which in turn represented a multilayered nationality when blended with his and other co-stars' nationalities. Throughout his previous roles, Statham predominately interacted with British co-stars. With the exception of the lacklustre *Ghosts of Mars* (2001), which did not reach a wide audience, his preceding characters and co-stars remained firmly rooted in 'Britishness'. Statham's former characters had been shaped by British directors and appeared in productions that featured personalities that portrayed a stereotypical British persona. Both Guy Ritchie's *Lock, Stock and Two Smoking Barrels* and *Snatch* created an ambience that appealed to the British sense of humour. This detail, coupled with setting the film locations around the streets of London, embodied 'Britishness'. Indeed, both Statham/Bacon's (*Lock Stock and Two Smoking Barrels*) and Turkish's (*Snatch*, 2000) wit – along with Statham's own sense of humour – created scenes that epitomised and indulged the British Monty Python-esque jocularity. For example, in *Lock, Stock...*, a scene that involved a traffic warden and a stolen car, which the group of friends had acquired after a heist, highlighted the uniquely British distaste for the man's occupation. Likewise, in *Snatch* Turkish's sarcasm found vent when he opened the door to his caravan, which breaks in his hand as he declares that it was in 'tip-top' condition. However, Ritchie's movies predominately casted British actors and all the characters had an equal part to play. To that end, Besson's ingenious casting of largely unknown international actors demonstrated to the audience and other film makers that Statham was more than just a mock-cockney body. By selecting unfamiliar actors to support Statham, Besson ensured that they did just that – supported Statham's star turn, while also from a character point of view, their characters helped to cement the reality and genuineness that Martin is supposed to employ.

But interestingly, their global identities were fundamental to removing the Britishness border of Statham's personality. His co-stars elevated Statham's identity to something more than a British actor and provided credibility to his new identity. His transnational character was constantly supported by his fellow actors. Statham's co-performers humanised Martin, their engagement increased his believability and placed him in context. For example, Martin made madeleines for Lao, he played riddles with Jack and he personally introduces himself to Valentina. Also, all of the challenges Martin confronted he did with other international movie stars and their cultural and nationality differences which added a contextual layer to Statham's presentation as the calm-under-pressure Transporter.

Conclusion

Interpreting Jason Statham's role as Frank Martin has provided tangible proof of his transnationality. The evidence would suggest that his performance of a highly masculine identity reinforces all of the themes discussed, from the internationally recognisable dark-suited uniform to the globally recognised combat style, to his patriarchal and paternalistic self-sacrificial yet heroic identity.

Prior to the *Transporter* movies Statham's immutable movie characters ensured his identity remained British. Besson's trilogy catapulted his fictional and personal character into more enduring international stardom. Significantly, the transnational character of Martin empowered Statham's own identity. All of the evaluated elements and themes provided a platform that a global audience could easily recognise. Hollywood's formula for their leading men's manliness produced a hegemonic Hollywood version of masculinity, whether male or female, whereby the cultural codes of heterosexual masculinity are understood universally. By using a combination of heterosexual masculinity, combined with chic 'Frenchness' and coupled with obvious Hollywood style, this formula permanently secured Statham's transnational identity. Succeeding the *Transporter* series, he continued to perform an almost identical role in other films and franchises, including lead characters in *Parker* (2013), *The Mechanic* (2011), *Mechanic: Resurrection* (2016), *The Expendables* (2010, 2012, 2014) trilogy and, finally, in *Fast and Furious 6* (2013), *Furious 7* (2015) and *The Fate of the Furious* (2017). Indeed, these last two franchises highlight just how transnational a star Statham had become. The character of Frank Martin offered Statham a world without borders. But Statham did not just act out the part, he embodied the part – Statham and Martin represent one persona. Without doubt, the role of Frank Martin propelled Statham into a world that went beyond the shores of Great Britain; it even went further than the European oceans. It made it all the way to Hollywood.

References

Anderson, K., Domosh, M., Pile, S. and Thrift N. (2003). *Handbook of Cultural Geography*. London, Thousand Oaks, CA and New Delhi: SAGE.
Bird, S. (1996). 'Welcome to the men's club: homosociality and the maintenance of hegemonic masculinity'. *Gender and Society*, 10(2), 120–132.
Bond, T. (2017). 'How *The Fast and the Furious* franchise used cars to symbolize the American dream'. *Guardian* (12.04.17).
Brod, H. and Kaufman, M. (eds). (1994). *Theorizing Masculinities*. Thousand Oaks, CA, London and New Delhi: SAGE.
Craig, S. (ed.) (1992). *Men, Masculinity and the Media*. Thousand Oaks, CA, London and New Delhi: SAGE.
Godfrey, R., Lilley, S. and Brewis, J. (2012). 'Biceps, bitches and Borgs: reading *Jarhead*'s representation of the construction of the (masculine) military body'. *Organization Studies*, 33(4), 541–562.
Green, D. (2009). *Manhood in Hollywood from Bush to Bush*. Austin, TX: University of Texas Press.
Messner, M. A. and Sabo, D. F. (1990). *Sport, Men and the Gender Order: Critical Feminist Perspectives*. Champaign, IL: Human Kinetics Books.

Morrison, T. G. and Halton, M. (2009). 'Buff, tough, and rough: representations of muscularity in action motion pictures'. *Journal of Men's Studies*, 17(1), 57–74.

Mulvey, L. (1999). 'Visual pleasure and narrative cinema', in Braudy, L. and Cohen, M. (eds). (2009). *Film Theory and Criticism: Introduction Readings*. New York: Oxford University Press. pp. 833–844.

Neale, S. (1993). 'Masculinity as spectacle', in Cohan, S and Hark, I. R. (eds). *Screening the male: exploring masculinities in Hollywood cinema*. London and New York: Routledge.

Niekrenz, Y., Witte, M. D. and Albrecht, L. (eds). (2016). 'Transnational bodies: embodiment of transnational settings'. *Transnational Social Review*, 6(1–2), 124–140.

Presner, T. S. (2007). *Muscular Judaism: The Jewish Body and the Politics of Regeneration*. London and New York: Routledge.

Woodward, K. (2006). *Boxing, Masculinity and Identity: The 'I' of the Tiger*. New York: Routledge.

10

The avatar hero: exploring the virtualisation of the Statham brand

Dean Bowman and Erin Pearson

Introduction

Despite his firm grounding in the action film genre, Jason Statham is a star brand constructed and constituted at the intersection of the film, videogame and promotional industries. Outside of the multiplex cinema, Statham's image proliferates in posters, trailers, websites, billboards and print features promoting the latest releases, and also in the free-to-play mobile game *Sniper X with Jason Statham* (Glu Mobile 2015). Elsewhere in the digital sphere it is dispersed and spread across social media by film distributors, his own management and millions of followers and fans; at the time of writing, Statham's own Instagram page boasts 15.3 million followers, while his Facebook page boasts an impressive 54,759,301 followers. Statham has also infiltrated the field of console gaming with appearances in the highly popular first-person shooters (FPS) *Red Faction II* (as 'Shrike', THQ 2002) and *Call of Duty* (as 'Sergeant Waters', Activision 2003). In this chapter, drawing on *Crank* (Dir. Mark Neveldine and Brian Taylor 2006) and *Sniper X*, we analyse the crucial role that his transferability across film and game texts has played in rendering the particular virtual and kinetic dynamic of his stardom; and, how the transmedial qualities of his brand work to forge new consumer relationships across those converging markets.

We take the view that celebrity is a form of branding which, in a similar manner to the broader concept of brand, can exemplify the relations between products and services to their consumers (Hackley 2015: 462; Lury 2004: 1). For Matthew Thomson, it is the way that the celebrity is professionally managed by a range of interests – along with the additional associations and connotations that become inextricably linked with the celebrity over time – that determines their status as brand (Thomson 2006: 105). Statham is therefore considered here as a human brand – a 'well-known persona who is the subject of marketing communications efforts' (Thomson 2006: 104). We focus on the aspects of the Statham brand that circulate within a transmedia environment between game and film texts within and through which his celebrity has emerged. According to Henry Jenkins such transmedia texts 'contribute to a larger narrative economy' (Jenkins 2006: 124) through a process of transmedia storytelling, in which 'integral elements of a fiction get dispersed systematically across multiple delivery channels for the purpose of creating a unified and coordinated entertainment experience' (Jenkins 2011). Within this transmedia process, we consider Statham's brand to be the 'fiction' that is generated, organised and extended into the public consciousness largely through the work of the promotional industries across multiple media platforms.

While the specificity of the medium in question is important, it is also vital to note that no medium exists in isolation; as Jay David Bolter and Richard Grusin (2000) argue, each medium remediates other forms in a bidirectional process. This is especially the case for new media like videogames, which depend for their aesthetics and cultural significance on convergence with prior-existing media (Grusin 2000: 56). In this context, videogames have tended to borrow the stylistic and aesthetic trappings of cinema in an effort to draw on that medium's established cultural prestige and acceptability, while also positing themselves as 'better than film', since they generate a particular kind of interactive immediacy by 'allow[ing] the player to intervene in the action and so to define a role unlike the one offered by film' (Grusin 2000: 101). Indeed, it is the specific ways in which Statham remediates aesthetic devices associated with the videogame and its uniquely interactive qualities that renders his transferability across these media as potent, and full of emerging potential.

By drawing explicitly on the aesthetic, stylistic and ideological tropes of videogames, Statham's brand can be considered as 'hypermediated', to borrow Bolter and Grusin's terminology (2000). That is to say, Statham's brand – formed through film and videogame appearances, along with a wide range of promotional texts – explicitly foregrounds a process of remediation, rather than attempting to render it as transparent and invisible. For Lorrie Palmer (2012), this is most evident in Statham's appearance in *Crank*, a film which she finds to demonstrate an interrelated aesthetic regime of hypermediation and hypermasculinity. Here, we further extend the concept of hypermediation to consider the dynamics of Statham's star brand, exploring not only Statham's transferability across the arena of film and gaming, but also the ways that his brand celebrates and embodies the virtual. We argue that this implies a mutually productive relationship with videogame aesthetics; and, further, that it is illustrative of a cultural break with traditional visions of the action hero in the popular imaginary. Throughout this process, Statham has been consistently positioned as a new kind of action hero throughout both his films *and* his games: what we term an avatar hero.

The Statham brand

In film promotional materials, Statham's image acts as a recognisable logo that highlights and reinforces the physical virtuosity and kinetics that situate him within the action film genre. Film posters, in particular, demonstrate a remarkable consistency for images of Statham frozen in various states of hypercharged action: precariously clinging from a skyscraper (*The Mechanic*, 2011); his body contorted mid-leap, guns pointing at an unknown assailant (*The Transporter*, 2002; *Transporter 2*, 2005; *Transporter 3*, 2008); or, walking away from an explosion, frozen mid-stride (*Crank*, 2006). The posters for *Crank*, *Transporter* and *Mechanic* franchises all offer full-body images, captured in a perpetual state of motion, uniformly wearing tailored black clothing that highlight Statham's slim and agile physique.

Whereas the redundancy and repetitive nature of this highly proliferated image could, for others, lead to the kind of typecasting that limits the career of a star (Marshall 2010), in this instance it is this unification of the 'Statham brand' that is fundamental to his constantly evolving transmedia presence. Indeed, according to Janet Murray (1997: 188), such patterning, repetition and redundancy of information are core traits of the computer and central to the kinds of narratives they produce; a formulaic or algorithmic approach to storytelling that she relates back to the participatory qualities of the oral, bardic tradition. This repetition can also be seen in the concept of the gameplay loop (Momoda 2016), a core structuring principle of game design which sees players repeating the same actions over the course of the game; just as Statham runs, jumps and shoots his way through the obstacles that separate him from his goal. Statham's positioning throughout the course of film promotion, and indeed in the films themselves, thus clearly resonates with the aesthetic regime of the videogame; a defining characteristic of which is fluid traversal through and mastery over virtual spaces.

With this repetition and redundancy in mind, this chapter borrows P. David Marshall's terminology to note how Statham's image comes with a distinctive 'over-coding' that unifies the conceptualisation of his brand (Marshall 2014). This particular organisation, simply put, revolves around the foregrounding of Statham's unique physical presence, situating Statham in a category that Marshall (drawing on Richard De Cordova) terms the 'physical performer', by emphasising the 'physical characteristics that make him or her unique' in the absence of other extratextual knowledge about the actor (Marshall 2014). Given the apparent stability of his brand image, Statham could be read as being somewhat arrested in this stage of star development. However, this unification of image-based branding enables Statham's star text to operate in a manner akin to a much broader conceptualisation of brand. Namely, Statham is 'able to secure the recognition of the brand as a constantly shifting series of (variously related) products through its positioning' (Lury 2004: 11). In other words, Statham's image and its association with the genre of the action film and gaming forms a common recognisable link between like-products. For Jenkins, Sam Ford and Joshua E. Green (2013: 198), in order for content to be spread it must be 'quotable (editable by the audience) and grabbable (easily picked up and inserted elsewhere by the audience)'. It is precisely the over-coding of Statham's brand image that has enabled him to become 'grabbable', and 'quoted' in promotional materials and games such as *Sniper X*. This image-coding lends to his transferability between media forms, with action in particular being particularly transferable to the video game space, where crucially players may participate in the text and interact with Statham's persona.

The hyperviolent and macho nature of Statham's brand image also aligns him to the ideology of games, particularly in light of their tendency towards 'militarised masculinity', a condition observed by Stephen Kline *et al.* as a core constituent of videogames, which they define as a 'bias [that] privileges themes and representations of warfare, fighting, combat, and conquests along with the subject positions of aggressive, active male characters' (Kline *et al.* 2003: 194). For instance, his character poster as Lee Christmas for *The Expendables 2*, dressed in full military bulletproof gear and holding an assault rifle, is distinctly echoed in the promotion for the *Sniper X* game that sees a militarised, cartoonish Statham threateningly posed with weapon-in-hand. The past associations of the Statham brand, carefully curated and redundantly over-coded with symbols of militarism, masculinity and action, enable *Sniper X* not just to offer a recognisable avatar of Statham, but to form a transmedia link between military-style action films and games. Through playing a soldier and a sergeant in both films and games, and finally appearing (as a version of himself) as leader of an elite private military company in *Sniper X*, this particular aspect of Statham's career can be termed 'militainment'; a strand of popular culture that focuses on war games, military interventions, the organisation of political violence, and the focus on the armed forces (Stahl 2010). Drawing on the deeply embedded nature of the action genre, kinetic mobility and this emerging militarism, *Sniper X* crucially embeds and extends militainment into what can be termed the 'larger narrative economy' (Jenkins 2006: 124) of Statham's brand; but in doing so, appeals to not only a media literate and mobile audience, but also to a young male gamer audience weaned on the interactive qualities of (particularly, military-style) videogames.

In *Sniper X*, players are assigned to Statham's Private Military Company, Spearhead, where they are tasked with carrying out a series of missions as a lone wolf sniper. Missions take the form of timed shooting galleries in realistically rendered 3D environments across a variety of war-torn settings. In this, Statham's avatar acts as a supportive figure or mentor for the player: guiding them as they navigate the game world, training them and offering insights (and insults) while also helping to push forward the key narrative thrust of the game. His perceived position of authority on this front comes entirely from his carefully cultivated action man persona, built up in films and games. Ultimately, Statham's macho, militaristic cinematic persona, already heavily inflected as it is with a gamer aesthetic, is a perfect fit for a believable virtual performance. This is particularly evident in the statements of Glu Mobile's CEO Niccolo De Masi in interviews at the time of the *Sniper X* release, which are telling of the ways in which Statham's image is deployed in their wider commercial strategy:

> As Glu's *first male celebrity partner*, Jason Statham's over 55 million social followers *add a new demographic to the company's celebrity gaming platform*. Mr. Statham's creative input throughout the game's development has ensured a unique and authentic action-adventure experience his fans will enjoy worldwide. (Shaul 2015. Our emphasis)

Clearly the casting of Statham is partly motivated by the access to the celebrity's extensive social media network, demonstrating that at least part of the added value a star brings to a product is their followers. Statham's brand creates links between audience groups across platforms – here, the audiences for military-style gaming, casual social network games and action films – within what Brownlie, Hewer and Kerrigan term 'networks of affiliation and belonging' (2015: 455). De Masi's explicit foregrounding of Statham's gender, by noting he is their 'first male celebrity partner', illustrates a desire to return to the male gamers the studio had sought to appeal to in its early days when their catalogue consisted of a ruggedly masculine line of games such as *Gun Bros* (2010), *Deer Hunter Challenge* (2010) and *Big Time Gangsta* (2011). It also makes a marked distinction from the studio's recently successful Kardashian product, *Kim Kardashian: Hollywood* (2014), which was seen to appeal to a much broader audience (Farokhmanesh 2014), and was a significant breakthrough hit for the studio (Rose 2014). This started the company off in a profitable new direction of celebrity tie-ins that have included: Nicki Minaj (*Nicki Minaj: The Empire*, 2016), Gordon Ramsay (*Restaurant Dash with Gordon Ramsay*, 2016), Taylor Swift (*The Swift Life*, 2017) and of course, Jason Statham. As De Masi's statement shows, such celebrity tie-ins are strategically chosen to reach out to specific demographics. In this context, not only is Statham's brand acknowledged as being able to cross national boundaries to reach fans 'worldwide', but further, this militaristic and avatar-like aspect of his persona is deemed to lend to the 'authentic' action-adventure experience in a military game. This strategy attempts to attract the adolescent male audience, which is still deemed to be the core demographic that the commercial games industry seeks, as exemplified through the continued popularity of the military FPS genre (Payne 2012: 311). It is this genre that *Sniper X* remediates, albeit in a stripped-down abstracted manner suitable for mobile devices, giving players the empowered feeling of being able to reach out into a virtual world via the barrel of a high-tech sniper rifle and, through a series of dexterous finger movements, pluck a life from an unsuspecting enemy.

The consistency of Statham's branding, therefore, forms an 'at-a-glance' measure for consumers that may otherwise be spread out, disparate, across a range of platforms and devices. Yet, although Statham provides significant symbolic/celebrity capital for Glu's project – his digitised face giving the game both the novelty and military authority it needed to stand out in a crowded market place – the value exchange between star and studio, like the nature of remediation itself, is a reciprocal one, with Statham crucially able to use the game as a platform to showcase his own ludic qualities, which we will now explore.

Statham as 'avatar hero'

We contend that the hypermediated nature of Statham's brand, compounded by its consistent and over-coded emphasis on his mobility and dynamism, positions Statham as an avatar in film and games alike. The avatar is a core aspect of videogames that conceptualises the protagonist as a vessel for the player's embodied subjectivity within the game space, which is seen to be central to the notion of immersion at the heart of the game experience (Murray 1997; Calleja 2011). In his book on immersion in games, Gordon Calleja summarises the avatar thus:

> Avatar control games ... beckon the player to inhabit their worlds by *anchoring her in the figure of the avatar* ... Controlling a single avatar creates a more direct link between the player and the in-game entity. Pressing a key or waving a Wii controller will result

in an immediate reaction from the avatar (Calleja 2011: 60–61. Our emphasis).

With its etymological links to Hinduism as a god made manifest on Earth, the concept of the avatar carries with it considerable connotations of empowerment and domination, which links it clearly with the empowering concept of militarised masculinity. In a critical reading of the celebration of interaction within the emergence of virtual reality, C. Richard King and David J. Leonard see this notion of empowerment as a 'delusion' of the powerful: 'It allows the powerful and privileged to "play God" ... we can invent enemies, frontiers, geographies, consequences (or lack thereof), or historical narratives all towards our own empowerment' (King and Leonard 2010: 93). *Sniper X* clearly proceduralises these experiences of empowerment and control by allowing the player to select missions from a disembodied and omniscient gods-eye-view of the battlefield that, when chosen, immediately transitions to sequences in which the player is ideally situated to gun down his enemies on the ground. The transition between these two privileged points of view – one a macro strategic overview through the vantage point of a virtual drone camera, and the other a fetishised microsurgical command of the scene through the scope of a high-tech sniper rifle – takes place without any inconvenient questions about how the player came to be inserted so easily in enemy territory.

Bolter and Grusin characterise two strategies of remediation that work to create a sense of immediacy: transparency and hypermediation. While the former 'dictates that the medium itself should disappear and leave us in the presence of the thing represented' (Bolter and Grusin 2000: 6), as in the dream of virtual reality that King and Leonard rail against, the latter seeks to proliferate and draw attention to the act of mediation itself; 'seek[ing] the real by multiplying mediation so as to create a feeling of fullness, a satiety of experience, which can be taken as reality' (Bolter and Gruisin 2000: 53).

Paradoxically, this fullness of the hypermediated experience depends on the emptiness of the character the player inhabits in the game space; an emptiness that defines it as an avatar. The avatar thus performs the function of remediating the player into the game space, allowing them to pour themselves into the empty vessel of the character. By taking on some of these qualities of the avatar, Statham performs a similar function for the viewer of the films he stars in. This is immediately apparent in the unusual opening of *Crank*, which utilises the rarely used cinematic technique of point-of-view shots to place the viewer in the shoes of the protagonist, clearly foregrounding the film's link to videogame aesthetics through its hypermediation of the embodied perspective of the first-person shooter. This recasts the protagonist clearly as an avatar, and explicitly invites the audience to immerse themselves within his subjectivity. In a sequence that players of modern story-driven games will be well familiar with, here Chev Chelios wakes up and roams his apartment, splashing water in his (and the audience's) face before his eyes rest on the DVD entitled 'Fuck You' through which antagonist Ricky Verona delivers the monologue that reveals that Chelios has been poisoned. This use of a DVD to deliver the McGuffin that drives the plot on is highly reminiscent of the narrative audio-logs players find in games like *Bioshock* (Irrational 2007), which are typically used to deliver contextual information (referred to as 'lore' by gamers) about the virtual world, while minimising disruption to the player's control of the game. Such logs themselves remediate the audio form of the podcast or a telephone conversation, and thus this scene becomes a complex *mise en abyme* of older audio/visual media being remediated by games, and then remediated back again by film.

This infamous sequence makes it clear how Statham's brand embraces the new realm of the virtual avatar in counterpoint to traditional notions of action film masculinity, which have been defined by Yvonne Tasker (1993) as focusing on the material and natural. Indeed, Statham's virtuoso (virtual also) kineticism is a distinct departure from common conceptualisations of the classic 1980s action hero, distinguished by the overdetermined and statuesque bodybuilder physique (Tasker 1993: 87). Sylvester Stallone's character John Rambo acting as a human gun-turret, immobile and muscles bristling as he fires endlessly into the jungle, is offered by Tasker as a case-in-point (1993: 87). In contrast, Statham is slim, dexterous and well known for a certain high-speed, violent virtuosity. He is more in keeping with what Tasker terms the 'elaborate, quick-fire, physical performance' that is part of the Hong Kong action tradition (1993: 73), which is supported by his appearance alongside renowned martial arts actor Jet Li in *The One* (2001) and *War* (2007). Indeed, Statham's reported martial arts training in mixed martial arts and Brazilian Jiu Jitsu, along with a propensity for performing his own high-octane stunts (Palmer 2012; Blunden 2016; Chen 2017), only serves to reinforce this kinetic brand image.

Statham's acting style also demonstrates avatar-like qualities, which have supported his transferability to the gaming platforms while also embodying his uniqueness in the film industry. With his bald, bullet-shaped dome, Statham not only looks like the part of the clichéd 'scruffy white male' that has come to define the videogame hero in the popular imaginary (Kaiser 2014) but, like the hero of a videogame, Statham's blankness provides the negative space needed for the player/viewer to pour their own subjectivity onto the character. Statham's everyman persona, with his highly affected London working-class accent, eases this transition into the avatar, and throughout his films Statham has cultivated a persistently blank and emotionless action hero facade. Such 'blankness' can be understood to reduce the distance between the spectator and Statham's on-screen presence, creating a sense of embodiment and immediacy that is a key requirement for the concept of immersion. Calleja (2011: 3) describes this as 'the blending of a variety of experiential phenomena afforded by involved gameplay'.

Another example of this avatar style in adaptation from game to film is the game *Hitman: Codename 47* (Eidos Interactive, 2000) and its sequels, and the later films *Hitman* (Gens: 2007) and *Hitman: Agent 47* (Bach 2015), which present a character remarkably similar to Statham in both costuming (a black suit) and in look (a bald white man). Here, players control the stone-faced and impenetrable Agent 47 to carry out a series of assassinations – much like Statham's assassin character, Arthur Bishop, in *The Mechanic*. Like Agent 47, Statham's single-faceted identity becomes a digital prosthesis for the player's agency. This is only enhanced by the incredible regularity with which his image is rendered and positioned across the promotional sphere, where Statham-as-brand appears to respawn, videogame-like.

It is perhaps the film *Crank*, however, that most prominently and self-reflexively exemplifies the videogame qualities of Statham's back catalogue. In *Crank*, Statham's character, Chev Chelios, has been poisoned with a drug that threatens to stop his heart unless he receives the required shocks and volts to kickstart it. Of course, this is similar to many game narratives that require 'power-ups' or charges to replenish either health, stamina, or otherwise throughout the course of gameplay. At the end of *Crank*, a bonus extra is footage of Statham as a video game character, in a platform-style game; a moment of clear self-reflexivity concerning the hypermediated aesthetics of the film and its relationship to games. The type of spectacle at work in Statham's movies maps very well on to a notion of gameplay, and so it is no surprise to see such stunts emphasised in the films so that they appear more as a series of spectacles strung together; such as viewers might imagine themselves playing through such a series of set pieces with Statham as their avatar. The self-referential elements of *Crank* enhance this sensation. This is an interesting inversion of the typical view that narratively motivated AAA videogames typically ape cinema and its conventions (Eskelinen 2001). The flow between cinema and videogames is, instead, far from one-sided; with modern films remediating ludic qualities of videogames, just as games remediate the cinematic qualities of films.

Exploring the film's high-octane style and deployment of Statham as an example of hypermediated masculinity, Lorrie Palmer (2012: 2) notes how a variety of aesthetic techniques (such as split screens, animated inserts, 360-degree camera rotation and smash cuts; to name just a few) are utilised by directors Neveldine and Taylor to create a sense of immediacy and immersion that are a hallmark of videogames (Calleja: 2011). *Crank* utilises an 'aggressive camera style' specifically developed by the directors who formerly worked as stuntmen and makers of extreme motorcycle videos, and sees them filming on handheld cameras while moving at high speed on rollerblades, emphasising the mobility and fluidity of Statham's performance and its game-like aesthetic (Palmer 2012: 17). According to Palmer, the highly mobile digital video camera becomes a prosthesis, much like the prominence of the gun in a FPS, hovering in front of the player and extending into the game space to define the exclusively violent terms of their interaction with the world (Lukas 2010). Here the body and technology become fused into a state that 'frames a particular mode of production in new media as a gendered technological expression' (Palmer 2012: 8). Like any good videogame protagonist/avatar acting as a kind of prosthesis for the player, Statham often has an outlandish and comically exaggerated level of agency upon the world around him, which seems to bend to his will. He is seemingly incapable of becoming tired or being mortally wounded, as summed up perfectly by the tagline to *Crank: High Voltage* (2009): 'He was dead ... But he got better'.

Statham's particular rendition of the action hero, which combines physical performance with game-like aesthetics, resonates with the breakthrough success of films such as *The Matrix* (1999), which Palmer sees as initiating a new aesthetic and thematic regime in contrast to the action movies of the 1980s. The genre of cyberpunk thematically displaces the material and natural evocations of the action hero in favour of a transhumanist quality of 'physical ephemerality', which has, 'reimagined human avatars of digital technology ... in the cultural imaginary' (Palmer 2012: 6). The emergence of this techno-humanist genre significantly bridges the traditional action beefcake hero with the virtual nature of Statham. As a visual precursor to *Crank*, *The Matrix* offered scenes of bullet-time slow motion that fetishised the movements of Neo (Keanu Reeves), and placed him not only within the domain of the virtual (the game *Max Payne* (2001)) remediated this aesthetic as a core mechanic less than two years later) but also the technological, not only through the narrative concept of the matrix itself (the notion that the world is merely a simulation that enslaves humans), but also within the high-tech production context of the sophisticated camera rigs the Wachowski Brothers used to achieve their aesthetic. This resonates with the position of the videogame player via Espen Aarseth's influential notion of the cybertext, which positions games as, 'cyborg relationship[s] between organic and inorganic processes' (Aarseth 1997: 55). Both Statham and Reeves, in the context of *Crank* and *The Matrix*, are placed in a very material sense within a cybernetic feedback loop; a composite of flesh and optics rendered virtual to the cinematic audience through digital compositing, just as in the narrative layer both Chelios and Neo are composites of physical and virtual.

James Newman (2013) discusses how games are divided into playable interactive sequences and non-interactive cut-scenes that typically move on the story. He notes that although a character's emotional traits are emphasised in cut-scenes or transmedia adaptations (specifically, film adaptations of the game), 'during interactive sequences of the videogame, the individuality and autonomy of the character is subsumed to the game-specific techniques and capabilities that the player uses, or embodies within the world' (Newman 2013: 126). Such cut-scenes thus remediate the typically cinematic techniques of action cinema and the spectacle of the body that Tasker sees operating therein. However, in the surrounding playable sequences the sense of the hero as protagonist gives way to a sense of immediacy as the agency of the player takes hold. Statham's films are thus far closer to the dynamic, player-driven interactive segments of videogames, than their static, reflective and cinematic cut-scenes. As has been shown, this is essentially down to his action persona as a transmedia avatar hero. Statham's films build immersion and immediacy not only through the myriad highly stylised shots that, as Palmer notes, hypermediate videogame aesthetics into the stylistic regime of film, but also brings the viewer into the film space through his open acting style that renders him as an avatar for viewer embodiment in a cybernetic feedback loop.

Conclusion

Considered together, Statham's film, promotional and videogame presence unifies an image of physicality, virtuality, action and militarism. Through this unification, Statham's brand also works to organise the market; Statham is a symbol of meaning, a recognisable image that fuses together a network of associations between action films, console and casual gaming. Unlike the action heroes who came into their prime in the 1980s within the Reaganite era of Hawkish politics and bodybuilding culture, Statham's career developed alongside the growth of social media and videogames, particularly the era of the home console and the AAA videogame with its emphasis on narrative and kinetic violence. While in the symbolic systems of many 1980s action movies it is thus common for the hero to rail against technology (Tasker 1993: 105), Statham typically embraces it. Rather than natural, Statham is technological. Rather than material, he is virtual; the very epitome of the action hero for a generation weaned on the transhumanism of cyberpunk and the immersive and interactive qualities of the videogame.

Statham can thus be understood as first among a new breed of action hero; one influenced by the embodied avatars of videogames as much as the ephemeral, kinetic fighters of the martial arts film. Perhaps Statham is the clearest indicator of a larger movement in films towards the medium of the game, not simply in the form of adaptation (which is a common process in both directions), but in the much more integrated form of hypermediation. In essence, the kinetic violence of his movements, and the generic nature of his characters that evoke the interchangeability of the macho, white, male game protagonist, also positions him as a transmedia brand that is uniquely able to vacillate between the realms of game-like action films and film-like action games. Explicit references to game-like aesthetics, rather than breaking immersion in his films, deliberately import the promise of immediacy videogames embodied through their dual-logics of interactivity and immersion (Murray 1997). No medium exists in a pure form; instead, it builds the sense of immediacy it strives for through a careful renegotiation of remediated forms (Bolter and Grusin 2000); in this context, Statham has mastered such a recourse to videogames in his films, both through rendering his film persona in games like *Sniper X* and in turn importing the operational logics of the avatar from videogames to cinema.

References

Aarseth, E. J. (1997). *Cybertext: Perspectives on Ergodic Literature*. Baltimore, MD: Johns Hopkins University Press.

Blunden, F. (2016). '15 male actors with serious martial arts skills'. *Screenrant*. https://screenrant.com/male-actors-serious-martial-arts-skills/ (22.06.16, accessed 26.02.18).

Bolter, J. D., and Grusin, R. (eds). (2000). *Remediation: Understanding New Media*. Cambridge, MA: MIT Press.

Brownlie, D., Hewer, P. and Kerrigan, F. (2015). 'Celebrity, convergence and transformation'. *Journal of Marketing Management*, 31.

Calleja, G. (2011). *In-Game: Immersion to Incorporation*. Cambridge, MA: MIT Press.

Chen, A. (2017). '6 Hollywood actors with serious martial arts skills'. *Martial Tribes*. www.martialtribes.com/practitioners/general-en/6-hollywood-actors-serious-martial-arts-skills/ (22.08.17, accessed 26.02.18).

Eskelinen, M. (2001). 'The gaming situation'. *Gamestudies.org*. www.gamestudies.org/0101/eskelinen/ (01.07.01, accessed 26.02.18).

Farokhmanesh, M. (2014). 'The most progressive game of the summer is the one you're probably not playing'. *Polygon*. www.polygon.com/2014/7/24/5930655/kim-kardashian-game-progressive (24.07.14, accessed 03.01.18).

Hackley, C. (2015). *Advertising and Promotion, 3rd edition*. London, SAGE.

Jenkins, H. (2006). 'Game design as narrative architecture', in Wardrip-Fruin, N. and Harrigan, P. (eds). *First Person: New Media as Story, Performance and Game*. Cambridge, MA: MIT Press). pp. 118–130.

Jenkins, H. (2011). 'Transmedia 202: further reflections'. *Confessions of an Aca-Fan: The Official Weblog of Henry Jenkins.* http://henryjenkins.org/blog/2011/08/defining_transmedia_further_re.html (20.11.08, accessed 25.02.18).

Jenkins, H., Ford, S. and Green, J. E. (2013). *Spreadable Media: Creating Value in a Networked Culture.* London: New York University Press.

Kaiser, R. (2014). 'The curse of the scruffy white male: why representation matters in videogames'. *IndieWire.* www.indiewire.com/2014/07/the-curse-of-the-scruffy-white-male-why-representation-matters-in-video-games-23990/ (07.14, accessed 26.02.18).

King, C. R. and Leonard, D. J. (2010). 'Wargames as a new frontier: securing American empire in virtual space', in Huntemann, N. B. and Payne, M. T. (eds). *Joystick Soldiers: The Politics of Play in Military Videogames.* London: Routledge. pp. 91–105.

Kline, S., Dyer-Witheford, N. and de Peuter, G. (2003). *Digital Play: The Interaction of Technology, Culture and Marketing,* 2nd edition. Montreal: McGill-Queen's University Press.

Lukas, S. A. (2010). 'Behind the barrel: reading the videogame gun' in Huntemann, N. B. and Payne, M. T. (eds) *Joystick Soldiers: The Politics of Play in Military Videogames.* London: Routledge. pp. 75–90.

Lury, C. (2004). *Brands: The Logos of the Global Economy.* London: Routledge.

Marshall, P. D. (2010). 'The promotion and presentation of the self: celebrity as marker of presentational media'. *Celebrity Studies,* 1(1), 35–48.

Marshall, P. D. (2014). *Celebrity and Power: Fame in Contemporary Culture.* Minnesota, University of Minnesota Press.

Momoda, J. (2016). 'The importance of core game loops'. *Game Analysis* [Blog]. http://jerrymomoda.com/the-core-loop-key-to-an-engaging-game/. (accessed 25.02.18).

Murray, J. H. (1997). *Hamlet on the Holodeck: The Future of Narrative in Cyberspace.* Cambridge: MIT Press.

Newman, J. (2013). *Videogames,* 2nd edition. London: Routledge.

Palmer, L. (2012). '*Cranked* masculinity: hypermediation in digital action cinema', *Cinema Journal,* 51(4), 1–25.

Payne, M. T. (2012). 'Marketing military realism in *Call of Duty 4: Modern Warfare*', *Games and Culture,* 7. pp. 305–327.

Rose, M. (2014). 'Kim Kardashian helps Glu Mobile to record profits'. *Gamasutra.* www.gamasutra.com/view/news/229040/Kim_Kardashian_helps_Glu_Mobile_to_record_profits.php (accessed 26.02.18).

Shaul, B. (2015). 'Glu Mobile launches Sniper X with Jason Statham on mobile'. www.adweek.com/digital/glu-mobile-launches-sniper-x-with-jason-statham-on-mobile/ (accessed 03.01.18).

Stahl, R. (2010). *Militainment, Inc.: War, Media, and Popular Culture*. London: Routledge.
Tasker, Y. (1993). *Spectacular Bodies: Gender, Genre and the Action Cinema*. London: Routledge.
Thomson, M. (2006). 'Human brands: investigating antecedents to consumers' strong attachments to celebrities'. *Journal of Marketing*, 70(3) (July), 104–119.

11

Ageing Statham: expendable Expendable?

Natasha Parcei

I'm moving better than I used to. I'm feeling pretty nimble. It's about the whole thing: training, eating, sleeping ... all of those have a massive impact on how you feel. And I'm doing better at all of those things. Sly Stallone's got 20 years on me and still looks good, so he's part of my inspiration.

Jason Statham (*Men's Health*, April 2017)

The Expendables (2010, 2012 and 2014) is a film series that is light on narrative and character development. It places its emphasis on action set pieces, violence, destruction and gung-ho machismo. By utilising an ensemble cast of quintessential action stars from the past and embracing ones from the present (including former professional athletes), the franchise is a homage to the iconic action films of the 1970s and 1980s. From the figurehead of the franchise, Sylvester Stallone, to Arnold Schwarzenegger, Bruce Willis, Dolph Lundgren and Wesley Snipes, newer action stars and former professional athletes such as ex-NFL star Terry Crews, and Randy Couture take to the silver screen in their battle against despots, villains and ne'er do wells. It is in this collection of hard-bodied representations of masculinity that Jason Statham fits as part of *The Expendables* ensemble cast. He is positioned as the modern incarnation of the classic hypermasculine action stars of his fellow cast members, with his combination of an elite athletic history and his own iconic hardboiled characters, as discussed in other chapters elsewhere in this volume.

This chapter investigates how Jason Statham's role as Lee Christmas in *The Expendables* franchise constructs and frames age identity through various theoretical approaches in order to understand how ageing can be represented in modern action cinema. The hypermasculine ageing body of the franchise's lead actor, iconic action star Sylvester Stallone playing Barney Ross, is the main spectacle of the film series. This is in keeping with the historic critical focus that Stallone's muscular body has received throughout his film career, as 'Reviewers have on the whole refused the attempt at a shift in Stallone's image, retaining the emphasis on the body' (Tasker 1993: 86). While Ross's ageing body is constructed as the main spectacle of the franchise, the construction of Christmas' age identity as a middle-aged man displays the unstable cultural position of middle-agedness, whereby the character is presented as constantly oscillating between representations of youthfulness and agedness. The construction of an unstable age identity presents Christmas as the most expendable of *The Expendables* group, due to his uncertain value position within the group dynamic. This on-screen representation of the instability of middle age speaks to a wider perception of how middle-agedness is understood as a precarious age identity unless bolstered by other cultural traits that signify value, such as wealth, class or social position. By focusing on how Christmas's age identity is constructed through the franchise to date, this chapter will consider how his age trajectory aligns with ageing theories of decline, prowess and the culture of the Third Age.

Each entry in the series showcases a post-millennial approach to the action genre and its stars, as the narrative follows the ensemble cast as a mercenary-for-hire group embarking on dangerous missions. Of course, the missions never run smoothly and more action ensues. The first film is centred on Ross and Christmas scouting a small South American island before deciding to accept the job of executing the island's dictator. Yet not all is as it seems. The dictator is a puppet for rogue CIA agent, James Munroe (Eric Roberts), who uses the island as a front for his drug and money laundering operations. The action in *The Expendables 2* is instigated by a rival mercenary group killing a member of Ross's team. *The Expendables 3* also follows a revenge narrative as an old foe of Ross's injures a group member. However, in this narrative Ross decides to retire his original mercenary group, including Christmas, for a much younger replacement team. Later in the plot the original team come to the rescue of their replacements after they have been captured. Throughout the series' overarching narrative Christmas remains (for the most part) Ross's right-hand-man, keeping intact the buddy movie style set up for the pair. However, while Ross's position and value within the group remains constant, Christmas's age identity is fluid, and by tracking the fluidity of Christmas's age construction throughout the narrative, this chapter is able to consider how ageing and agedness are presented to the young target audience.

The premise of the franchise, as indicated by the title, is that the ensemble group of mercenaries are no longer valuable to society due to their age; highlighted with a young counterpart to the group in each movie. The head of the team, Barney Ross is a retired US marine who leads the mercenary group on freelance jobs, partnered by his right-hand-man Lee Christmas, a former SAS solider. The pair are framed within the ensemble cast in a buddy movie set-up, where Christmas is initially positioned as the youthful counterpart to Ross's agedness in the first film.

As the films' casts are composed of famous action stars, much of their characterisation plays on an audience's existing cultural knowledge of the cast's celebrity personas, including their past roles and public personal history. So heavily is this done at times that some of the actors appear in what almost verges as thinly veiled cameo performances. This is most distinctively done with Arnold Schwarzenegger's character, Trench Mauser, a mysterious figure and rival from Ross' past. Not only does Ross state that Mauser 'wants to be president', thus gently mocking Schwarzenegger's position as former Governor of California, but the actor himself proclaims 'I'll be back' in the final fight scene of *The Expendables 3*, which evokes his most-iconic role as *The Terminator* (1984). Much like the film's narrative, the action stars themselves are positioned as expendable to the Hollywood action movie genre, as ageing theorist Dolan (2017: 91) notes of the franchise's cultural existence:

> These star names effectively establish expectations of the action genre and the associated macho masculinity routinely exhibited

by this acting crew. But, at the time of production, the cast had variously reached chronological ages that might be deemed 'past it' for the physicality of action heroics and the performance of hardboiled machismo.

Yet, despite their social understanding of being chronologically 'past it' for action stars, their agedness functioned as a novel mechanism to attract cinema audiences. It is particularly visible in the box office success of the first *Expendables* film grossing over $274 million worldwide. This financial success allows the franchise to reassert the cultural value of the older stars as legitimate action heroes and enabling for the two sequels to be made.

Ageing theory

The field of cultural gerontology, or critical age theory, invites its audience to view age as a social construct (Gullette 2004). This approach moves past the purely biomedical perspective of understanding ageing through the physical changes to the human body over time, and to recognise how this biological process is socialised to contain other meanings (Gilleard and Higgs 2000). The arbitrary further meanings attached to how the ageing body is understood by society shows how age is not simply a biological process but also a social one that gains subjective connotations as assigned by the culture it inhabits. In considering how ageing is constructed into cultural understanding, reading the way ageing is represented in popular media is important in both reflecting current cultural understandings of ageing as they exist in society, while also adding meaning to ageing in how it frames the process in its narrative. In other words, how ageing is understood in society is not solely dependent on the physical biological changes that affect the human body over time, but rather how these changes are also given meaning by the culture and (popular) media that adds to it.

The Third Age

The cultural understanding of ageing and old age has visibly shifted over the past thirty years, particularly in western culture, resulting in the construction of Third Age culture as the new dominant narrative for later life. Indeed, Higgs and Gillard both provide a clear historic track of the understanding of old age, at least in the UK. They speak of the wider demographic shifts that contribute to the framing of old age such as Industrialisation and the emergence of later life urban poverty. Following a traditional political economy understanding of the typical human life course, a person who is retired from working life was constructed as an old-aged pensioner. This concept of the 'old-aged pensioner' was born of good intentions as a propaganda tool in the campaign for a national state pension to alleviate later life poverty. But this propaganda had the unintentional effect of attaching attention almost exclusively upon the disabilities and helplessness of the 'old' (Laslett 1987: 156).

Moving on from this outdated understanding of later life, older people are now framed more as being engaged in post-retirement activities, and therefore are constructed as remaining valuable to society. This 'new category' is often considered as wealthy consumers who continue to support the dominant culture of capitalist consumerism with their leisure focused later-lifestyles. This post-retirement focus on lifestyle is often referred to as the Third Age (Laslett 1987), where the theorist saw the Third Age emerging from the mid-twentieth century. When he wrote his inaugural works on the Third Age in the late 1980s and 1990s, the cultural shift in understanding old age was visibly shifting. This Third Age is understood to be a period of self-fulfilment once freed from the pressures of their past responsibilities, which allows the older person to shift their focus to engaging in their interests along with other retired people in a communal way. That is, the focus on a collective of older people engaging in self-fulfilling activities together leads to the Third Age being understood as a 'cultural space' (Gilleard and Higgs 2000; 2005). This sense of a communal space of self-fulfilment is how the mercenary-for-hire group in *The Expendables* franchise is positioned to the audience. Made up of former, or retired, military and athletic personnel, the group exists as a post-work community for people with mercenary skills in which they can engage in covert operations with their peers.

The group members are shown as being retired from their formative professions, yet they are still not at the correct chronological age to comply with the usual cultural understanding of retirement. This creates a void of understanding around the construction of their age identities. From a political economy perspective, the life course, and one's position in it, is understood in direct relation to their career status. With this in mind, *The Expendables* team are displayed to have aged-out of their professional use in their primary career. However, having not yet reached the cultural chronological norm for perceived retirement age, they inhabit an unstable age presence. This premature retirement is also seen in other areas of popular culture such as athletics, when professional athletes retire at a much younger chronological age than the usual understanding of retirement age. They are framed as anomalies to the standard life course in the construction of working life. Their retirement from their past duties highlights ageing as a social and cultural construction, and in this instance the life course does not comply to a chronological understanding from a political economy perspective. This leaves the young retirees positioned to engage in Third Age self-fulfilment, which often manifests in a secondary, more leisurely, career with their peers – like commentating, coaching or, in the case of Ross, Christmas *et al.* mercenary-for-hire.

As a film that weaves an intertextual narrative with celebrity culture, it is worth noting that Statham himself is a retired professional athlete. He was signed by Britain's national diving team to compete at the 1990 Commonwealth Games in Auckland, New Zealand, in which he did not place and did not compete again. This draws a parallel between Statham and his character Christmas, as both are engaged in secondary self-fulfilling careers that stemmed from their formative profession. For Statham, this is a more glamourous lifestyle than his character counterpart, yet Christmas earnestly feels fulfilled by his engagement in the mercenary-for-hire group of the narrative. When Ross retires the group in *The Expendables 3*, a montage follows displaying the former group members as unable to adjust to 'retired' life. Their days are now void of purpose, signalling the loss that Christmas and company experience at the group's dissolution, as it disrupts their ability to engage with the fulfilling Third Age culture.

The growing visibility of Third Age culture as the prominent manifestation of post-retirement and later life is positive in that Third Agers are framed as remaining active and useful members of society, and in doing so removes some stigma from the cultural understanding of later life. However, it has not actually removed the negative connotation associated with oldness; only shifted the focus. While the success of the ageing action hero as displayed in *The Expendables* franchise marks a positive shift in the action genre being inclusive of older cast members, it does still rely on a youthfulness that the culture of the Third Age promotes. This includes a compulsory able-bodiedness and sharpness of mind, which further alienates those who do not fit in Third Age's youthful presentation of agedness, as displayed through the film's ageing action heroes. Those who are not able-bodied and/or have declining mental cognisance are marginalised even further into the shadowy depths of cultural knowledge as the truly old. Higgs and Gilleard (2015) refer to this as the Fourth Age; an embodiment of the widely held fears of agedness.

So, with Third Age culture focusing more on a continuation of youthfulness in agedness, *The Expendables* franchise is less about promoting later life itself, but rather presenting a 'stretching of middle age', where this term was first coined (in this context) by Jones' (2008) scholarly work on cosmetic surgery. In displaying a continuation of the youthful action hero traits in its older protagonists it speaks of a 'they've still got it' representation of the ageing action hero. The stretching of middle age 'implies less a denial of age and more its careful supervision and design' (Raisborough *et al.* 2014: 1078). The muscular physiques of the characters and their ability to continue to meet the physical and mental demands of their mercenary work is presented as being due to their careful ageing by which they maintain their middle-age prowess into later life. While this is particularly seen in Ross as the main protagonist and Stallone as the leading star, it also exists in Statham's prolonged success as an action star. Interestingly, his character, Christmas, does not follow the same construction, as he has an oscillating age construction throughout the series which leads him to be displayed in an insecure value position within the group.

Ageing as decline

The unstable social value of middle age, as displayed by Christmas, is indicative of the cultural understanding of ageing as decline. The decline narrative that accompanies ageing comes from a social understanding of a young/old binary whereby youth is the dominant binary and cultural superior. This dynamic displays youth and youthful attributes as desirable traits, so that as a person ages, their perceived social value decreases. Yet, the decline narrative is not a blanket concept. The understanding of social value also considers the intersection of other identity facets, like race, gender and class. Boyle and Brayton acknowledge this in their analysis of *The Expendables* as a labour text, in which the physical labour of the professional mercenary aligns with the traditional physical work associated with a working-class identity (Boyle and Brayton 2012). Therefore, the biological decline of the ageing body signifies a concurrent decline in professional value, and in turn societal value. Intertextually, this also aligns with the ageing action hero, whose cinematic value is situated in physical prowess and a youthful virility.

In order to understand how the franchise frames ageing, the fluid construction of Christmas's age identity throughout the three movies must be considered. While there are no explicit ages assigned to the characters within the narrative, by taking an intertextual understanding to the characterisation of Christmas, his age can be considered to align with Statham's. In the core mercenary group Christmas is the youngest character and is over twenty years younger than his buddy Ross. This mirrors Statham and Stallone's ages in real life. Using this real-life age difference, the first movie frames Christmas as the group's youngster, whose positioning as a young counterpoint to Ross naturally creates a sense of friendly rivalry between the two. Part of the opening scene displays Ross and Christmas discussing which of the villainous pirates each will kill, with Christmas advising Ross, 'You should take the two on the right. You're not that fast anymore,' to which Ross replies, 'The only thing faster is lightning.'

This initial dialogue clearly shows that from the outset of the series ageing will be presented as decline, with Christmas occupying the position of youth to Ross's agedness. In the context of the opening scene, the dialogue is used to draw attention to the older age identity of Stallone, so that he can subsequently present his mercenary prowess as a counter to the decline narrative present throughout the film. Even with the main action displaying Ross's proficiency as a mercenary, the decline narrative of the film is adhered to at the climax of the film. This is seen when Ross and Christmas simultaneously kill the villain and decide to 'call it a tie' even though it is not displayed as an evenly weighted achievement. Following the kill, Christmas goes on to reinforce the film's framing of age as decline, and through this promote his own youthful superiority as Ross's counter, mirroring their introductory exchange by noting, 'You know you're not as fast as you think,' to which Ross concedes, 'I'm beginning to sense that.' In addition to the scene's dialogue the decline narrative is underscored by the presentation of Ross's battle worn body against Christmas, who remains unscathed. This presents the difficulty that Ross has had in meeting Christmas's battle standard and displays the value of the youthful body in the mercenary-for-hire business.

The decline narrative remains the dominant framing of ageing into *The Expendables 2*, but this time Christmas is no longer occupying the dominant youthful space. This movie introduces Billy 'The Kid' (Liam Hemsworth, himself twenty-three years younger than Statham) as a new addition to the mercenary group. He is considerably younger than all of the original team, including Christmas, and becomes the youthful counterpart to the older mercenaries. Billy's presence disrupts Christmas's age identity as dominant youngster and leaves him without a fixed age position in the group's dynamic. Billy's introduction to the group displays his value as a proficient mercenary, easily saving Ross and Christmas as they are surrounded by enemies. This is an action that is reminiscent of Christmas displaying his value by coming to rescue Ross in the first outing. Billy is presented as occupying both the age and value position in the group that was previously occupied by Christmas, thus leaving him now displaced within the group dynamic.

Following the action-packed opening sequence Billy continues to display his youthful prowess, but it does not last long, allowing Christmas to partially regain his age position and its associated value within the group. As the mercenaries set out on another mission and make their way through a misty forest, Ross instructs Billy to lead the group to their destination. As Billy impresses the group by racing ahead, Christmas tries to take up his mantle as Ross' youthful counter by teasingly asking, 'Remember when you could do that?' But his age identity no longer allows him to be excluded from the connotations of agedness as Ross quips back, 'No. Do you?' By turning the question back on Christmas, it signals that his previous age identity as the youngster is no longer valid in comparison to Billy. Unwilling to resign his previous position, Christmas retorts, 'Could blow him away if I wanted to' but Ross is not convinced, betting 'one-thousand bucks you can't catch him'.

This important exchange displays how Christmas's age identity has shifted with the introduction of Billy to the group, and clearly articulates the depreciation of his mercenary value to Ross following the decline narrative of ageing presented in the film. Shortly after this exchange Billy is killed by a rival mercenary group, sparking the revenge plot of the narrative, and granting

Christmas a brief reprieve to regain his youthful age identity. However, the reprisal of his youthful position in the group is not fully realised again as it has been notably challenged and the youthful prowess he previously extolled has been thrown into doubt, leaving Christmas in a vulnerable and unstable position within the group dynamic because he has no fixed value.

As the series' narrative continues into *The Expendables 3*, Christmas's position as the young mercenary is completely overturned as Ross 'retires' the original group, and replaces them with a 'young and hungry' team. The new young mercenary group is considerably younger than the original ensemble and refer to their predecessors as 'a bunch of has-beens still trying to be hard'. Ross's retiring and replacing of the group, along with the ageist terminology used by one of the young mercenaries clearly presents ageing as decline, which is emphasised off-screen by the ages (twenty-seven and twenty-nine) of the cast members playing the young replacement mercenaries some twenty years younger than, the then forty-seven-year-old Statham.

Even when the original group come to the rescue of their young replacements, the stigma of the decline narrative still frames the representation of ageing as a key theme in the franchise. This is confirmed in the film's closing scene as all the mercenaries enjoy a social event to celebrate defeating the villain and Christmas bests his older friendly rival Doc (Wesley Snipes) in a knife throwing contest. Both throw their knives onto the target of a dartboard bullseye but Doc's knife falls off and Christmas's remains in place, evoking phallic imagery and the superiority of youth through sexual prowess as the value of masculine virility is presented. This sequence concludes the series to date with a confirmation of decline narrative as the primary framing of ageing.

Ageing as prowess

Ageing as decline is not the only ageing narrative present in *The Expendables* series. With Stallone at the franchise's helm there is a promotion of the value in lived experience which displays a positive framing of agedness. Throughout the series, the value of life experience presents a counter narrative to ageing as decline. This is visible as, despite the presentation of Christmas's youthful superiority, Ross remains the group's leader and commands respect due to his lived experience – displaying his prowess in agedness.

In *The Expendables 3*, ageing as decline exists alongside this counter narrative of prowess in agedness, which allows for the experienced mercenaries to ably perform the narrative's action and save their younger counterparts. This promotion of the value of lived experience displays a positive attribute of ageing. It not only allows for Ross's position as undisputed leader, but it also functions to destabilise Christmas's age identity further by positioning a challenge to his value not only from his younger counterparts but from the older ones too.

In the introductory action sequence of the third film the mercenary group are shown rescuing Doc from imprisonment. Once safely aboard the group's private plane Doc displays an ambivalence to Christmas's occupation in the group dynamic as Ross's right-hand-man, as this was once his own position. Threatened by Christmas's status, Doc asserts his dominance by bragging, 'I'm the knife before Christmas', a play on the well-known phrase 'night before Christmas', indicating his previous involvement in Ross's mercenary team and presenting Christmas as an imitation to his own identity as an authentic member of the group. He continues to goad Christmas by proclaiming that he was 'Probably free-stylin' with a blade while you were still sucking on your daddy's titty, tryin' to learn how to eat with a spoon' in an attempt to undermine Christmas's value in the group due to his youth (despite Snipes being only eight years older than Statham; and the dialogue seems to emphasise that there is a greater age difference between the two). Here the instability of Christmas's oscillating age-based-value is clearly articulated as the previous source of his value, his youth, is now framed as his weakness.

Conclusion

The two opposing ageing narratives presented throughout *The Expendables* series frame ageing both as decline and advocating its value in acquiring lived experience. This allows for Ross to be revered by the young replacement mercenary group in *The Expendables 3*, while they simultaneously denounce the agedness of Christmas and the other members of the original group. So, the two ageing narratives present Ross's agedness positively and Christmas's negatively. Indeed, Ross's social value is also linked to his position as 'manager' of the group rather than the standard mercenary; thus his value is not solely understood by his advanced age but also his by elevated position.

With juxtaposing framings of ageing displayed in the series' narrative, Statham's character Lee Christmas embodies the constant oscillation between youth and agedness, and their associated values, depending on the situation. This insecure age identity plagues the construction of Christmas' middle-agedness as it is never able to secure a fixed age identity or stable value. It is particularly prominent in his fraught relationship with Doc in the third film, where the power dynamic between the pair constantly fluctuates. While the film does conclude with Christmas's youthful virility triumphing over Doc's lived experience, it is not a solidified occupation of superiority. This besting indicates only the temporary prevalence of the decline narrative of ageing, as Doc's earlier contestation to Christmas's value based on his relative youth leaves an insecure framing of Christmas's age value as the middle-aged mercenary.

Indeed, the unfixed value created by Christmas's middle-agedness is most prominent in *The Expendables 3* when his value is simultaneously threatened by Doc's superiority in his agedness, and its associated accumulation of valuable experience, as well as being positioned as an inferior to the young replacement mercenaries and their youthful physical prowess. This leaves Christmas in an insecure value position due to his fluid age identity, where he is constantly needing to prove his value or risk losing his worth in the group dynamic.

At the time of this chapter being written various media reports suggest that *The Expendables 4* may start shooting in 2019. This exciting prospect promises more adrenaline-filled action from the fifty-year-old Statham and Stallone, now in his seventies, and the continued construction of the ageing action hero as a fixture in Hollywood cinema.

So, in conclusion, this chapter set out to consider and understand how the age identity of Lee Christmas has been constructed in *The Expendables* series to date. The provocative title of this chapter speaks of the precarity of his value in the group dynamic due to his fluid age identity and oscillating social value. Throughout and over the course of the series, Christmas has transformed from the second-hero to protagonist Stallone, into being the member of *The Expendables* that is the most expendable to the group dynamic due to his lack of a fixed value in his age identity. It is this that makes Lee Christmas a fascinating character within the action film genre, and although Statham clearly has an incredibly masculine physique, it will be interesting to see where further *Expendables* series entries take him. Whether that will be to a South Sea Island where he can rescue the traditional 'damsel in distress' or into a retirement home for washed-up ex-mercenaries, whatever the outcome, the journey will be a fascinating one we all will watch with bated breath.

References

Boyle, E. and Brayton, S. (2012). 'Ageing masculinities and "muscle work" in Hollywood action film: an analysis of *The Expendables*'. *Men and Masculinities*, 15(5), 468–485.

Dolan, J. (2017). *Contemporary Cinema and 'Old Age': Gender and the Silvering of Stardom*. London: Palgrave Macmillan.

Gilleard, C. and Higgs, P. (2000). *Cultures of Ageing: Self, Citizen and the Body*. Essex: Pearson Education Limited.

Gilleard, C. and Higgs, P. (2005). *Contexts of Ageing: Class, Cohort and Community*. Cambridge: Polity Press.

Gullette, M. M. (2004). *Aged by Culture*. Chicago: The University of Chicago Press.

Higgs, P. and Gilleard, C. (2015). *Rethinking Old Age: Theorising the Fourth Age*. London: Palgrave Macmillan.

Jones, M. (2008). *Skintight: An Anatomy of Cosmetic Surgery*. London: Berg.

Laslett, P. (1987). 'The emergence of the Third Age'. *Ageing & Society*, 7(2), 133–160.

Raisborough, J., Barnes, M., Henwood, F. and Ward, L. (2014). 'Stretching middle age: the lessons and labours of active ageing in the makeover show'. *Media, Culture & Society*, 36(8), 1069–1083.

Tasker, Y. (1993). *Spectacular Bodies: Gender, Genre and the Action Cinema*. London: Routledge.

12

Crank it up! Scoring Statham

Shelley O'Brien

The diverse approaches to the work of Jason Statham in this book reveal much about his on-screen persona and how he functions as a film star. It is evident that a great deal of his work is situated within the action genre; a genre which is able to make the most of his talents. As Lorrie Palmer notes, 'Jason Statham is a former model, footballer, and diver who has seriously studied a number of martial arts, including kickboxing; certainly he is able to do many of his own stunts as an actor' (Palmer 2012: 8). These physical skills mark Statham out as a significant presence in action films along with his engaging witty, hardman persona which is further developed in *Crank* (2006) and *Crank: High Voltage* (2009), both written and directed by Mark Neveldine and Brian Taylor (credited as Neveldine/Taylor). They were well received by audiences and have garnered some critical attention – Palmer's article (2012) which focuses on the films and their representation of hypermasculinity is particularly noteworthy.

However, one aspect that has been largely neglected, and yet is extremely significant, is how music score and pre-recorded tracks are used in both films. Action films in general will use fast-paced rhythms, fragmented melodies and bold orchestration to mirror the set pieces on-screen, typically to create tension. Although these techniques do occur in Statham films (often alongside carefully chosen pre-recorded tracks) the difference in the *Crank* movies is how remarkably these particular tracks and the original scores cohere with his persona. In light of this, then, a close analysis of how the music operates in relation to narrative and style will be discussed, as well as considerations into how it functions as a sonic signifier of Statham's image.

Crank and *Crank: High Voltage* feature Statham as the seemingly invincible hitman, Chev 'Chevy' Chelios. The premise in both films is his race against time to stay alive. In *Crank*, Chev – who works for Triad boss, Don Kim – is injected with poison by a small-time gangster, Ricky Verona, who wants to advance his criminal career. The 'Beijing Cocktail' will prove fatal unless he manages to maintain a high level of adrenaline in order to keep his heart pumping. Hence, he then proceeds to stave off the effects via numerous outrageous means – cocaine, energy drinks, nasal sprays, a defibrillator charge, a huge shot of Epinephrine, sex with his girlfriend in a crowded street, fist fights and, of course, driving fast cars and a motorcycle.

In *Crank: High Voltage*, falling foul of villains yet again – this time a combination of Mexican gangsters and the Triads – Chev has his heart removed and replaced with a battery-powered one. In order to stay alive on this occasion he must keep charging the artificial heart, until he can track down who received his. This includes sticking his hand in a waffle iron and his finger into a car lighter socket, generating static electricity, 'hot-wiring' himself and, not unexpectedly, having sex in front of a crowd. Notably, both films are styled as high-octane videogame narratives and make the most of Statham's on-screen persona, which allows for suspension-of-disbelief even in such outlandish events as witnessed here. Similarly, the frenetic pace and kinetic energy common to videogame play is further generated and emphasised by the original scores (by Paul Haslinger and Mike Patton respectively) and numerous pre-recorded tracks.

In order to consider how the music functions in these films it is useful to take a summary from Kathryn Kalinak (2010: 1) on what film music can do in relation to the image. She takes her cue from Aaron Copland's five functions of film music and extends it somewhat, stating that,

> It can establish setting, specifying a particular time and place; it can fashion a mood and create atmosphere; it can call attention to elements onscreen or offscreen, thus clarifying matters of plot and narrative progression; it can reinforce or foreshadow narrative developments and contribute to the way we respond to them; it

can elucidate characters' motivations and help us to know what they are thinking; it can contribute to the creation of emotions, sometimes only dimly realized in the images, both for characters and audiences to feel (Kalinak 2010: 1).

Music can also help characterisation as well as maintaining continuity and aiding closure. Furthermore, on the subject of a compilation film score – where songs or instrumental tracks are chosen specifically to work with the image – Kalinak notes (2010: 87) that, 'Lyrics can be used to specifically express emotion, for example, or they might tie directly to the action or events on-screen. But they can still perform the same sort of functions as specially composed film scores.'

Similarly, even if the lyrics do not have a specific meaning for the image, the idiom or style of music may well have. This is significant for the two *Crank* films in several ways. The films certainly conform in many respects to the above, but arguably the music goes even further by becoming an integral part of the videogame experience. Indeed, a form of interactivity is created via the intensity of the musical forms used, and the often-repeated concept of action film as rollercoaster ride (Palmer 2012: 21) is taken to another level here. The adrenaline rushes experienced by Chev Chelios are presented in such a way – via cinematography and editing – that they are intended to create an actual physiological effect on the viewer. The music, then, also works to intensify this experience as well as to fulfil the other functions outlined by Kalinak. It is important to note here that in using a videogame style narrative there is far less importance attached to the plot or character development, and yet in order to engage with the plot and, more importantly, the character of Chev it is necessary to generate some measure of alignment. Neveldine/Taylor therefore create something which is a series of set pieces linked entirely by, and focused on, Chev and his race against time. There is a sort of sensory overload of action due to the constant movement of Chev which conforms to some degree to Palmer's assertion that, 'In varying collaborations since the 1980s, Bruckheimer, Bay, and Scott have branded Hollywood action movies with a collective style that, for many critics, has come to symbolize an abandonment of plot and character in favor of excess and spectacle, the centrality of surface over substance' (Palmer 2012: 4).

Similarly, the films owe something to the 'MTV aesthetic', which Kay Dickinson notes is 'now a pervasive stylistic element of television, of adverts, and, in particular, of feature films' (Dickinson 2003: 144). This is, indeed, an overt feature of the *Crank* films. No attempt is made to present this aesthetic in a serious manner either. There is a very knowing sense of the ridiculousness on show which is heightened further by the black humour in evidence throughout. Another aspect of this, as Palmer notes, is that, 'the filmmakers use digital technology to emphasize the larger-than-life masculinity of their central character' (Palmer 2012: 12). This is a noteworthy point because it also ties into the ways in which music is used in both films and, in particular, how it relates to this 'larger-than-life' quality of Statham's image.

Haslinger's score for *Crank* and Patton's for *Crank: High Voltage* are major factors in the characterisation of Chev and the Statham comic/action star persona. Similarly, the pre-recorded tracks in both films are a mixture of styles and are used specifically to reinforce the frantic pace of the editing, the plot and the movement and psychology of Chev. The range of styles – punk rock, speed metal, rock, 'urban', Mexican and Puerto Rican hip-hop and pop – have evidently been chosen to work with Chev's situation as well as to underscore and reinforce the videogame style. For example, the use of loud, fast, aggressive punk rock and speed metal are primary styles tied to Chev's character and his actions in the film.

In order to extend these ideas and analyse sequences from the films in more detail, it is useful to note that traditional film scoring commonly utilises a range of musical forms along with elements found in orchestral composition, such as tonality, harmony, rhythm, tempo, dynamics, timbre and instrumentation. These are all features that will be referred to in the analysis. Of course, film composers sometimes eschew one or more of these elements, just as not all scores feature the use of leitmotif (the linking of a person, place or thing with a recurring musical phrase). In the case of the *Crank* films, though, all of these musical elements can be found either in the score itself or in the track compilation supervised by the music editors.

By examining key sequences, mostly from *Crank*, it will be clearly demonstrated as to how significant the music is in underscoring the action and also how a range of sonic signifiers are tied directly to the character of Chev. In doing this, it will also become clear how these sonic signifiers are representative of Jason Statham's comic/action persona. Palmer asserts that,

> Statham seems built for sheer velocity, and he is thus perfectly cast in movies about motion and machines; he has become marked as a generic identifier within the context of a particular set of action films. Statham is about cars, violent physicality, and moving at high speed…[and]…his fighting style is sharp and brutal, not balletic, which makes his body an ideal visual motif for Neveldine/Taylor's fast cutting and hypermediated shooting style. (Palmer 2012: 9)

The focus on 'cars, violent physicality, and moving at high speed' are all major aspects of his persona, especially in the *Crank* films, but so is the deadpan delivery and ability to make fun of that persona. So, exactly how are these aspects represented by music?

The opening sequence of *Crank* immediately sets the tone for the rest of the film. A videogame style image appears and a shot of a pounding heart to the song lyrics 'Bang Your Head'. Rapid cuts from close-ups of hands to stumbling point-of-view shots are accompanied by the sound of heavy, laboured breathing. The effect is disorientating and it is a stylistic feature that returns on several occasions throughout the narrative. On-screen, time is variously slowed down and speeded up as electronic synthesised sounds begin to intrude and we are introduced to this stumbling figure. It is Chev Chelios. Palmer neatly sums up the image of Jason Statham asserting that, 'His onscreen persona is rough around the edges and blunt. He's a streetwise tough guy with a London accent, which lends his characterizations a working-class believability' (Palmer 2012: 8). Statham's ability to combine these traits with the deadpan delivery of absurd dialogue, make him the ideal performer to create Chev. (In the outtakes, though, Statham can be frequently seen collapsing in hysterical laughter, thereby highlighting the difference in his on-screen persona.) This bluntness is further reinforced as he sees a note and a DVD taped to his TV set, saying 'Fuck you!' On the disc is low-life Chinese criminal, Ricky Verona, who proceeds to explain that he has poisoned Chev and he only has an hour to live. Chev responds defiantly by shouting, 'tick tock' – a sound which is then emulated by the score as a fast, electronic pulse begins. Accordingly, this is linked with Chev's predicament regarding his heart and is set up to be a form of leitmotif.

From this point on, this rhythmic ticking sound is always associated with Chev's heart; it is in constant flux and features in tandem with how slow or fast his heart is beating. It may not be a musical leitmotif in the traditional sense, but it still functions as a signifier of Chev. This is built upon as ominous swelling electronic drones and wobbly guitar chords develop tension further. The tension is suddenly released when Chev yells, leaps up and picks up the TV to smash it. Immediately, the music shifts gear, accelerates and kicks into action along with Chev. A punk rock track with a heavy 4/4 beat on drums and bass mirrors the action. It is loud, fast and angry and underscores the combination of fast/jerky/slow-motion camerawork as Chev runs away wildly. The action becomes disorientating again as images are cut up and shots of the heart beating rapidly inside Chev are accompanied by cymbals and tom-toms being hit hard and fast, punctuated by riffs on bass and guitar. It is only after he has screeched off in his car and phones his girlfriend, Eve, that there is a brief respite from the berserk events which have just occurred, and the music decelerates and calms slightly.

At this point, the character, Doc, is introduced to the strains of a sexually suggestive hip-hop track, 'Take It', as he cavorts with three women. The scene is played for laughs as he talks to Chev on his mobile phone. Doc promises to try and help him as Chev screeches off in his car again to the wild tempo of the thrashing punk rock track. Other characters are swiftly introduced – Chev's friend, Kaylo, and a black gangster, Orlando – as the ticking element in the score keeps recurring. While he is at Orlando's Hood (shown in superimposed lettering on-screen) he desperately snorts cocaine and then starts a fight in order to try and generate adrenaline. Once again, these outrageous actions are underscored with fast punk rock, which is, by this point, cemented as the sound of Chev's crisis.

Once he is back in the car, a chase ensues as an electric bass plays a form of tension ostinato (i.e. shifting between two pitches constantly), which is often typically used as a technique in horror/thriller scoring. The tension is even greater due to the fact Doc tells him on the phone the effects of the drug saying, 'If you stop, you die!' The ostinato quickly changes to a rapid 4/4 beat on drums as Chev is chased through a shopping mall. He smashes the car on to an escalator and begins to run as a repeated bass riff accelerates with him, once more imitating and reinforcing the pace of his movement.

Chev hails a taxi and continues his desperate urge to stay alive by telling the driver to make the music loud, 'Crank it!' In this darkly hilarious sequence, the country music track 'Achy Breaky

Heart' plays as Chev's heart pounds on the soundtrack and he 'headbangs' violently in the back of the car, thereby fulfilling the functions which Kalinak describes in relation to song use. There is the expression of emotion through the lyrics – in this case used ironically – and the underpinning of the events on-screen. The feel of constant movement continues as he yells 'pull over!' and rushes into a store to get Red Bull energy drinks in a bid to keep his adrenaline flowing. Frenzied drumming and rapid staccato beats on the high-hat cymbal emphasise the overall tempo of the scene, and, at the same time, strengthens our alignment with Chev and his catastrophic situation.

Chev continues his journey in the taxi via Carlito's penthouse (yet another gangster), when Doc phones and tells him he must find some Epinephrine (adrenaline shot). The sound of 'kerranging' heavy metal guitar punctuates the order from Doc. As Chev journeys onward, a range of videogame style sounds – electronic glissandos, bass ostinato and high-pitched sustained electronic notes – are employed to create more tension. Chev is pursued by Ricky Verona's armed brother through a restaurant kitchen and spies a meat cleaver, which he suddenly uses on Verona's brother in the alleyway, chopping off his hand. The fast-ticking sound is evident throughout and maintains continuity, as well as the heavy metal guitar timbre which is repeatedly associated with Chev's violent actions. This musical device, combined with the dispassionate black humour which underpins the brutality, also serves to strengthen the on-screen persona of Statham as comic/action star.

The combination of over-the-top violence and humour continues apace as Chev heads to a hospital to find Epinephrine. The guitar sound symbolising Chev returns as he ends up using nasal sprays stolen from the pharmacy as they contain the Epinephrine drug he needs. Aggressive, presto speed metal drumming bursts in at fortissimo level in support of Chev's desperation. Oddly, there is a break from the frenzy and noise when he hides in a private ward room and puts on a hospital gown – the silence therefore mirroring how he behaves in this situation. The tranquillity does not last long, however, as he gets chased by security guards down a corridor with the gown flapping wildly and exposing his bare backside. The tempo increases again as frantic staccato quaver beats are played on snare drum, rising to a crescendo when Chev commands a male nurse to shock him with a defibrillator machine, 'Juice me!' The shock thrusts him into the nearby elevator and chaos ensues on-screen which is 'Mickey-Moused' (a musical device which directly mimics the action on-screen as in cartoons) by frenetic speed drumming and then a slow electronic descending glissando as the nurse injects him with Epinephrine. The adrenaline kicks in and Chev is off and running again and being chased as the agitated punk song 'Trix Are For Kids' mimics his pace.

Yet again, the 'MTV aesthetic' is foregrounded in the scene and, although there is little development of plot, there is a further cementing of Chev's character and Statham's tongue-in-cheek hardman image. This is developed further as the chase continues in videogame style where everything is speeded up and disorientating, and the hefty shot of Epinephrine has the side-effect of giving Chev a huge erection. As he steals a police motorcycle the rhythm becomes uptempo on cymbals, and in a hilariously bizarre moment the Harry Nilsson song 'Everybody's Talkin' plays while Chev rides oblivious to everything and 'I don't hear a word they're saying' rises on the soundtrack as he starts to both physically and mentally slow down. In order to combat this, he stands up on the bike, arms outstretched, as the hospital gown flaps in the wind again revealing his bare backside before he crashes and somersaults onto a nearby cafe table as the lyric 'I won't let you leave ...' crescendos to end the outlandish set piece.

This intense level of off-the-wall humour continues once Chev goes to meet Eve. The same musical devices recur in line with his quest to stay alive pumped up with adrenaline. As he shoves his hand in a hot waffle iron and has yet another mass fight, throbbing bass beats and noisy punk rock return again. In the next sequence of events, Chev and Eve go to Chinatown, where he confesses that he is a hitman, but he is retiring for her. It is a charming, quieter moment in a narrative which has very few. Of course, this calm does not last long as his heart starts to slow down again. This prompts another outrageous set piece, as Chev persuades Eve to have sex with him in a crowded street. As the uninhibited action proceeds, the track 'Let's Get It On' plays on the soundtrack and segues into an upbeat funk style complete with brassy horn riffs, strong rhythmic bass, syncopated guitar licks and insistent grooving cymbals. The music, again, underpins movement and is stylistically appropriate; Marvin Gaye's song is an invitation to make love and the rhythms and sounds of funky music are often regarded as having sexual connotations.

Here, while people look on incredulously, the funk beat literally plays in time with Chev's thrusting motion. This is, then, a further development of his character in relation to music – we have witnessed his deadpan humour, his bluntness, his violence and, now, his sexual prowess preceded by a sort of gruff tenderness.

Therefore, this persistent use of appropriate music is both tied to and develops Chev's character and it also functions as a way of aligning viewers with Chev and his plight. Similarly, the blackly comic tone which pervades the entire film works because of Statham's rather incongruous London accent and his frank delivery of absurd dialogue. And so, these seemingly ridiculous scenes do serve a purpose in terms of how they add to the figure of Statham as comic/action star. In particular, the sonic signifiers – the musical idioms and their stylistic traits – quite literally work to beef up his image and even go so far as to represent him in musical terms. Instrumentation and musical styles are well known to have specific connotations and it is no different in *Crank*. The heavy timbres of bass, thrashing guitar, occasional shouted vocals and speed drumming entirely match the figure of Chev Chelios. Equally, the additional styles such as funk and recontextualised songs successively develop that image in ways that the dialogue cannot.

Once the film shifts into its final phase the constant repetition of all these musical devices is further proof of their significance for Chev/Statham. Kaylo is unceremoniously murdered by Verona, and yet the one emotion not allowed for Chev is grief. The musical answer to this is not melancholic piano or strings (which might seem incongruous), it simply shifts to tense musical drones and dissonant guitar riffs as a forerunner to Chev having a shoot-out with more gangsters and another car chase before his heart starts to slow down again.

When he eventually finds Doc, he gets a shot of fake Ephedrine as a temporary fix. There is suddenly an unexpected tonal shift when he tells Chev he is going into a coma. This is the only time in the score where a conventional musical device is used to underscore emotion. Doc says he could give Chev a drug to simply let him slip away into a dream before his death. An electric piano plays a soft melody in a minor key to accompany this rather sad moment as a generic and somewhat clichéd way of manipulating audience emotions. Unsurprisingly, this melancholy does not last and Chev says, 'I want one hour!' In other words, he wants to go out with a bang, the same way as he has lived his life as a hitman. What keeps him going is the thought of getting his revenge on Verona. Eventually he catches up with him and the mobster, Carlito, whom Chev had been involved with. In the final sequence a huge shoot-out ensues as Don Kim and his Triad cronies arrive in a turn of events to help Chev. The now-familiar, loud and aggressive punk rock plays in fast 4/4 time as chaos descends and the atmosphere is completely demented. Chev is injected again and Verona kills Carlito as a kerranging guitar effectively functions as a 'stinger' to punctuate the action. Suddenly, the sound of helicopter blades become dominant in this soundscape of havoc as Chev and Verona end up hanging onto the chopper as it starts to take-off. The fight continues until Verona is pulled out and falls (we assume) to his death. Chev follows suit and the music 'Mickey-Mouses' his descent in blatant cartoonish fashion – a final musical nod to the videogame aesthetic.

Chev calmly takes out his mobile and calls Eve only to be greeted with her ditsy answerphone message. The music becomes mellower as the song 'Miracles' by Jefferson Starship accompanies his slow-motion fall as well as predicting the ending of the film. Chev's body bounces off a car into the street seemingly dead, but then the sound of a heartbeat leads into the speed metal track 'Bring Us Bullets' indicating that Chev is not only alive but that he will return to dole out more mayhem. Which indeed he does in the sequel.

However, rather than continuing with a close analysis of *Crank: High Voltage* it should suffice to flag up a few key points that confirm the extent to which music plays a major role in terms of characterisation of Chev and underscoring the narrative and style of the film. Basically, the premise of the film is the same as in *Crank*, except Chev's heart has been removed and replaced with an artificial one which he has to keep charging while he tracks down the culprits. In fact, the sequel replays almost everything that happens in the first film, including sex with Eve in public (on a horse racetrack), car chases and shoot-outs.

Even though the score is composed by Mike Patton, not Paul Haslinger, the general style and feel of it is very similar, with the addition of a few notable elements. In line with the fact that this time Chev is involved with both the Triads and a group of Mexican gangsters, musical devices are used which have a different vibe along with the punk rock, speed metal and recontextualised songs which featured heavily in *Crank*.

So, there is use of the Chinese pentatonic scale in certain scenes related to the Triads and, more interestingly, the addition of music with a Latin American feel. Indeed, there is a musical phrase in a Latin groove which recurs on a regular basis in conjunction with Chev. The phrase contains three notes ascending and three notes descending at a moderato tempo, and because it recurs so often and is sometimes played on different instrumentation, it clearly functions as an additional leitmotif linked to Chev. Sometimes the phrase is played on a synthesiser and at other points it is more instrumentally layered and has a heavier texture – usually when Chev is performing outrageous acts to charge the battery – and therefore adds to his characterisation over and above the loud and aggressive punk rock. It also 'beefs up' his image even further.

There are other musical elements that create a more light-hearted and comical atmosphere, such as the upbeat, major key melody played on flute and the track 'Heard It In A Love Song' during the racetrack sex scene. Much of the time, though, the score and pre-recorded tracks follow a similar pattern to the first film. There is a range of punk rock and speed metal, electronic sounds and techno-pop, and, rather than hip-hop, the addition of Tex Mex music and Latin American orchestration and instrumentation which fulfil the function of establishing settings such as the Rancho Del Dude Club. Notably, the score often follows a more traditional pattern when generating suspense, albeit using the Latin feel. For example, when Chev is searching for Johnny Vang, the Triad who was responsible for his heart being stolen, tension is created with low drones, guitar chords, and a güiro (Latin American percussion instrument played with a stick rubbed across grooves cut into it). The instrument makes a 'ratchet' sound when played and, here, is literally ratcheting-up the tension. There is an occasional shift in tempo and dynamics, plus whistling enters the score and generates a mood reminiscent of Ennio Morricone's compositions for his work in numerous 'spaghetti westerns'. This is also evident in the scene where the gangster 'El Hurón' aka 'The Ferret' is revealed to be the brother of Ricky Verona; a harmonica enters the score which immediately has connotations of western films, especially as this is now shown to be a feud situation.

The humour also follows on from the first film, for example, when Chev is kidnapped by Don Kim and his cronies. Chev shoots everyone in the car as the three-note ascending/descending leitmotif plays and his parting shot is to shout 'Chicken and broccoli!' at the dead gangsters. He also variously 'hot wires' his artificial heart, steals an electronic dog collar used for training to give him shocks, and even uses jump leads to power up the heart – a replay of the defibrillator scene in *Crank* as he yells 'Just juice me!' All of these events are accompanied by the fast tempo punk rock or speed metal as they were in the first film. Other absurd events are scored using synthesised electronic sounds, such as a fight between Chev and Johnny Vang at a power plant. Filmed as a kind of Japanese kaiju sequence, exaggerated animated versions of them blunder around like Godzilla, before shifting back to live action. This sequence continues to reinforce the fact that the films are extremely tongue-in-cheek and also that Statham does not take himself too seriously either. In line with this, and the videogame aesthetic, there is a return to the device of 'Mickey-Mousing' when Chev is dragged behind a speedboat by Vang. Prestissimo guitar, bass and drumming all generate a sense of frenzy and match the movement of Chev in the water.

The ending of this film is even more over the top and bizarre than the first. Ricky Verona's head is revealed to have been kept alive in a pseudo fish tank and loud operatic music plays to accompany El Hurón whipping Chev in a moment of farcical high drama. After one more shoot-out to up tempo punk, the action shifts into slow motion as Chev's artificial heart starts to lose its charge. The final moment of riotous excess ensues as he climbs a telegraph pole and gives himself an enormous electric shock, resulting in him being set on fire. While he burns, he imagines that Eve is with him. As they embrace, REO Speedwagon's 'Keep On Loving You' plays in an unironic manner underscoring his genuine feelings for her. Then he walks to camera, on fire, and gives 'the finger' defiantly to the audience in an ultimate, knowing Chev Chelios gesture.

In conclusion the score and pre-recorded tracks for both *Crank* films have an extremely important role to play in underscoring narrative events, contributing to the videogame aesthetic of both films, while maintaining the excessive and humorous tone delivered by Neveldine/Taylor. Similarly, the music works in a traditional way to aid the characterisation of Chev Chelios through the use of leitmotif, instrumentation, and a variety of musical forms. These elements also aid alignment with Chev and the predicaments he finds himself in, although it could also be argued that the music subsequently becomes a sonic signifier of

Jason Statham's tongue-in-cheek hardman image and, therefore, contributes significantly to his star persona. While other similar film stars such as Stallone may use a more traditional score for his *Rambo* outings, and Schwarzenegger's *Terminator* films use a mix of electronic and orchestra, the two *Crank* films use their music 'scores' as both accentuators of Statham as a character/star while simultaneously propelling the story through its videogame style narrative. It is this dual approach – at once chaotic and yet not chaotically reflective of Statham/Chev – that makes the music deployed in the narrative, when combined with the visual elements, such an overwhelmingly immersive experience.

References

Dickinson, K. (2003). 'Pop, speed, teenagers and the "MTV aesthetic"', in Dickinson, K. (ed.). *Movie Music: The Film Reader*. London: Routledge.

Kalinak, K. (2010). *Film Music: A Very Short Introduction*. New York: Oxford University Press.

Palmer, L. (2012). '*Cranked* masculinity: hypermediation in digital action cinema'. *Cinema Journal*, 51(l4), 1–25.

13

Clothes make the man: Jason Statham's sartorial style

Steven Gerrard

Ha! These public labels, the things the media like to paint you as, I don't really look at them. I see myself as a pretty standard sort of chap, really.

Jason Statham (*Men's Health*, April 2017)

In his article, 'Getting it right: the Statham', Simon Doonan puts forward the case that if a post-millennial man has a shaved head, CrossFit body, wall-to-wall tattoos, and wears dirty and slouchy denims, then that man could be a candidate for the Jason Statham tribe. Doonan argues that 'the charismatically grunty British star of numerous violent movies' has a fashion style that is easy and inexpensive to maintain, where nothing is fancy or elitist. The Statham "look" is tough, edgy and with whiffs of sadism. The mixing of Rag and Bone jeans with Viberg work boots, James Perse T-shirts or Ralph Lauren polo shirts – preferably in navy or black – are offset by a storm-proof, waxed-cotton, Belstaff Citimaster jacket' (Doonan, 2016).

As far as the Statham wannabe is concerned, Doonan sees them as the Statham *de coiffure*, where gay hairdresser Stathamites have bigger muscles than straight hairdresser ones, and included in this wannabe tribe are 'yeehaw Stathamites' who are dressed down and gritty, much unlike their past electric horsemen and rhinestone cowboy counterparts. Likewise, the pampered

Hollywood star look – helped by actors such as Ryan Gosling and Brad Pitt – remains popular with A-listers when seen by paparazzi as the actors are photographed drinking coffee, shopping or having a date-night with their spouses. Doonan argues that the reason why 'blokes' prefer the Statham look is simple: he sees it as unimpeachable and hater-immune. As he states, '[the] tough-guy simplicity of the Statham look provides an iron dome of social media protection to those who might otherwise be subject to endless critical bombardment'. By concluding his article with, 'The Statham look is dirty. It's clean dirt, but it's dirty nonetheless,' he raises the question: do clothes really make the man?

As has been seen in other chapters in this collection, gender and masculinity theories are arguably the cornerstone to understanding Jason Statham as both a concept (actor, star, father) and as a recognisable set of 'constructed values' that can be critiqued through the investigation of 'Statham' via this set of theories. Such concepts could include the roles he plays in his films, his modelling work, diving at the 1990 Commonwealth Games, or his media-savvy persona as both Tough Guy and husband-and-father-figure. However, across all these roles and constructions, one thing remains fundamentally the same: Statham, himself. With his chiselled looks, hard body, and mock-cockney accent he has become a 'product' – Jason Statham. The following chapter will briefly discuss ideas about fashion, the body image, dress and fashion's role, and Statham's body of work.

The body image

Our bodies can be read as a complex set of both physical and social constructions. The first, the *physical* is that which includes the daily ritual that we subject them to (the food we eat, when we eat, where we eat, the fitness regimes we undertake). The second is as a social and cultural 'text' from which information can be gathered and interpreted to produce a new meaning. This textual, or 'surface' reading comes from the individual's body, art, piercings, hair colour, hair style (or lack of hair), jewellery, cosmetics and cosmetic surgery, and dress sense (Hall 2014: 22).

Stern and Russell (2004: 371–394) argue that our bodies have taken on late-capitalist cultural constructs. As such, a fascination with the consumption of different cultures through the adornment of clothing, tattoos, etc. has become so apparent that the 'window dressing' of the male has taken centre stage in the pursuit of both new fields of consumerism and through the reimagining of the 'male' as a means of negotiating ideas of masculinity in an age when scrutiny remains all-important to how 'others' see 'us'. Indeed, the media are constantly offering discourses that encourage people to adopt styles and fashions. Although this is nothing new – Mary Quant's mini-skirts of the 1960s remain arguably the ultimate example of fashion via media-tailoring – the emphasis on concepts of 'perfection' remain at the core of advertising, whether it is for the combating of ageing (grey hair, saggy skin, wrinkles) to the correcting of appearance flaws (pimples, acne and scarring) (Clarke and Griffin 2008: 653–674). The target audience (and for that matter, the non-targeted one, too) is encouraged to buy products which combat all these imperfections, thus changing 'I' from 'I-natural-imperfect' into 'Other-not-natural-(im)perfect' or 'Other-perfect'. According to Coupland (2007: 37–61), the maintenance work required to move from normal to perfect is presented through a series of discourses that produce positive, self-confident and sexually self-assured recognition for the individual and for the larger society. This positivity, according to D'Alessandro and Chitty (2011: 843–878), Featherstone (2010: 193–221) and Grogan (2010: 757–765) implies that the media-created image of perfection, where belief in the perfect-individual is paramount, indicates that buying the right product promotes the 'looking good, feeling good' factor that 'everyone' desires and wishes to attain.

Hall (2014: 23) argues that there has been a recent trend in compartmentalising the body into sexualised bodies: teens and adolescents, young adults, adults, older aged, healthy/unhealthy, fit/unfit, fat/slim, beautiful/ugly, etc. He indicates that the once-static body has become much more flexible, and as such is able to move across culturally determined boundaries. By saying that the body is not a totally fixed space and can change in size, shape, colour and age, it can, to a degree, be controlled by such things as dieting, fitness regimes and even surgical procedures to halt the ravages of time. In this postmodern designer body culture, there is a refusal to accept the body as unchanging and natural. The body is seen as an unfixed point, where personal design of one's own body – through cosmetic, diet, etc. – opens up infinite possibilities of identities (Hall 2014: 24). This suggests that identities of the individual are fluid, shifting constantly according to the needs of the individual, the constraints of society and the culture that produces it, and the media that promotes the change/s within these boundaries.

Body image is fundamental to the dissemination of a construction like Jason Statham and is central to ideas about masculinity, and arguably men's interest in their appearance has been spurred on due to the dominance of media-promoted ideology (Henwood and McLean 2005: 39–62). Men's lifestyle magazines such as *Health* and *GQ*, and billboard posters advertising David Beckham's range of toiletries, etc. clearly establish the idea that men's bodies are now as actively fetishised and sexualised as women's have been. While Osgerby's (2003) historical study of 'dandy', 'dude' and 'playboy' suggests that men of the past may have managed their consumption of style through a 'robust heterosexuality', there is the idea that this robustness has been challenged since the 1980s through both the female and homo-erotic gaze. This has become more noticeable when seen through the promotional adverts in that decade's rise in consumerist power. This increase in eroticisation and cross-boundary scopophilia suggests that there is a tension between the 'product' (the body and persona of the actor) and those that consume that 'product'. Where there was once a male or female gaze, there is now a combination of male-heterosexual, male-homosexual, female-heterosexual, female-lesbian, and transgenderised viewpoints. Now that the modern media makes little differentiation between all categories, where *metrosexual* now covers a wider range of sexual categories, it becomes apparent that not only is the showing of the (near) naked male form now a part of everyday life, the image of the clothed man remains just as potent a symbol of (changing) ideals of masculinity as it always has been. With that in mind, it is not just the individual body that is reflective of such deconstructions, but also the fashions that cocoon it.

Dress and fashion

Dress and fashion are used for two functions: the first is as a modifier of body processes, whereby clothes protect the body from external environments; the second is that dress is used as a medium for communication (Roach-Higgins *et al.* 1995). Dress has no actual meaning per se, but it is given meaning when used/worn/discussed by individuals. Crane (2000) sees clothing as performing one of the major social constructions of identity, no matter what class or society the individual 'belongs' to, and that gender and status can be 'confirmed' from the clothes worn by individuals and groups; although, Kaiser (2012) argues that children from the age of two divide people into respective genders through the clothes they wear.

It could be argued that social and power relations are expressed through the body and therefore the fashions worn. While the differences between male and female bodies are obvious, this is accentuated through dress codes and conventions: traditionally, males wear trousers, females wear skirts. However, as Nicolson (2005: 43) ponders, 'the need for certainty in differentiating between the sexes is so important [that it] reveals the political significance of the gendered meanings given to the subjectivity of the person occupying the body.'

Although gender 'norms' in fashion have become naturalised, it is only when there is something out of the ordinary that people notice. When gender 'norms' are broken, social dislocation occurs (Lorber 1996). Clothing becomes a communication tool, and this social construction becomes part and parcel of society's determining males from females – the aforementioned 'normal' male wears trousers, while 'normal' females wear skirts. However, if these rules no longer apply gender barriers become eroded. It was only with the short-lived Peacock revolution in the 1960s that trousers for women became accepted (Victoria and Albert Museum). The trend of peacocking, where men wore colourful and shiny suits, often with patterns set off with frilly shirts, embroidered waistcoats and high-heeled boots, was an attempt to attract females by standing out in the crowd, much as a peacock displays its feathers to attract a mate. The alternative to the Peacock was the more traditional, though still stylish and classically designed 'Perfect Suit'. This Perfect Suit was seen as synonymous with masculinity: for example, Sean Connery's James Bond wore tailored suits that clearly reflected his 'cool' sophistication – where the sharp creases, tight trousers and crisp, white shirt with black tie reflected his character.

Provocative fashion trends reflected the rising wave in gender politics. When gender stereotypes began to be questioned in the 1960s and 1970s, so the fashion industry reacted to these questions. Hippy styles and unisex fashions questioned conservative ideas on how males and females were represented.

Musicians like David Bowie and Marc Bolan pushed these boundaries of representation out into the cultural arena, where their androgynous costumes, make-up, hair and clothing suggested a melding of both male and female into one unit, while the 1980s saw further changes in fashion where unisex mixed alongside yuppie pinstripes. However, it must be remembered that clothing does not, in itself, have a meaning. It is the culture that uses it that assigns it a cultural value. Therefore, trousers (as an example) do not have a masculine meaning on their own. Rather, the physical trousers are given a cultural meaning by: a) who is wearing them; b) the person viewing the person wearing them; c) the dominant culture that produces 'meaning' from them; and, d) any alternative outlook to the 'accepted norm'.

The role of dressing

Fashion is a reflection of the zeitgeist, and while gendered styles from the post-millennium onwards are leaning more towards de-gendered fashions, where gender neutrality and unisex are often seen as blurring fashion lines, the role of dressing remains important to the construction of Jason Statham. The body can be regarded as the visible outer limit of the Self, but when viewed by the individual or collective, becomes a part of that societal construct. Yet the body can also be hidden, and therefore protected from the outside. This means that 'clothing' becomes the accepted face of 'social skin', consisting as it does of garments, bodily gestures, attitudes, etc. (Turner 1980; Fisher and Loren 2003: 225–230). This accepted face goes further in referring to the social fabric of both similarities and differences in appearance, whereby clothes express aspirations, dreams, fantasies and realities (Butler 1993).

Dressing is an important way of communicating one's status, persona and attitudes to others. It is a way of sharing one's own personal values, even though it could be argued that this personal approach is often 'regulated' by the society that produces such values. Clothing communicates ideas of social identity, and by association reflects the class character of contemporary society. It is justifiable to argue that Statham's clothing (ranging from khaki pants and T-shirts to his Perfect Suit) reflect the concentration of power in the narratives of his films while simultaneously emphasising his prestige in his work across numerous fashion magazines (Davis 1988).

For the majority, clothes highlight the wearer's own characteristics. Clothing becomes a visual and tactile language with its own vocabulary. The code of that language often remains ambiguous, maybe not in meaning but in the outlook and projected viewpoint of the wearer. For example, uniforms may be alike in the cultural ideals they promote, yet the individual wearer may not have that culture's outlook. Perhaps it is the capricious nature of fashion that enables this to occur. In the case of Statham, his heavily manicured and designed fashions, casual designer wear, toned physique and cropped hair remain a statement of intent for the actor/persona/character. As fashions change, and his dress sense alters to accommodate these trends, it remains clear that clothing (and the lack of it) remains a vital component in understanding how he 'fits' into the various media worlds that his canon has embraced.

Statham: Adonis

According to Emma Garland's (2016) satirical deconstruction of Jason Statham, he is a saviour and an inspiration to modern UK men. She argues that he is Britain's most beloved hardman. While his 'hair seems to have been thinning since birth', he does his own stunts, 'has a neck the width of three tyres' and 'constantly looks about two seconds away from curb stomping you for eating his Snickers out of the fridge'. Garland says that Statham does not play characters but manipulates them until they become *him*, and that he is 'an archetype of British masculinity that leaves men across the nation emotionally torn between wanting to be him and wishing he was their dad.' But Garland was not introducing Statham as a film star or media icon. She was setting his contextualisation as a dancer in two electro-synth-pop videos during the early-1990s.

Katie Calautti's (2015) ode to Statham focused on his work in these two videos, where he took centre stage of the image. According to Carol Vernallis, the major component of the pop video, then still in its burgeoning infancy, was not the actual song itself. It was the image of the solo artist or group that was of paramount importance. The video was designed primarily to promote the artist, and not the song (Vernallis 2004). However, Vernallis also argued that when it came to this promotion the singer/band was given a 'privileged space' within the music video's *mise en scène* through which the artist's ideology was promoted.

By the early 1990s, Statham had already become known through his high-board diving at the 1990 Commonwealth Games, where he competed at the ten, three and one-metre competitions. He was a member of Britain's National Swimming Squad for twelve years, and during his tenure he was placed twelfth in the world and third at Olympic trials on three separate occasions. He was spotted by an agent working for French Connection clothing and hired for one of their campaigns. He was signed for Tommy Hilfiger, Levis and various modelling contracts during this period. Statham was also asked to appear in three pop videos. The final video saw Statham in a blink-and-you'll-miss-him cameo for 'Dream a Little Dream for Me' by The Beautiful South in 1995, in which he sits next to a woman in a cinema. The first was for Scottish electro-dance band The Shamen, and their song 'Coming On'; the second was for English electro-pop band Erasure, and the song 'Run to the Sun'. He did not sing in either; he danced.

'Coming On' begins with a backdrop of a rocky outcrop, on which are numerous repeated images of two of the band's singers. As they sing 'Hey! Yeah!' the image cuts to a psychedelic montage of the lead singer against a backdrop of swirling patterns. The image then cuts back to the rocky outcrop backdrop. There are small images of the band members singing at the front of the screen. However, on-screen left and right are gigantic, Olympian images of Statham. His well-toned physique has been wet-shaved, his body oiled, his muscles bulging, his sinews rippling, and his gold-tinted, leopard-print lamé hot-pants are straining to contain any hints of masculinity.

As the music pumps out, Statham's physicality dominates the entire image, becoming a set of symbols. Despite the video returning to the band, it is Statham's work in this privileged space that becomes *the* focal point of the video. Even though Statham is heterosexual, the images that are presented are done in a *faux* but knowing campness. The hot-pants are deliberately kept in shot throughout Statham's appearance, and when linked with his hefty working-class boots, the juxtaposition of his own heterosexuality combined with the images reveals the excess of the era. Indeed, while he might resemble Talos, the Man of Bronze from antiquity, he represents a hybridised form of male 'Other' and is therefore 'dangerous' to the 'norms' of society inasmuch as he is a heterosexual man dancing in highly fetishised/sexualised ways that appeal to a variety of audiences across a variety of sexual platforms.

This Olympian detachment becomes further evident in Erasure's 'Run to the Sun'. Set against the backdrop of Berlin's iconic Alexanderplatz television Tower landmark, Statham appears atop the square's World Clock. As Andy Bell sings and the music blasts, Statham again takes up the privileged space. The image of the clock turning around, with its giant spheres acting as platforms for him to stand against, project this image of Statham as an Olympian figure, who twists and turns in time to the clock's revolutions. Painted in silver from head to toe and again wearing hot-pants, Statham's body becomes the focal point of the video. A crowd looks up at him as he slowly turns and contorts his body much in the way bodybuilders show off their physique. As one man takes a photograph, the image cuts to Statham looking sternly at the camera; he folds his arms, and his body turns around in a way as to suggest a form of scopophilic narcissism. The reading here is that Statham has achieved the Olympian ideal and attained his goal of reaching Mount Olympus.

Fashions change rapidly, and Statham's early career as a model saw him modelling fashions dictated by the era and its requirements. One image shows him walking down a fashion show catwalk wearing black glasses, a cream bomber jacket, baggy black chinos, no socks and walking sandals, all of which are topped off by his naked chest on display. Another shows him wearing a bright orange T-shirt, pink wristband, cream combats and undone brown working boots. Neither suggest sartorial elegance in the given sense, but rather the fashion constructs of the early to mid-1990s. His fashion catalogue shots see him advertising Timberland's range of outdoor clothes, where he wore masculine-affirming colourful waterproof jackets, chinos and hiking boots. To confirm his masculinity another shoot saw him wearing an Adidas 'Brave' blue tracksuit, with white stripes on the arm and red on the legs, coupled with his sullen stare off-camera he remains blandly uninviting in the way that only catalogue modelling can achieve.

Once his film star status is confirmed, Statham's sartorial appearance began altering. He began to wear/advertise casual or high-end tailored suits. Creases became sharper. Suits became tighter. Ads for IDS show that his fashion is 'of the now' – trendy, stylish (for the era) and affordable: in other words, *attainable*. His friendship with film director Guy Ritchie certainly helped cement this image as a 'modern man': a paparazzi shot of Ritchie and Statham walking down a street shows the two chatting. Ritchie wears a padded jacket, open shirt, khaki trousers and brown brogues, topped off with a tweed cloth cap; Statham has a dark grey cloth cap, long black woollen coat, T-shirt, jeans and sneakers. While Ritchie is promoting ideals of *faux* middle/upper class gentility, Statham's look is more working class.

However, Statham does have a particular 'look' and 'style'. As his career progressed from modelling into film, so his photoshoots reflected that progression. Although he is at home off-screen in T-shirt, jacket, smart jeans and trainers, the cover for *Details* magazine shows him in his most-traditional attire: sharp black suit, crisp white shirt, and black tie. He remains stubbled, and his hair is short. It could be reasoned that this Perfect Suit creates both an ambience of sophistication and 'danger' in that it represents a repressed air of menace. While the image of Statham 'suited and booted' remains defiantly heterosexual and there is a toughness that enables Statham's persona and image to carry on the tradition of James Bond, it adds to the canon of well-dressed British men such as Michael Caine, Stanley Baker, Terence Stamp, Jude Law, Clive Owen and Daniel Craig who remain both attainable and yet charismatically *unattainable*.

Due to his film work constantly emphasising his physique, a magazine like April 2017's *Men's Health* emphatically highlighted the Olympian status that Statham now has. A black and white image of Statham is central of the front cover. He stands side on, topless and wearing tracksuit bottoms. His stature, with chiselled jaw, abs and rippling muscles accentuated, scream traditional masculinity at the reader. Statham's body has become ingrained with the ideals of a capitalist society, whereby ideas of men's interest in their appearance is down to media-promoted ideologies (fittest is best). The headlines 'Get the Jason Statham Formula! *Ripped* at 49' and 'BUILD ARMS LIKE THIS! The Stath's Own Training Secrets for Growing Stronger with Age' are clearly aimed at enticing readers of numerous demographics to buy the magazine through the ideological implication that *all men* want to be Statham.

If Hall's viewpoint is taken into account, then Statham has been compartmentalised: he is approaching middle age, healthy, fit, slim, and therefore beautiful. Although Statham's image is one of media-formed masculinity, the fact that boundaries change or blur means that his approach to his own body seems to offer a postmodern version of masculinity, where image remains important, but bears a myriad of readings. Statham's body has not only developed into a Perfect *Birthday* Suit in its own right, but has also become a conduit through which identity, shape, physique and ideological implications remain important. These components are projected outwards to a postmodern male audience that will accept him as a role model (fit father), reflection of themselves or an unattainable Zeus.

Statham's 'Perfect Suit'

When examining Statham's film career, especially in its later years, one thing becomes apparent: the narrative and his character 'type' and trajectory remain virtually intact from film to film. In films like *The Transporter* (2002, 2004, 2008) series, *The Mechanic* (2011) and its sequel *Mechanic: Resurrection* (2016) and *Killer Elite* (2011) Statham is a loner, has limited friendships, and is called into action unwillingly. Movies like *War* (2007), *Safe* (2012) and *Homefront* (2013) may have Statham in a position of authority, with a family and children, but his family is either destroyed (and so he must seek vengeance) or be placed into danger. In all of these movies, he has a set of 'special talents' (through his FBI, police or army training) that he relies on to vanquish his enemies. Even though he has a family in some of his films, it is the metaphorical family in which Statham appears to feel most at home. As Lee Christmas in *The Expendables* trilogy (2010, 2012, 2014) he is the 'son' to Sylvester Stallone; in his outings in *The Fast and Furious* franchise (2013, 2015, 2017) he transforms from the villainous Deckard Shaw to 'brother' of Dwayne 'The Rock' Johnson.

While his appearances in earlier movies like *Lock, Stock and Two Smoking Barrels* (1998), *Turn It Up* (2000) and *Mean Machine* (2001) offered Statham cameo appearances or limited roles, there are definite beginnings of the two Styles of Statham: the (usually) black suit and tie, with (usually) white shirt, that became his most recognisable outfit appeared in *Snatch* (2000); and, the more casual combination of leather jacket, T-shirt/jumper, jeans and boots that appeared in later films like *Revolver* (2004) and *Chaos* (2005). Whether he wears combats in *Ghosts of Mars* (2001) and *The Expendables* franchise, Frankenstein's Death Mask in *Death Race* (2008) or the street-smart casuals of 1970s fashions in *The Bank Job*, each outfit reflects both the actions and outlook of these characters.

Statham wears the outfit. The outfit becomes the character. The character *is* Statham. Therefore, Statham, outfit and character remain both physically and psychologically linked as one single unit.

A study of Statham's outfits reveals the following statistics – black suit, white shirt, black tie: eight appearances (*Snatch, The Transporter, Transporter 2, Transporter 3, The Mechanic, Mechanic: Resurrection, Parker, Hummingbird*); casual suit and shirt: eleven (*Turn It Up, The One, Revolver, The Bank Job, The Mechanic, Mechanic: Resurrection, Parker, Hummingbird, Fast and Furious 6, Furious 7, The Fate of the Furious*); sports/leather jacket, T-shirt, and jeans combinations: eighteen (*Lock Stock, The One, Revolver, London, Chaos, War, The Bank Job, The Expendables, Expendables 2, Expendables 3, Blitz, Killer Elite, Wild Card, Hummingbird, Fast and Furious 6, Furious 7, The Fate of the Furious, The Meg*); military: four (*Ghosts of Mars, The Expendables, The Expendables 2, The Expendables 3*); other: thirteen (*Mean Machine, Chaos, Crank, Crank: High Voltage, In the Name of the King, Death Race, Hummingbird, The Mechanic, Mechanic: Resurrection, The Bank Job, Parker, The Fate of the Furious, The Meg*). In each instance, the outfit not only places Statham into the 'real' world of the film, they begin to then reflect the persona that his character is projecting.

This melding of actor/persona to character/outfit is evident most notably in the *Transporter* trilogy, where his trademark black suit, white shirt and tie clearly emphasises his character (Frank Martin) and his unemotional detachment from his job, while his peacocking prowess in his Perfect Birthday Suit seduces the women he rescues. Arguably the scene that encapsulates this is in *Transporter 3*. Frank Martin, an ex-Special Forces mercenary, is assigned to deliver a Ukrainian minister's daughter, Valentina to a hidden destination within a given time, otherwise: a) a conference on nuclear fuel disposal will be in jeopardy; and, b) a wristband that Frank wears will explode.

As Frank's mechanic begins to deactivate a bomb in his highly polished black Audi, a group of thugs attempt to beat him up. As they look at him, he says: 'In my profession, a man is only as good as the car he drives. Take care of the car, and the car will take care of you,' emphasising his attachment to both the vehicle and his professionalism. As the men attack, Frank's balletic smashing, kicking, punching, high-kicking, tripping and tying-up with a hose, beating with a fire extinguisher, slapping, karate-chopping and smashing a face with a shovel appeal to Valentina's desire for him. This is then emphasised further when Frank's jacket and tie are used as a garrotte and bolas. An assailant pushes a pole through Frank's shirt, which is quickly removed to reveal his muscular frame. Frank finally confronts a thug who calls himself 'the big one' and through a series of wide, medium and close-up shots, each treating his body as both a work of art, much in the way that the statue of David is, and a vessel of absolute (sexual) power, it becomes apparent that Frank/Statham becomes a mix of both Perfect Suit and Perfect Birthday Suit. The aftermath of the fight sees Frank reaching into the boot of his car and removing a crisp white shirt, black tie and jacket. The car, Frank and Statham are completely interlinked, and while Statham is at ease in displaying his body, Frank is not and prefers to immerse himself back into the safety of his suit-cocoon.

Interestingly, later in the film Valentina seduces Frank when she holds his car keys (themselves a sign of his masculinity) and will only return them if he strips off. Clearly uneasy at her dominance, Frank tries to get the keys back. She tells him that she wants to see him strip for her, finding his fighting 'a turn on':

> *Valentina:* You want the keys?
> *Frank:* I want you to stop fooling around.
> *Valentina:* Maybe this is your first chance to play around.
> *Frank:* This is not the time or place for playing.
> *Valentina:* I get the feeling that, with you, it's never the time or place.
> *Frank:* If I want to get analysed, I'll see a psychiatrist. Now give me the keys.
> *Valentina:* Now, Frank Martin. Make playtime for me!

Frank backs away and slowly, reluctantly takes his jacket and tie off.

> *Valentina:* This is supposed to be sexy. You know. Move your ass a little.
> *Frank:* You know what I'm going to do to you after I've done this?
> *Valentina:* Spank me!
> *Frank:* For starters.
> *Valentina:* Tie me up?
> *Frank:* Really?

As his shirt comes off, and his hairy, muscular chest revealed, he grabs Valentina around the waist. She gasps and says, 'Not too rough. A new game. A kiss for the keys.' Frank kisses her quickly but she says, 'Like you mean it! Do you kiss like you mean it, Frank? Maybe not. You live alone. Inside and outside. It's not dying you're afraid of. It's living. Live with me. Just this once.' The two embrace and Frank's hand reaches up and takes the keys from Valentina. The car, Frank's extra component to his sexual prowess and masculinity remains more important than her. The next scene sees Valentina and Frank sitting on the bonnet of the car. They are both fully dressed. She nestles into him, and he comforts her as she tells him her personal story. It is in this moment, with his suit put back into its rightful place as his cocoon, that Frank's masculinity is revealed: his Perfect Body Suit – despite its toned musculature – remains second-best to his Perfect Suit of black jacket, black tie and white shirt.

However, this Perfect Suit also proves problematic. In *Hummingbird* Frank plays an AWOL British soldier, Joey Smith, on the run from Helmand Province living as a down and out in London. The narrative sees Joey assume the identity of another man while trying to find the killer of his friend. As a tramp, Joey wears a grey nylon jacket and trousers, with both his beard and hair long. When he breaks into an unoccupied apartment, he looks at himself in the mirror: the duality of his character becomes apparent, and he shaves his head and changes into smart clothes, eventually wearing his Perfect Suit in which he despatches numerous villains in violent ways. However, while he is still in his Perfect Suit, he gets injured. As he staggers into the London night, his jacket torn, his shirt covered in blood, and his tie loose around his neck, a police sky patrol helicopter spots him. A voice on the radio says, 'We are closing in.' If the Perfect Suit has become his armour, as it has in so many of his films, with it now in tatters it represents a different aspect to Statham's complex and richly rewarding portrayal of a man under physical and mental siege. It offers an image of failure. As such *Hummingbird*, which deals with masculinity and duality, affords Statham arguably his best performance and most-complicated role to date, where his Perfect Suit is now Imperfect.

This is the importance that clothing brings to Statham's image/persona/character. There is a tailored-ness to his T-shirt, black jacket, blue jeans and boots. While they may seem as if they are retro-complimentary to Marlon Brando, they demonstrate that his media-savvy knowledge of promotion is well in evidence, and this is why he picks his clothes with care. His chiselled looks and physique offer his audience an almost-impossible-to-attain image of masculinity on to which many ideas can be displayed. However, in *Crank* his naked posterior sticking out of an ill-fitting hospital gown reveals his masculinity under threat and he crashes the bike he has stolen. In its sequel, his masculinity is almost-curtailed when his captors try to sever his penis, which has apparently mystical properties, and his chest has a massive scar ripped across it, something which he hides. When showing off his body in *Transporter 3*, Frank seems ill at ease away from areas of violence and needs his Perfect Suit to reassert his dominance over others and the narrative. In his biggest box office successes, *The Expendables* and *Fast and Furious* films, he remains fully clothed. While he may have been a victim of fashion during his modelling days, and for that he cannot be blamed, his move from pop video to catalogue modelling, and then into cinema is a logical step to take for an actor of Statham's physique.

What makes Statham so interesting is that he uses clothes in his films to both reflect and accentuate his characters' actions and mental state. It is this that makes Statham's sartorial style so compelling. For Jason Statham/Chev Chelios/Frank Martin/Lee Christmas and all his other roles, clothes (and even the lack of them) really do make the man.

References

Butler, J. (1993). *Bodies That Matter: On the Discursive Limits of Sex*. New York: Routledge.

Calautti, K. (2015). 'Watch a '90s shirtless Jason Statham dancing in leopard-print underwear'. *MTV News*. www.mtv.com/news/2137352/jason-statham-comin-on-video/ (19.04.15, accessed 01.04.18).

Clarke, L. H. and Griffin, M. (2008). 'Visible and invisible ageing: beauty work as a response to ageism'. *Ageing & Society*, 28, 653–674.

Coupland, J. (2007). 'Gendered discourses on the 'problem' of ageing: consumerized solutions'. *Discourse & Communication*, 1, 37–61.

Crane, D. (2000). *Fashion and its Social Agendas: Class, Gender and its Identity in Clothing*. Chicago: Chicago University Press.

D'Alessandro, S. and Chitty, B. (2011). 'Real or relevant beauty? Body shape and endorser effects on brand attitude and body image'. *Psychology & Marketing*, 28, 843–878.

Davis, F. (1988). 'Clothing, fashion and the dialectic of identity', in Maines, D. and Couch, J. (eds). *Communication and Social Structure*. Springfield, MO: Charles & Thomas.

Doonan, S. (2016). 'Getting it right: the Statham'. *Slate*. www.slate.com/articles/life/doonan/2016/05/a_fashion_guide_to_the_careless_masculinity_of_jason_statham.html (26.05.16, accessed 01.04.18).

Featherstone, M. (2010). 'Body, image and affect in consumer culture'. *Body & Society*, 16(1): 193–221.

Garland, E. (2016). www.noisey.vice.com/en_uk/article/rnwrmg7/remember-when-jason-statham-was-the-go-to-hot-bod-of-90s-music-videos (19.02.16, accessed 01.04.18).

Gill, R., Henwood, K. and McLean, C. (2005). 'Body projects and the regulation of normative masculinity'. *Body & Society*, 11(1), 39–62.

Grogan, S. (2010). 'Promoting positive body image in males and females: contemporary issues and future directions'. *Sex Roles*, 63(9): 757–765.

Hall, M. (2014). *Metrosexual Masculinities*. London: Palgrave Macmillan.

Lorber, J. (1996). *Paradoxes of Gender*. New Haven, CT: Yale College Publishing.

Nicolson, P. (2005). *Gender, Power and Organisation*. London: Routledge.

Osgerby, B. (2003). 'A pedigree of the consuming male: masculinity, consumption and the American "leisure class"'. *Sociological Review*. May. pp. 1–29.

Roach-Higgins, M. E., Eicher, J., Johnson K. K. P. (eds) (1995). *Dress and Identity*. New York: Fairchild Books.

Stern, B. B. and Russell, C. A. (2004). 'Consumer responses to product placement in television sitcoms: genre, sex and consumption.' *Consumption, Markets & Culture*, 7, 371–394.

Turner, S. (1980). 'The social skin', in Cherfas, J. and Lewin, R. (eds). *Not Work Alone: A Cross-Cultural View of Activities Superfluous to Survival*. Beverly Hills, CA: SAGE.

Vernallis, C. (2004). *Experiencing Music Video: Aesthetics and Cultural Context*. New York: Columbia University Press.

Victoria and Albert Museum (2011). 'The Perfect Suit'. London: V&A.

Conclusion

Steven Gerrard and Robert Shail

While the tabloid culture and online forums of the post-millennium years have focused on creating 'stars' through virtual reality TV shows and social media, where 'being famous for being famous' seems to be an accepted norm, stars still remain the cornerstone of the film industry. Genre fortunes may fluctuate, and directors have assumed more 'legendary' status than ever before (and often for their visual aesthetics rather than the more traditional *auteur* status afforded to their predecessors). But film *needs* stars.

Richard Dyer recognised the importance of film stars to the film industry. He saw them as being at the forefront of a business led along capitalist lines, where stars such as John Wayne, Clint Eastwood, Jane Fonda and others were the main reason to watch a movie, and in turn helped create profits for the studios. But times change. The contemporary film star, although not too removed from their forerunners, still plays a vital part in the film industry. They remain the outward face of it, appearing on talk shows to promote their latest efforts, giving magazine interviews, using social media. But Jason Statham is different to, say, Tom Cruise or Sylvester Stallone. Their careers have remained relatively fixed, despite the odd stepping out of their usual roles, whereby 'a Tom Cruise film' remains fixed in an audience's preconceptions. Admittedly, the same could be argued about Statham – but as this collection has clearly demonstrated, he is a new style of film 'product'. This clearly shows that while Dyer's model for film stars is justifiably important, it remains limited inasmuch as he focuses on the stars working in cinema, and through limited exposure in film magazines, and not through other forms of media. Of course, this is not Dyer's failure – after all, his superlative work was written long before other forms of promotion through the internet were made available – but it does show that there is still room, and indeed *need* for further work to be done on the *modern* film star whose work may run across both multimedia and interdisciplinary platforms. This collection of chapters will hopefully be the first that will embrace and, indeed, highlight just how these two approaches now 'work' for the individual film star in this era of social media.

Above all else, Jason Statham is a film star. He has worked across a variety of media, and while critics have sometimes been unfair to dismiss his work, he remains among Britain's most popular (at least in box office terms) film stars. His persona is one of gritty toughness, of no-nonsense action and derring-do. His Statham-physique adorns numerous magazines. Unless promoting his latest project, Statham remains remarkably quiet and shuns the limelight, fame and self-publicity that other stars may crave. Even then he seems markedly reticent about talking about himself on camera. And yet this elusiveness marks him out as a film star in Dyer's mode: attainable yet unattainable, present yet absent, where his rags-to-riches story seems to reflect the ultimate ideals of Hollywood. There is an ambiguity here that contradicts the certainties of his apparently traditional masculinity.

But what does the future hold for a star like Statham? His latest film, *The Meg*, is the first where he is not only a leading man, but a leading man in a $130million movie. Although he has appeared in other blockbusters such as the later outings of *The Fast and Furious* franchise, this is the first time he has headlined a summer blockbuster. A lot rides on the success of this film for Statham: his box office bankability, his credibility to carry a big-budgeted movie, and his ability to reach out to new audiences would be tested. *The Meg* was released on 10 August 2018. According to boxofficemojo.com, the film had an opening weekend of $45,402,195. The film was ranked No.1 at 4,118 theatres, with an average 'take' of $11,025 per screening. Through the course of its run, *The Meg* performed well, with its domestic (USA) gross figure of $142,598, 364, and international gross was $383,400,000 forming a combined box office gross of $525,998, 364. The secondary release – through Blu Ray, digital download, and 4K – is to be in late-2018, and no doubt will prove equally as popular.

Although the film had a clear marketing strategy – giant, prehistoric shark battling Jason Statham – it also showed that *he* could 'open' a big-budget film without the need for other big-name action actors to help him. The advertising for the film was canny: the posters had images of the megalodon's jaws barely perceptible rising from the depths to devour hundreds of unwary surfers, while the tagline 'Opening Wide' emphasised the gigantic shark. The trailer begins with a serene view of underwater life at an aquatic research centre. As a little girl walks through its chrome-and-glass corridors, the megalodon spies on her and attempts to break through the glass separating them. The image then cuts to a quick series of shots showing Statham running, other people shouting, and back to Statham, the child and her mother. The little girl, comforted by her mother, says that 'There's a monster outside.' There is some explanatory dialogue between the research centre's scientists (and for modern audiences to grasp) about just what the shark is, before it cuts to a close-up of Statham, who exclaims, 'My God! It's megalodon!' As the trailer continues highlighting some of the action and set pieces to come, Frank Sinatra's version of *Beyond the Sea* plays. Statham's voice is heard: 'That thing's out there. We need to kill it.' There are more action sequences, including the megalodon rising out of the water before settling once again on Statham. This time the audience is shown Statham the *action hero*: piloting a submarine, swimming, running, being pulled along under the water, and walking through the research centre. An off-screen voice says. 'He looks heroic. But he's kinda got a negative attitude.' At this moment, in a wonderful close-up, Statham's character looks back at the person who's just said this. It is this tongue-in-cheek approach to the material, and especially at the way that Statham's persona has been openly – though gently – mocked ensured that audiences were completely 'in on the joke'. That is, *The Meg* was boldly brash, it had a genuine sense of *joie de vivre* about it, and that not only was Jason Statham the (human) star of the movie, he was prepared to, as he had done in *Spy* before him, offer a caricature (while simultaneously keeping the original intact) of himself.

At the time of this edited collection being completed, Jason Statham has numerous productions in the pipeline. The first, *Hobbs and Shaw* is due for release in 2019. Directed by David Leitch, the film is an offshoot from the *Fast & Furious* franchise. It clearly showed that despite the franchise showing no signs of abating in their original format/style, the inclusion of Statham into the series was a shrewd move. While he may have been seen as a villain in his few outings in the movies, it would appear that in this there is more of a buddy-buddy feel to this venture. Time will tell. Moving away from film, Statham has been both starring in, and producing, a TV series. The series, shot in London, is called *Viva La Madness*. It is a sequel to the Daniel Craig vehicle, *Layer Cake* (2004). Written and adapted from his own novel by J. J. Connolly, the TV series will focus on the anonymous narrator's further journeys through the drug-fuelled underworld of London. Statham will take over the role originated on the big screen by Craig. This is an interesting move for Statham. He has embraced working in new areas of media, including gaming platforms, pop video promos and, of course, cinema. But this is a new challenge: the small screen. In the post-millennial world of Netflix, streaming, HBO, Amazon Prime and many more, perhaps this is an assured and astute move to branch the Statham product out even further. But what is more interesting is this: Daniel Craig has announced that he is to retire from his role as Ian Fleming's 007 James Bond, and Statham has indicated that he would like to take on the role, albeit vastly different from previous incarnations. With him taking over a role that Craig has already played in *Layer Cake*, perhaps we can speculate that this is the next logical step in Statham's career trajectory?

Whatever happens, and as the reader has been able to see from this collection, Jason Statham is a bona fide *British* film star who has made the transition from street seller to pop video Adonis, cameo guest star to video gaming voice-over artist, to become the hero of numerous cult films to the star of both independent and mainstream productions. That Statham starred in a summer blockbuster, and one that performed well at the box office, clearly shows his prowess at moving across a variety of media, and his popularity with a media-savvy public. As Chev Chelios rides off, on fire, into the distance shouting 'Chicken and broccoli!', Frank Martin coolly despatches his parcels to villainous clientele, Lee Christmas knifes another soldier of misfortune, and Jonas Taylor punches a shark, we are reminded that Statham is a new type of film star that embraces all forms of media resulting in the production of the Statham brand. This is why Jason Statham is important in the study of film stars.

Select bibliography

Books

Babington, B. (ed.). (2001). *British Stars and Stardom: From Alma Taylor to Sean Connery*. Manchester and New York: Manchester University Press.
Benwell, B. (ed.). (2003). *Masculinity and Men's Lifestyle Magazines*. Oxford: Blackwell Publishing/Sociological Review.
Braudy, L. and Cohen, M. (eds) (2009). *Film Theory and Criticism: Introduction Readings*. New York: Oxford University Press.
Brod, H. and Kaufman, M. (ed.) (1994). *Theorizing Masculinities*. Thousand Oaks, CA, London and New Delhi: SAGE.
Brown, L. (2011). *Jason Statham: Taking Stock*. London: Orion.
Butler, J. (1993). *Bodies That Matter: On the Discursive Limits of Sex*. New York: Routledge.
Cassell, J. and Jenkins, H. (eds) (2000). *Barbie to Mortal Kombat: Gender and Computer Games*. Cambridge, MA: MIT Press.
Cohan, S. and Hark, I. R. (eds). (1992). *Screening the Male: Exploring Masculinities in Hollywood Cinema*. London: Routledge.
Cornea, C. (ed.). (2014). *Genre and Performance in Film and Television*. Manchester: Manchester University Press.
Craig, S. (ed.). (1992). *Men, Masculinity and the Media*. Thousand Oaks, CA, London and New Delhi: SAGE.
Crane, D. (2000). *Fashion and its Social Agendas: Class, Gender and its Identity in Clothing*. Chicago: Chicago University Press.
Dickinson, K. (ed.). (2002). *Movie Music: The Film Reader*. London: Routledge.
Dolan, J. (2017). *Contemporary Cinema and 'Old Age': Gender and the Silvering of Stardom*. London: Palgrave Macmillan.
Dyer, R. (1998). *Stars*. London: BFI Publishing.
Egan, K. and Thomas, S. (eds). (2012). *Cult Film Stardom: Offbeat Attractions and Processes of Cultification*. Basingstoke: Palgrave Macmillan.
Elliott, P. (2014). *Studying the British Crime Film*. Leighton Buzzard: Auteur Publishing.

Gilleard, C. and Higgs, P. (2000). *Cultures of Ageing: Self, Citizen and the Body*. Essex: Pearson Education Limited.
Gilleard, C. and Higgs, P. (2005). *Contexts of Ageing: Class, Cohort and Community*. Cambridge: Polity Press.
Green, D. (2009). *Manhood in Hollywood from Bush to Bush*. Austin, TX: University of Texas Press.
Hackley, C. (2015). *Advertising and Promotion, 3rd Edition*. London: SAGE.
Hall, M. (2014). *Metrosexual Masculinities*. London: Palgrave Macmillan.
Hayward, S. (2000). *Cinema Studies: The Key Concepts, Second Edition*. London and New York: Routledge.
Holmlund, C. (2014). *The Ultimate Stallone Reader: Sylvester Stallone as Star, Icon, Auteur*. London: Wallflower Press.
Huntemann, N. B. and Payne, M. T. (eds) (2009). *Joystick Soldiers: The Politics of Play in Military Videogames*. London: Routledge.
Hunter, I. Q. (2016). *Cult Film as a Guide to Life: Fandom, Adaptation and Identity*. London: Bloomsbury.
Jaeckle, J. (ed.). (2013). *Film Dialogue*. London and New York: Wallflower Press.
Jameson, F. (1992). *Postmodernism: Or, the Cultural Logic of Late Capitalism*. London: Verso.
Jancovich, M., Lazaro Reboll, M., Stringer, J. and Willis, A. (eds). (2013). *Defining Cult Movies: The Cultural Politics of Oppositional Taste*. Manchester: Manchester University Press.
Kaiser, S. B. (2012). *Fashion and Cultural Studies*. London: Bloomsbury.
Kline, S., Dyer-Witheford, N. and de Peuter, G. (2003). *Digital Play: The Interaction of Technology, Culture and Marketing, 2nd edition*. Montreal: McGill-Queen's University Press.
Lee, D. (2014). *The Heist Film: Stealing with Style*. London and New York: Wallflower Press.
Lorber, J. (1996). *Paradoxes of Gender*. New Haven, CT: Yale College Publishing.
Lury, C. (2004). *Brands: The Logos of the Global Economy*. London: Routledge.
Marshall, P. D. (2014). *Celebrity and Power: Fame in Contemporary Culture*. Minnesota: University of Minnesota Press.
Mathijs, E. and Sexton, J. (2011). *Cult Cinema*. Oxford: Wiley-Blackwell.
Messner, M. A. and Sabo, D. F. (1990). *Sport, Men and the Gender Order: Critical Feminist Perspectives*. Champaign, IL: Human Kinetics Books.
Meuf, R. (2017). *Rebellious Bodies Stardom, Citizenship, and the New Body Politics*. Houston, TX: University of Texas Press.
Newman, J. (2013). *Videogames, 2nd edition*. London: Routledge.
Nicolson, P. (2005). *Gender, Power and Organisation*. London: Routledge.

Redmond, S. and Holmes, S. (eds). (2003). *Stardom and Celebrity: A Reader*. Los Angeles and London: SAGE.
Roach-Higgins, M. E., Eicher, J. and Johnson, K. K. K. (eds) (1995). *Dress and Identity*. New York: Fairchild Books.
Ryan, M. (ed.). (2008). *Cultural Studies: An Anthology*. Oxford: Blackwell.
Sconce, J. (ed.). (2007). *Sleaze Artists: Cinema at the Margins of Taste, Style and Politics*. London: Duke University Press.
Shail, R. (2008). *Stanley Baker: A Life in Film*. Cardiff: University of Wales Press.
Shaviro. S. (2010). *Post Cinematic Affect*. Winchester: O-Books.
Shingler, M. (2012). *Star Studies: A Critical Guide*. London: Palgrave Macmillan.
Spicer, A. (2001). *Typical Men: The Representation of Masculinity in Popular British Cinema*. London: I. B. Tauris.
Stahl, R. (2010). *Militainment, Inc.: War, Media, and Popular Culture*. London: Routledge.
Tasker, Y. (1993) *Spectacular Bodies: Gender, Genre and the Action Cinema*. London: Routledge.
Taylor, A. (ed.). (2012). *Theorizing Film Acting*. New York and London: Routledge.
Vernallis, C. (2004). *Experiencing Music Video: Aesthetics and Cultural Context*. New York: Columbia University Press.
Wardrip-Fruin, N. and Harrigan, P. (eds). (2006). *First Person: New Media as Story, Performance and Game*. Cambridge, MA: MIT Press.
Woodward, K. (2006). *Boxing, Masculinity and Identity: The 'I' of the Tiger*. New York: Routledge.

Journals

Body & Society, Vol.11, No. 1.
Body & Society, Vol.16, No.1.
Celebrity Studies. Vol.1, No.1.
Cinema Journal. Vol.48, No.4.
Cinema Journal. Vol.51, No.4.
Consumption, Markets & Culture. Vol.7.
Discourse & Communication. No.1.
Games and Culture. No.7.
Gender and Society. Vol.10, No.2.
Journal of Communication. No.62.
Journal of Contemporary History. Vol.19, No.1.
Journal of Marketing. Vol.70, No.3
Journal of Marketing Management. No.31.
Journal of Men's Studies. Vol.17, No.1.
Men and Masculinities. Vol.15, No.5.
Psychology & Marketing. No.28.

Quarterly Review of Film and Video. Vol.27, No.4.
Sex Roles. No.63.
Sight and Sound. Vol.16. No.1.
Sight and Sound, Vol.16. No.10.
Sight and Sound. Vol.18. No.3.
Sight and Sound. Vol.19. No.7.
Sight and Sound. Vol.23. No.26.
The Sociological Review. No.51.
Westminster Papers in Communication and Culture.

Websites

www.adweek.com/digital
www.bbc.co.uk/films
www.chicagoreader.com
www.cinemablend.com
www.denofgeek.com
www.digitaljournal.com
www.digitalspy.com
www.empireonline.com
www.entertainmentweekly.com
www.esquire.com
www.forbes.com
www.gamasutra.com
www.gamestudies.org
www.gurubaftta.org
www.henryjenkings.org
www.heyguys.com
www.hollywoodreporter.com
www.huffingtonpost.com
www.independent.co.uk
www.indiewire.com
www.kftv.com/news
www.leonardmaltin.com
www.martialtribes.com
www.mensfitness.com
www.mtv.com
www.nytimes.com
www.observer.com
www.rogerebert.com
www.screendaily.com
www.screenrant.com
www.skysports.com
www.smh.au/news
www.spectator.com

www.telegraph.com
www.theguardian.com
www.time.com
www.usatoday.com
www.vanityfair.com
www.variety.com
www.vulture.com
www.whatculture.com

Jason Statham filmography

Lock, Stock and Two Smoking Barrels 1998, 106 mins, col. UK
Director: Guy Ritchie
Production company: Handmade Films, SKA Films, The Steve Tisch Company, Summit Entertainment
Producer: Matthew Vaughan
Script: Guy Ritchie
Cinematography: Tim Maurice-Jones
Film editing: Niven Howie
Music: David A. Hughes, John Murphy
Cast: Nick Moran (Eddy), Jason Flemyng (Tom), Dexter Fletcher (Soap), Jason Statham (Bacon), Vinnie Jones (Big Chris)

Snatch 2000, 102 mins, col. UK
Director: Guy Ritchie
Production company: SKA Films
Producer: Matthew Vaughn
Script: Guy Ritchie
Cinematography: Tim Maurice-Jones
Film editing: Jon Harris
Music: John Murphy
Cast: Jason Statham (Turkish), Stephen Graham (Tommy), Brad Pitt (Mickey O'Neil), Benicio del Toro (Franky 'Four Fingers'), Jason Flemyng (Darren)

Turn it Up 2000, 86 mins, col. USA
Director: Robert Adetuyi
Production company: New Line Cinema (Dist.)
Producer: Guy Oseary, Happy Walters
Script: Ray Daniels, Chris Hudson, Kelly Hilaire
Cinematography: Hubert Taczanowski
Film editing: Jeff Freeman
Music: Frank Fitzpatrick
Cast: Pras (Diamond), Ja Rule (David 'Gage' Williams), Jason Statham (Mr B), Tamala Jones (Kia), Vondie Curtis-Hall (Cliff)

Ghosts of Mars 2001, 98 mins, col. USA
Director: John Carpenter
Production company: Storm King Productions
Producer: Sandy King
Script: John Carpenter, Larry Sulkis
Cinematography: Gary B. Kibbe
Film editing: Paul C. Warschilka
Music: John Carpenter
Cast: Ice Cube (James 'Desolation' Williams), Natasha Henstridge (Lt Melanie Ballard), Jason Statham (Jericho Butler), Pam Grier (Cdr Helena Braddock), Joanna Cassidy (Dr Arlene Whitlock)

Mean Machine 2001, 99 mins, col. UK
Director: Barry Skolnick
Production company: SKA Films
Producer: Matthew Vaughn
Script: Tracy Keenan Wynn (original), Charlie Fletcher, Chris Baker, Andrew Day
Cinematography: Alex Barber
Film editing: Eddie Hamilton, Dayn Williams
Music: John Murphy
Cast: Vinnie Jones (Danny Meehan), David Kelly (Doc), Jason Statham (Monk), Danny Dyer (Billy the Limpet), David Hemmings (Governor), Jason Flemyng (Bob Likely), Ralph Brown (Burton)

The One 2001, 87 mins, col. USA
Director: James Wong
Production company: Revolution Studios, Hard Eight Pictures
Producer: Steve Chasman, Glen Morgan, Charles Newirth, James Wong, Todd Garner, Lata Ryan, Tom Sherak, Greg Silverman, Happy Walters
Script: Glen Morgan, James Wong
Cinematography: Robert McLachlan
Film editing: James Coblentz
Music: Trevor Rabin
Cast: Jet Li (Gabriel Law), Jason Statham (MVA Agent Evan Funsch), Delroy Lindo (MVA Agent Harry Rodecker), Carla Gugino (T. K. Law)

The Transporter 2002, 92 mins, col. France
Director: Corey Yuen
Production company: EuropaCorp, TF1 Films Production, Current Entertainment, Canal+
Producer: Luc Besson, Steve Chasman
Script: Luc Besson, Robert Mark Kamen
Cinematography: Pierre Morel

Film editing: Nicolas Trembasiewicz
Music: Stanley Clarke
Cast: Jason Statham (Frank Martin), Shu Qi (Lai Kwai), François Berléand (Inspector Tarconi), Matt Schulze (Darren 'Wall Street' Bettencourt), Ric Young (Mr. Kwai)

The Italian Job 2003, 110 minutes, col. USA
Director: F. Gary Gray
Production company: De Line Pictures
Producer: Donald De Line
Script: Donna Powers, Wayne Powers
Cinematography: Wally Pfister
Film editing: Richard Francis-Bruce, Christopher Rouse
Music: John Powell
Cast: Mark Wahlberg (Charlie Croker), Charlize Theron (Stella Bridger), Edward Norton (Steve Frazelli), Donald Sutherland (John Bridger), Jason Statham ('Handsome' Rob)

Cellular 2004, 94 mins, col. USA/Germany
Director: David R. Ellis
Production company: Electric Entertainment
Producer: Dean Devlin, Lauren Lloyd
Script: Chris Morgan
Cinematography: Gary Capo
Film editing: Eric Sears
Music: John Ottman
Cast: Kim Basinger (Jessica Kate Martin), Chris Evans (Ryan), Jason Statham (Ethan Greer), William H. Macy (Sgt Bob Mooney)

Collateral 2004, 120 mins, col. USA
Director: Michael Mann
Production company: Parkes/MacDonald Productions, Edge City
Producer: Michael Mann, Julie Richardson
Script: Stuart Beattie
Cinematography: Dion Beebe, Paul Cameron
Film editing: Jim Miller, Paul Rubell
Music: James Newton Howard
Cast: Tom Cruise (Vincent), Jamie Foxx (Max Durocher), Jada Pinkett Smith (Annie Farrell), Mark Ruffalo (Ray Fanning), Jason Statham (Airport Man – cameo)

Chaos 2005, 106 mins, col. Canada/UK/USA
Director: Tony Giglio
Production company: Mobius International, Epsilon Motion Pictures, Current Entertainment, Rampage Entertainment, Chaotic Productions, Pierce/Williams Entertainment

Producer: Michael Derbas, Gavin Wilding, Huw Penallt Jones
Script: Tony Giglio
Cinematography: Richard Greatrex
Film editing: Sean Barton
Music: Trevor Jones
Cast: Jason Statham (Det. Quentin Connors), Ryan Phillippe (Shane Dekker), Wesley Snipes (Jason York)

London 2005, 92 mins, col. USA
Director: Hunter Richards
Production company: Samuel Goldwyn Films (Dist.)
Producer: Paul Davis-Miller
Script: Brian Richards
Cinematography: Jo Willems
Film editing: Tracey Wadmore-Smith
Music: The Crystal Method
Cast: Jessica Biel (London), Chris Evans (Syd), Jason Statham (Bateman)

Revolver 2005, 110 mins, col. UK/France
Director: Guy Ritchie
Production company: EuropaCorp, Isle of Man Film
Producer: Luc Besson, Virginie Silla, Marty Katz
Script: Guy Ritchie, Luc Besson
Cinematography: Tim Maurice-Jones
Film editing: James Herbert, Ian Differ, Romesh Aluwihare
Music: Nathaniel Méchaly
Cast: Jason Statham (Jake Green), Ray Liotta (Dorothy Macha), Vincent Pastore (Zach), André Benjamin (Avi)

Transporter 2 2005, 87 mins, col. France
Director: Louis Leterrier
Production company: EuropaCorp
Producer: Luc Besson, Steve Chasman
Script: Luc Besson, Robert Mark Kamen
Cinematography: Mitchell Amundsen
Film editing: Christine Lucas-Navarro, Vincent Tabaillon
Music: Alexandre Azaria
Cast: Jason Statham (Frank Martin), Alessandro Gassman (Gianni Chellini), Amber Valletta (Audrey Billings), Kate Nauta (Lola), François Berléand (Inspector Tarconi), Matthew Modine (Jefferson Billings)

Crank 2006, 88 mins, col. USA
Director: Neveldine/Taylor
Production company: Lakeshore Entertainment, @radical.media

Producer: Michael Davis, Gary Lucchesi, Tom Rosenberg, Skip Williamson, Richard S. Wright
Script: Neveldine/Taylor
Cinematography: Adam Biddle
Film editing: Brian Berdan
Music: Paul Haslinger
Cast: Jason Statham (Chev Chelios), Amy Smart (Eve), Jose Pablo Cantillo (Ricky Verona), Carlos Sanz (Carlito), Dwight Yoakam (Doc Miles), Efren Ramirez (Kaylo), Keone Young (Don Kim), Reno Wilson (Orlando)

In the Name of the King 2007, 127 mins, col. Canada/Germany/USA
Director: Uwe Boll
Production company: Boll KG Productions, Herold Productions, Brightlight Pictures
Producer: Uwe Boll, Dan Clarke, Shawn Williamson, Wolfgang Herold
Script: Doug Taylor
Cinematography: Mathias Neumann
Film editing: Paul Klassen, David M. Richardson
Music: Jessica de Rooij, Henning Lohner
Cast: Jason Statham (Camden Konreid), Leelee Sobieski (Muriella), John Rhys-Davies (Merick), Ron Perlman (Norick), Claire Forlani (Solana), Kristanna Loken (Elora), Matthew Lillard (Duke Fallow), Ray Liotta (Gallian), Burt Reynolds (King Konreid)

War 2007, 103 mins, col. USA
Director: Philip G. Atwell
Production company: Lionsgate, Fierce Entertainment, Mosaic Media Group
Producer: Steve Chasman, Christopher Petzel, Jim Thompson
Script: Lee Anthony Smith, Gregory J. Bradley
Cinematography: Pierre Morel
Film editing: Scott Richter
Music: Brian Tyler
Cast: Jason Statham (FBI Agent John Crawford), Jet Li (Rogue), John Lone (Li Chang), Mathew St Patrick (Wick), Luis Guzman (Benny)

Death Race 2008, 111 mins, col. Germany/UK/USA
Director: Paul W. S. Anderson
Production company: Relativity Media, Cruise/Wagner Productions
Producer: Paul W. S. Anderson, Jeremy Bolt, Roger Corman, Paula Wagner
Script: Paul W. S. Anderson

Cinematography: Scott Kevan
Film editing: Niven Howie
Music: Paul Haslinger
Cast: Jason Statham (Jensen Garner Ames/'Frankenstein'), Joan Allen (Claire Hennessey), Tyrese Gibson (Joseph Mason), Ian McShane (Coach), Natalie Martinez (Case)

The Bank Job 2008, 112 mins, col. UK
Director: Roger Donaldson
Production company: Mosaic Media Group, Relativity Media LLC, Skyline (Baker St) Productions
Producer: Charles Roven, Steven Chasman
Script: Dick Clement, Ian La Frenais
Cinematography: Michael Coulter
Film editing: John Gilbert
Music: J. Peter Robinson
Cast: Jason Statham (Terry Leather), Saffron Burrows (Martine Love), Richard Lintern (Tim Everett), Keeley Hawes (Wendy Leather), David Suchet (Lew Vogel), Peter Bowles (MI Executive Director Miles Urquhart), James Faulkner ('Major' Guy Singer), Peter de Jersey (Michael Abdul Malik/Michael X)

Transporter 3 2008, 104 mins, col. France
Director: Olivier Megaton
Production company: EuropaCorp, TF1 Films Production, Grive Productions, Apipoulai Entertainment, Canal+, CineCinema
Producer: Luc Besson, Steve Chasman
Script: Luc Besson, Robert Mark Kamen
Cinematography: Giovanni Fiore Coltellacci
Film editing: Camille Delamarre, Carlo Rizzo
Music: Alexandre Azaria
Cast: Jason Statham (Frank Martin), Natalya Rudakova (Valentina), François Berléand (Inspector Tarconi), Robert Knepper (Johnson), Jeroen Krabbé (Leonid Tomilenko)

Truth in 24 2008, 98 mins, col. USA
Director: Keith Cossrow, Bennett Viseltear
Production company: Intersport, NFL Films (Distributors)
Producer: Charles N. Besser
Script: Keith Cossrow, Bennett Viseltear
Cinematography: Jim Barry, David Dart, Matt Lyons, Dave Malek, Donald Marx, Hank McElwee, Allen Sandrow
Film editing: Keith Cossrow, Bennett Viseltear
Music: David Robidoux
Cast: Jason Statham (narrator)

Crank: High Voltage 2009, 96 mins, col. USA
Director: Neveldine/Taylor
Production company: Lakeshore Entertainment, @Radical.media
Producer: Gary Lucchesi, Tom Rosenberg, Skip Williamson, Richard Wright
Script: Neveldine/Taylor
Cinematography: Brandon Trost
Film editing: Fernando Villena
Music: Mike Patton
Cast: Jason Statham (Chev Chelios), Amy Smart (Eve), Jose Pablo Cantillo (Ricky Verona), Carlos Sanz (Carlito), Dwight Yoakam (Doc Miles), Efren Ramirez (Venus), Keone Young (Don Kim), Reno Wilson (Orlando), David Carradine (Poon Dong), Bai Ling (Rita), Corey Haim (Randy), Art Hsu (Johnny Vang)

13 2010, 97 mins, col. USA
Director: Géla Babluani
Production Company: Magnet Media Group, Overnight Films, Barbarian Films, Morabito Picture Company
Producer: Rick Schwartz, Aaron Kaufman, Valerio Morabito
Script: Géla Babluani, Gregory Pruss
Cinematography: Michael McDonough
Film editing: Géla Babluani, David Gray
Music: Alexander Bubenheim
Cast: Jason Statham (Jasper Bagges), Sam Riley (Vincent Ferro), Ray Winstone (Ronald Bagges), Curtis '50 Cent' Jackson (Jimmy), Mickey Rourke (Patrick Jefferson)

The Expendables 2010, 103 mins, col. USA
Director: Sylvester Stallone
Production Company: Millennium Films, Nu Image
Producer: Avi Lerner
Script: David Callaham, Sylvester Stallone
Cinematography: Jeffrey Kimball
Film editing: Ken Blackwell, Paul Harb
Music: Brian Tyler
Cast: Sylvester Stallone (Barney Ross), Jason Statham (Lee Christmas), Jet Li (Yin Yang), Dolph Lundgren (Gunner Jensen), Eric Roberts (James Munroe), Mickey Rourke (Tool), Bruce Willis (Mr. Church), Arnold Schwarzenegger (Trench Mauser)

Blitz 2011, 97 mins, col. UK
Director: Elliott Lester
Production Company: Davis Films, Lipsync Productions
Producer: Brad Wyman, Steven Chasman, Samuel Hadida, Zygi Kamasa
Script: Nathan Parker
Cinematography: Rob Hardy

Film editing: John Gilbert
Music: Ilan Eshkeri
Cast: Jason Statham (Det. Sgt Tom Brant), Paddy Considine (Porter Nash), Aidan Gillen (Barry Weiss), David Morrissey (Harold Dunlop), Mark Rylance (Chief Insp. Bruce Roberts)

Gnomeo & Juliet 2011, 84 mins, col. UK/USA
Director: Kelly Asbury
Production Company: Touchstone Pictures, Rocket Pictures
Producer: Baker Bloodworth, Steve Hamilton Shaw, David Furnish
Script: Kelly Asbury, Mark Burton, Andy Riley, Kevin Cecil
Cinematography: none listed
Film editing: Catherine Apple
Music: James Newton Howard, Chris Bacon
Voice Cast: James McAvoy (Gnomeo), Emily Blunt (Juliet), Michael Caine (Lord Redbrick), Jason Statham (Tybalt), Maggie Smith (Lady Bluebury), Patrick Stewart (William Shakespeare)

Killer Elite 2011, 114 mins, col. Australia/UK
Director: Gary McKendry
Production Company: Omnilab Media, Ambience Entertainment, Current Entertainment, Sighvatsson Films, Film Victoria, Wales Creative IP Fund, Agora Films, International Traders, Mascot Pictures Wales
Producer: Michael Boughen, Steve Chasman, Sigurjón Sighvatsson, Tony Winley
Script: Matt Sherring
Cinematography: Simon Duggan
Film editing: John Gilbert
Music: Reinhold Heil, Johnny Klimek
Cast: Jason Statham (Danny Bryce), Clive Owen (Spike Logan), Robert De Niro (Hunter)

The Mechanic 2011, 93 mins, col. USA
Director: Simon West
Production Company: Millennium Films
Producer: Irwin Winkler, Robert Chartoff
Script: Lewis John Carlino, Richard Wenk
Cinematography: Eric Schmidt
Film editing: T. G. Harrington, Todd E. Miller
Music: Mark Isham
Cast: Jason Statham (Arthur Bishop), Ben Foster (Steve McKenna), Tony Goldwyn (Dean Sanderson), Donald Sutherland (Harry McKenna)

Safe 2012, 95 mins, col. USA
Director: Boaz Yakin
Production Company: IM Global, Lawrence Bender Productions, Trigger Street Productions
Producer: Lawrence Bender, Dana Brunetti
Script: Boaz Yakin
Cinematography: Stefan Czapsky
Film editing: Frederic Thoraval
Music: Mark Mothersbaugh
Cast: Jason Statham (Luke Wright), Catherine Chan (Mei), Chris Sarandon (Mayor Danny Tremello), Robert John Burke (Captain Wolf), James Hong (Han Jiao)

The Expendables 2 2012, 103 mins, col. USA
Director: Simon West
Production Company: Millennium Films, Nu Image
Producer: Avi Lerner
Script: Sylvester Stallone, Richard Wenk
Cinematography: Shelly Johnson
Film editing: Todd E. Miller
Music: Brian Tyler
Cast: Sylvester Stallone (Barney Ross), Jason Statham (Lee Christmas), Jet Li (Yin Yang), Dolph Lundgren (Gunner Jensen), Chuck Norris (Booker), Liam Hemsworth (Billy the Kid), Jean-Claude Van Damme (Jean Vilain), Bruce Willis (Mr. Church), Arnold Schwarzenegger (Trench Mauser)

Fast and Furious 6 2013 130 mins, col. USA
Director: Justin Lin
Production Company: Relativity Media, Original Film, One Race Films
Producer: Neal H. Moritz, Vin Diesel, Clayton Townsend
Script: Chris Morgan
Cinematography: Stephen F. Windon
Film editing: Christian Wagner
Music: Lucas Vidal
Cast: Vin Diesel (Dominic Toretto), Paul Walker (Brian O'Conner), Dwayne Johnson (Luke Hobbs), Michelle Rodriguez (Letty Ortiz), Jason Statham (Deckard Shaw – cameo appearance)

Homefront 2013, 100 mins, col. USA
Director: Gary Fleder
Production Company: Millennium Films, Nu Image, Endgame Releasing
Producer: Avi Lerner, Sylvester Stallone
Script: Sylvester Stallone

Cinematography: Theo van de Sande
Film editing: Padraic McKinley
Music: Mark Isham
Cast: Jason Statham (Phil Broker), James Franco (Morgan Bodine), Winona Ryder (Sheryl Marie Mott), Kate Bosworth (Cassie Bodine Klum)

Hummingbird 2013, 110 mins, col. UK
Director: Steven Knight
Production Company: IM Global, Shoebox Films
Producer: Guy Heeley, Paul Webster
Script: Steven Knight
Cinematography: Chris Menges
Film editing: Valerio Bonelli
Music: Dario Marianelli
Cast: Jason Statham (Joseph Smith/Joey Jones), Agata Buzek (Sister Cristina), Christian Brassington (Max Forrester), Vicky McClure (Dawn), Benedict Wong (Mr Choy), Victoria Bewick (Isabel)

Parker 2013, 118 mins, col. USA
Director: Taylor Hackford
Production Company: Incentive Filmed Entertainment, Sierra Pictures, Sidney Kimmel Entertainment
Producer: Les Alexander, Steven Chasman, Taylor Hackford, Sidney Kimmel, Jonathan Mitchell
Script: John J. McLaughlin
Cinematography: J. Michael Muro
Film editing: Mark Warner
Music: David Buckley
Cast: Jason Statham (Parker), Jennifer Lopez (Leslie Rodgers), Michael Chiklis (Melander), Wendell Pierce (Carlson)

The Expendables 3 2014, 126 mins, col. USA
Director: Patrick Hughes
Production Company: Millennium Films, Nu Image, Splendid Film
Producer: Avi Lerner
Script: Sylvester Stallone, Creighton Rothenberger, Katrin Benedikt
Cinematography: Peter Menzies Jnr.
Film editing: Sean Albertson, Paul Harb
Music: Brian Tyler
Cast: Sylvester Stallone (Barney Ross), Jason Statham (Lee Christmas), Mel Gibson (Conrad Stonebanks), Harrison Ford (Max Drummer), Antonio Banderas (Galgo), Wesley Snipes (Doctor Death), Dolph Lundgren (Gunner Jensen), Jet Li (Yin Yang), Kelsey Grammar (Bonaparte), Robert Davi (Goran Vata), Arnold Schwarzenegger (Trench Mauser)

Furious 7 2015, 137 mins, col. USA
Director: James Wan
Production Company: Original Film, One Race Films, MRC, China Film
Producer: Neal H. Moritz, Vin Diesel, Michael Fottrell
Script: Chris Morgan
Cinematography: Stephan F. Windon, Marc Spicer
Film editing: Christian Wagner
Music: Brian Tyler
Cast: Vin Diesel (Dominic Toretto), Paul Walker (Brian O'Conner), Dwayne Johnson (Luke Hobbs), Michelle Rodriguez (Letty Ortiz), Kurt Russell (Mr Nobody), Gal Gadot (Gisele), Jason Statham (Deckard Shaw)

Spy 2015, 120 mins, col. USA
Director: Paul Feig
Production Company: Chernin Entertainment, Feigco Entertainment, TSG Entertainment
Producer: Peter Chernin, Paul Feig
Script: Paul Feig
Cinematography: Robert Yeoman
Film editing: Brent White, Melissa Bretherton
Music: Theodore Shapiro
Cast: Melissa McCarthy (Susan Cooper), Jason Statham (Rick Ford), Rose Byrne (Rayna Boyanov), Jude Law (Bradley Fine), Miranda Hart (Nancy B. Artingstall), Allison Janney (Elaine Crocker), Peter Serafinowicz (Aldo)

Wild Card 2015, 92 mins, col. USA
Director: Simon West
Production Company: Current Entertainment, Quad Films, SJ Pictures, Sierra/Affinity
Producer: Jason Statham, Steve Chasman
Script: William Goldman
Cinematography: Shelly Johnson
Film editing: Padraic McKinley
Music: Dario Marianelli
Cast: Jason Statham (Nick Wild), Sofia Vergara (DD), Michael Angarano (Cyrus Kinnick), Milo Ventimiglia (Danny DeMarco), Max Casella (Osgood), Jason Alexander (Pinky)

Mechanic: Resurrection 2016, 98 mins, col. France/USA
Director: Dennis Gansel
Production Company: Davis Films, Chartoff-Winkler Productions, Millennium Films

Producer: John Thompson, Robert Earl, David Winkler, William Chartoff
Script: Philip Selby, Tony Mosher
Cinematography: Daniel Gottschalk
Film editing: Michael Duthie, Todd E. Miller, Ueli Christen
Music: Mark Isham
Cast: Jason Statham (Arthur Bishop), Jessica Alba (Gina Thornton), Tommy Lee Jones (Max Adams), Michelle Yeoh (Mei)

The Fate of the Furious 2017, 136 mins, col. USA
Director: F. Gary Gray
Production Company: China Film, Original Film, One Race Films
Producer: Neal H. Moritz, Vin Diesel, Michael Fottrell, Chris Morgan
Script: Chris Morgan
Cinematography: Stephen F. Windon
Film editing: Christian Wagner, Paul Rubell
Music: Brian Tyler
Cast: Vin Diesel (Dominic Toretto), Dwayne Johnson (Luke Hobbs), Jason Statham (Deckard Shaw), Michelle Rodriguez (Letty Ortiz), Tyrese Gibson (Roman Pearce), Kurt Russell (Mr Nobody), Charlize Theron (Cipher)

The Meg 2018, 120 mins, col. China/USA
Director: Jon Turteltaub
Production Company: Warner Bros. Pictures, Gravity Pictures, Flagship Entertainment, Apelles Entertainment, Di Bonaventura Pictures, Maeday Productions
Producer: Lorenzo di Bonaventura, Colin Wilson, Belle Avery
Script: Dean Georgaris, Jon Hoeber, Erich Hoeber
Cinematography: Tom Stern
Film editing: Steven Kemper
Music: Harry Gregson-Williams
Cast: Jason Statham (Jonas Taylor), Li Bingbing (Suyin Zhang), Rainn Wilson (Jack Morris), Ruby Rose (Jaxx Herd), Winston Chao (Dr Minway Zhang)

Hobbs and Shaw 2019, col. USA
Director: David Leitch
Production Company: Universal Pictures; Universal Pictures International (UPI)
Producer: Steve Chasman, Dany Garcia, Hiram Garcia, Viet Luu, Kelly McCormick, Neal H. Moritz, Ethan Smith
Script: Chris Morgan, Gary Scott Thompson (based on characters created by)

Cinematography: Jonathan Sela
Cast: Jason Statham (Deckard Shaw); Dwayne Johnson (Luke Hobbs); Vanessa Kirby (Hattie Shaw); Idris Elba (Brixton)

Viva La Madness 2019, col. USA/UK (10 episodes)
Director:
Production Company: SJ Pictures, Gaumont International
Producer: Peter McAleese, Steven Chasman, Jason Statham
Script: J.J. Connolly
Cast: Jason Statham (XXXX)

Spy 2 2020, col. USA
Director: Paul Feig
Production Company: Feigco Entertainment
Producer: Paul Feig
Script: Paul Feig
Cast: Melissa McCarthy (Susan Cooper), Jason Statham (Rick Ford), Miranda Hart (Nancy B. Artingstall)

Videogames

Red Faction II 2002
Developer: Volition, Cranky Pants Games, Outrage Games
Role: Shrike
Call of Duty 2003
Developer: Infinity Ward
Role: Sgt Waters
Sniper X with Jason Statham 2015
Developer: Glu Mobile
Role: Team Leader

Music Videos

The Shamen, 1993, *Coming On*
Erasure, 1994, *Run to the Sun*
The Beautiful South, 1995, *Dream a Little Dream*
Calvin Harris, 2014, *Summer*

Index

Note: page numbers in *italic* refer to illustrations

13 (2010) 128, 131–134
  see also Tzameti (2005)

ageing 34, 185–197
arthouse cinema 127–138

Baker, Stanley 7, 8, 18–20, 25–27,
  103, 220
Baker Street bank robbery 99, 106
Banderas, Antonio 76–78
Bank Job, The (2008) 74, 75,
  99–110, *140*, *141*, 221, 222
Beautiful South, The 6, 218
Besson, Luc 151–155, 164
birth 6, 18
Blitz (2011) 110, *142*
Boll, Uwe 45
Bollywood cinema 102
Bourne franchise 26, 164
branding 29–31, 41, 169–182
Britishness 102, 151

Caine, Michael 8, 18, 19, 107,
  110, 220
Call of Duty 39, 169
cars 162–163
casting 46–50
Cellular (2004) 63, 130
Chaos (2005) 63, 110, 222
Chev Chelios *see Crank* (2006);
  Crank: High Voltage (2009)
Chinese market 37
class 25, 59

Clement, Dick 99, 107
cockney accent 59, 80
Connery, Sean 8, 18, 107, 215
costume 124–125, 211–225
Couture, Randy 73, 185
Craig, Daniel 75, 114, 164, 230
Crank (2006) 7, 8, 10, 20–27, 33, 45,
  47, 63, 72, *89*, *90*, *91*, *92*, *93*,
  110, 114, 118, 128, 169, 171,
  179, 198, 202–207, 222, 225
Crank: High Voltage (2009) 20–22,
  94, *95*, *96*, 113, 118, 124,
  134, 199, 207–210, 222
Crank 3 38
Crews, Terry 72, 76, 185
Cruise, Tom 29, 41, 227
cult movies 56–69

Damon, Matt 26, 75, 164
Death Race (2008) 20, 59, 64, 75,
  100, *141*, *142*, 221, 222
Death Race 2000 (1975) 64
Deckard Shaw *see Fast and the*
  Furious, The franchise
Die Hard franchise 17,
  34, 164
Diesel, Vin 56, 66
diving 6, 18, 29, 157, 190, 198,
  210, 218

Eastwood, Clint 16, 21, 34, 60,
  64, 227
Endfield, Cy 18

ensemble 71–84
Erasure 6, 218, 219
Evans, Luke 67, 82
Expendables franchise 2, 6, 7, 10, 20, 33, 34, 38, 65, 72–80, 115, 119, 122, 128, 134, 167, 185–197, 221, 222, 225
   Expendables, The (2010) 10, 18, 39, 64, 110, 117, 222
   Expendables 2, The (2012) 56, 60, 173, 222
   Expendables 3, The (2014) 222
   Expendables 4, The 196

Fast and the Furious, The franchise 6, 7, 38, 57, 63, 66–68, 71, 72, 74, 122, 221, 225, 228
   Fast and Furious 6 (2013) 82, 128, 167, 222
   Fate of the Furious, The (2017) 20, 38, 71, 82, 83, 84, 162, 163, 167, 222
   Furious 7 (2015) 34, 37, 38, 56, 71, 79, 80, 82, 83, 167, 222
feminism 17
Feig, Paul 8, 31, 37, 38, 125
film noir 82–83
Frank Martin *see Transporter, The* franchise

gender 113–126, 212, 215
genre 113–126
Ghosts of Mars (2001) 6, 75, 165, 221, 222
Glu Mobile 40, 174
Godzilla/Gojira franchise 22, 209
Great Train Robbery of 1963 103, 107

heist movies 99–110
heroism 29–41, 158–160, 166
Hobbs and Shaw (2019) 35, 38, 229
Homefront (2013) 33, 221
homoeroticism 136, 214
homophobia 24

Hummingbird (2013) 7, 26, 30, 37, 60, 110, 128, 135–138, *144*, *145*, 222, 224
   see also *Redemption* (2013)
Huntington-Whiteley, Rosie 61

In the Name of the King: A Dungeon Siege Tale (2007) 96, 140, 222
Italian Job, The (1969) 104, 108
Italian Job, The (2003) 20, 72, 74, 110

James Bond 9, 38, 50, 113, 114, 119, 124, 155, 159, 215, 220, 230
Johnson, Dwayne 34, 68, 75, 122, 221
Jonas Taylor *see Meg, The*
Jones, Vinnie 6, 32

Killer Elite (2011) 110, *143*

La Frenais, Ian 99, 107
Lavender Hill Mob, The (1951) 104, 105, 108
Layer Cake (2004) 39, 230
League of Gentlemen, The (1960) 104, 105
Lee Christmas *see Expendables* franchise
Li, Jet 73, 75, 118
Lionsgate Films 39, 99
Lock, Stock and Two Smoking Barrels (1998) 6, 18, 19, 32, 33, 45, 54, 58, 63, 72, 80, 81, 108, 109, 110, 151, 165, 221, 222
London (2005) 5, 80, 128–131
Losey, Joseph 18, 26

martial arts 156–157, 198
masculinity 15–27, 32, 40, 61, 116, 124, 153–157, 166, 212–214

Matrix, The (1999) 155, 180
McCarthy, Melissa 50, 54, 56, 75, 113, 120
Mean Machine (2001) 20, 63, 222
Mechanic, The (1972) 64
Mechanic, The (2011) 64, 75, 134, 143, 144, 167, 221, 222
Mechanic: Resurrection (2016) 38, 128, 167, 221, 222
Meg, The (2018) 1, 6, 37, 125, 147, 148, 222, 228–229
Meg: A Novel of Deep Terror (1997) 1
Mirren, Helen 20, 68
Mitchum, Robert 16, 18
modelling 18, 29, 210, 219–221, 225
monologues 79–83, 117
music score 198–210

national identity 25, 151–167
Norris, Chuck 72, 75, 77

One, The (2001) 6, 63, 157, 177, 222
Oscars 36

Payback (1999) 7
Parker (2013) 7, 20, 145, 146, 222
Pitt, Brad 29, 41, 212
Point Blank (1967) 7, 24
pop videos 18, 217–219, 225, 230
postmodernism 19

racism 21, 24
Rambo franchise 17, 34, 159, 177, 210
Red Faction II 7, 39, 169
Redemption (2013) 26, 30, 135
  see also *Hummingbird* (2013)
Revolver (2005) 63, 80, 110, 221, 222
Ritchie, Guy 6, 19, 21, 32, 33, 58
Rick Ford see *Spy* (2015)

Robbery (1967) 103

Safe (2012) 30–31, 221
Samouraï, Le (1971) 155, 160, 161
Schwarzenegger, Arnold 10, 17, 21, 29, 34, 56, 75–78, 116, 118, 122, 187, 210
Shamen, The 6, 218
Snatch (2000) 6, 32, 63, 72, 74, 75, 81, 151, 165, 221, 222
Sniper X series 7, 40, 169, 173–175
Snipes, Wesley 63, 76–79
social media 35, 40, 169
social realism 138
sound recording 80
Spy (2015) 8, 18, 31, 37, 48, 50–54, 64, 72, 80, 113–126, 146, 147
Spy 2 (2020) 37, 125
Stallone, Sylvester 10, 17, 21, 29, 33, 34, 35, 39, 56, 64, 73–79, 116, 138, 177, 210, 221, 227
star text 56–62
star typology 17, 29, 114
stardom 36, 114, 227–230
street hawking 29, 54–55
stunts 35–36, 61

Taken franchise 25, 161
Terminator franchise 17, 34, 187, 210
transnationalism 151–167, 166
Transporter, The franchise 2, 6, 9, 20, 38, 45, 72, 75, 101, 110, 115, 128, 151–167, 171, 221
Transporter, The (2002) 6, 33, 37, 63, 86, 222
Transporter 2 (2005) 87, 115, 118, 119, 222
Transporter 3 (2008) 88, 100, 113, 222, 225

Turn It Up (2000) 157, 221, 222
Tzameti (2005) 131–134

Ultimate Spider-man 7, 39
see also *13* (2010)

Van Damme, Jean Claude 72, 75, 77, 119
videogames 22, 39, 169–182
violence 156

Viva La Madness (2019) 39, 230
Vulture, The 7, 39

Walker, Paul 66, 71
War (2007) 177, 220, 222
Wild Card (2015) 220
Willis, Bruce 16, 17, 34, 60, 64, 75–78, 119

Yoakum, Dwight 20, 22

EU authorised representative for GPSR:
Easy Access System Europe, Mustamäe tee 50,
10621 Tallinn, Estonia
gpsr.requests@easproject.com

www.ingramcontent.com/pod-product-compliance
Lightning Source LLC
Chambersburg PA
CBHW070236240426
43673CB00044B/1812